CALE
SUPPORT | MATERIALISE

SCALE

SUPPORT | MATERIALISE

COLUMNS, WALLS, FLOORS

EDITORS
ALEXANDER REICHEL
KERSTIN SCHULTZ

AUTHORS
HENNING BAURMANN
JAN DILLING
CLAUDIA EULER
JULIUS NIEDERWÖHRMEIER

Birkhäuser
Basel

EDITORS' FOREWORD

Structure and material – without these two elements, architecture would be unthinkable and designs certainly not buildable. Structure and material are the elementary components of any construction and of any building. They form and shape it. For this reason, the third volume of the SCALE series is exclusively dedicated to these important elements, which are essential to a building and have to be considered at the beginning of a design. As in the previous volumes, the issue is that of the interaction between construction and design, which determines the appearance of a building.

This volume begins with an introductory section on the logic of structural systems in general – the structure – and goes on to describe the implementation of these principles using the respective construction material – the enclosing material. The last section of the book is dedicated to built examples, which demonstrate how the interaction between aesthetics and structure functions in practice. The illustrations include numerous drawings and plans to help the reader assimilate the process – from design to the completed building – and the resulting atmospheric quality.

The structural systems and developments illustrated here relate to the special structural and formal features of ideal structural systems. These structural principles are delineated so as to allow a general application, without requiring analysis and proof in terms of structural calculations. The idea is to create essential design tools that can be used in a successful design process – thus creating an interface that highlights the common ground between architects and engineers.

The structures are illustrated with their jointing details and principal dimensions and, at the same time, the range of materials best suited for a certain structural system is described. The selection of systems focuses on clear basic principles, such as skeleton and wall construction, in order to create clarity – and hence assist comprehension – in the knowledge that the complexity of modern building practice often involves hybrid structural systems, which could not be described, however, without this elaboration of basic principles. The quality of architectural expression, its general legibility and hence its acceptance by users is exemplified by the clear implementation of the different principles, such as column or girder, arch or frame, skeleton or wall construction.

The logic of the structure follows through in the selection of the material – as was stated by Louis Kahn in 1972. "When you talk to a brick and ask it what it wants, it will say: an arch. And when you reply: but look, arches are expensive, and it is simpler to use a lintel made of concrete, the brick will reply: I know that it is expensive, and I fear that currently it probably cannot be built, but if you ask me what I really want, it is still the arch." (From: Louis I. Kahn: *Writings, Lectures, Interviews.* New York, 1991). Using materials in a way that is appropriate to their properties is one of the basic prerequisites of sustainable building. This is the only way in which to achieve economic use of resources and to build a building with a long service life and low maintenance costs. The questions raised will have to be answered anew when new materials or new construction methods appear.

The relevant knowledge and background are introduced in detail in the main part of the book. Construction details and rules are illustrated for the different materials, i.e. masonry, concrete, timber and steel, using section drawings of selected buildings. With the help of the principles introduced, readers can pursue more detailed research on specific subjects and thereby arrive at a solution that suits their project. Building components such as walls, columns and floors, as well as bracing and jointing details, are illustrated at different scales and in different construction methods.

Not every material is suitable for every structure, and so it becomes apparent – when selecting the appropriate material – how important a detailed knowledge of the principles, jointing methods and special characteristics is, in order to ensure that material and structure form a homogeneous unit. The principles explained here supplement that part of the SCALE series of books that illustrates the construction principles of an independent building envelope. "Envelope and Construct" is that volume of the series in which the outer envelope, including roof and facade, is introduced in its multi-faceted architectural expression and, just as in this current volume, is shown with its design and construction details.

These two volumes are intended to document a variety of current architectural approaches while at the same time offering the basic principles leading to the synthesis of construction, form and shape. The quality of the architecture is the result of a process, which starts with a conceptual design and which is developed by applying a construction principle and selecting appropriate materials.

We thank the authors for their inspirational work in creating this book, Andrea Wiegelmann for her continuous conceptual support of the series and Birkhäuser publishers for the many years of consistent cooperation.

Darmstadt, Kassel, 31 March 2013
Alexander Reichel, Kerstin Schultz

SUPPORT | MATERIALISE
INTRODUCTION

INTRODUCTION

Architectural design is a continuous development process. In this process the structure, construction and material are decided, based on a number of different requirements, in conjunction with other people involved in the design. This 'checking and reviewing' – as the Italian architect Renzo Piano defines the strategy of designing – does not proceed in a straight line or an additive manner, but in a networked and integrated fashion, sometimes intuitively and improvised, and on the basis of a precise analysis of the brief. Consideration as to the available construction options does not necessarily have to be given at the beginning of the design process, but without an awareness of the possibilities and conditions of a construction system, the design will remain abstract. Implementing the design idea requires knowledge of construction: the design concept will be 'materialised' and assembled, it will have a dimension and an order of scale, texture and colour; it will integrate building components and elements, and it will enclose space. Therefore, familiarity with construction methods is one of the prerequisites of designing: design and construction cannot be separated. Design, as the materialisation of an idea, is inextricably linked with construction.

For this reason, what follows does not focus just on the structure in isolation, but on the connection between concept, material and structure. The structural system is responsible for the structural integrity of buildings and structures and therefore is the most important of all factors impacting on the design concept. The fact that the relationship between the structure and the appearance of the building is affected by many different factors, as well as constant and variable forces, becomes apparent when studying the history of design. In view of the breadth of impacting factors, weighting is necessary; therefore the focus here will be only on certain aspects and modes of development.

The history of structural systems is closely connected with the development of early building tasks: buildings – homes and places of worship (graves and temples) – on the one hand, and structures – transport structures and fortifications – on the other hand. Presumably, the first structure consisted of tree-trunk as a horizontal beam that was used for crossing ditches and ravines. ⌐ **1**

1 A tree trunk for crossing rivers or ravines – one of the earliest structures.

2 The original, archetypal branch-and-clay hut can still be found to this day in Mali. This simple construction combines a branch roof on posts with protective clay walls.

In buildings, the first structures can be found in shelters, which served the sole purpose of protecting against danger from the outside. According to the writings of Vitruvius, these were caves or huts of very simple construction using grasses or branches which, in the earliest times, were only fashioned with the hands as tools and, later, were coarsely worked on using sticks, bones or stones.

In contrast, the ceremonial buildings of early civilisations consisted of purely solid constructions, such as the graves of the Egyptians or Aztecs: constructions consisting of layers of natural stone, without tensile force, with the aim of limitless durability and structural integrity.

The original, archetypal branch-and-clay hut can still be found to this day in places such as Mali, Mesopotamia and Mongolia. While the huts in Mali may combine branch-and-leaf constructions with screening clay walls, the yurts found in Mongolia are held up purely by the central post, the radially arranged roof poles and the woven timber lattice work: a highly efficient construction, which has been refined over the centuries and which is easy to take apart to suit a nomadic lifestyle. These yurts have extremely simple joints and are very quick to erect and take down, demonstrating – with the separation of load-bearing structure and envelope or building skin – the key characteristics of skeleton frame construction. ⬩ 2, 3

When studying the process of 'materialisation' over millennia, it becomes apparent that construction methods and structural systems, with their relationship to the laws of physics, have been iteratively optimised over a long period of time.

Independently of the confines of construction methods, the conceptual characteristics of building have however changed much more rapidly under the impact of political,

3 Yurt, Mongolia. This highly efficient structure, which has been developed over centuries, is designed with simple joining methods so that it can be put up and taken down very quickly when the family moves on. The separation of supporting and enclosing elements, of structure and skin, is an early example of skeleton construction.

3

cultural and climatic influences. In the dichotomy between representative, social connotations and functional, technical requirements, the production facilities or railway stations of the 19th century illustrate this point. The increasing efficiency of new materials led structural systems and construction methods to become ever more sophisticated, particularly so under the modernising trends spawned by the Moderne movement. These buildings developed from fairly homogenous structures into heterogeneous, complementary ones. Their materials were chosen with less dependence on the dictates of the structure, such as in the first English iron structures, or the skeleton frame buildings of the Chicago School. ➘1

When studying the development of reinforced concrete construction, and shell construction in particular, it is noticeable how much – in addition to more efficient materials – new calculation methods have contributed to the optimisation of structures. One of the outstanding shell construction engineers was Ernst Neufert, who was involved in the construction of the new Test Institute for Hydrology at Darmstadt Technical University in 1955. For the large column-free space of 25 × 70 m, he and structural engineer Alfred Mehmel chose, in symbolic reference to the subject of the brief, a wave-shaped shell structure which affords both the structural and protective functions. The impression of utmost elegance, lightness and associative strength is characteristic of the project to this day; many of the buildings presented have benefited from such close cooperation between architect and engineer. For the construction of the Hydrology Hall, the shell construction method was developed further, the development being based on the earlier designs by structural engineers Franz Dischinger (1887–1953) and Ulrich Finsterwalder (1897–1988), who used the Zeiss-Dywidag (1923) system. The necessity of using materials sparingly resulted from the scarcity of raw materials and the need for economic efficiency in the 1950s.

The improvement in the quality of steel and cement constituted an important step in the development and a prerequisite for pre-stressed constructions. Although studies on the use of prestressed concrete methods had been carried out by the German engineer, Mathias Koenen (1849–1924) and the French engineer and inventor, Eugène Freyssinet (1879–1962) as early as the end of the 19th century, high-strength steel with a high elastic limit and high-quality Portland cement – which were required for prestressed constructions – did not become available until the 1930s. In addition, the design of structural shell systems was made more easy by simpler calculation methods such as the verification method used

by the engineers Alfred Mehmel and Wilhelm Fuchssteiner for cylindrical shells.

Although this reduced the complexity of the engineering design, shell constructions built with in-situ concrete remained the exception because, in the mid 1950s, shuttering the often complex shapes accounted for approximately half of the total construction cost. This work needed particularly qualified, skilled workers; likewise, bending and fitting the reinforcement was comparatively laborious and expensive. Wilhelm Fuchssteiner (1908–1982), working in cooperation with Alois Schader on the new building of the Technical Supervisory Association in Darmstadt, demonstrated how it was possible to achieve more cost-efficient construction of shell structures with significantly reduced formwork, shuttering and installation costs. They proposed a structure which was made up of six 44.50 m long shells with a cross section of only 10 cm thickness in the centre of the field. This resulted in a highly efficient solution for a structure that appeared light and elegant and to this day appeals through its unity of material, design and construction. ➘2-4

1

1 Reliance Building, Chicago, under construction (1890-1895), John Wellborn Root, Charles B. Atwood, Daniel Hudson Burnham.

2-4   TÜV building, Darmstadt, 1957, Wilhelm Fuchssteiner and Alois Schader. The idea for this elegant shell structure had its origin in the economic shortages of the 1950s; at the centre of the field, the shell is only 10 cm thick. Isometric projection and sections, 1:500

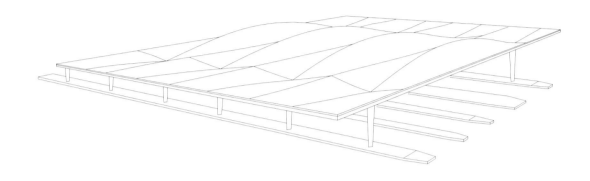

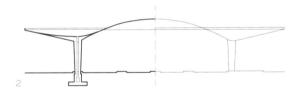

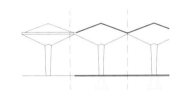

STRUCTURE AND LOCATION

Every building is built for a specific function at a specific location. The context of the respective location impacts in many ways on the design concept: considerations include those of urban design, the natural environment, the topography, the energy supply and construction law. When looking back at the origin of structural systems and their importance in building construction, it becomes clear that the structure of anonymous and autochthonous buildings in particular grew directly from the materials available at the location.

Examples are the historic timber structures found in medieval cities or the stone houses of the villages in the high Alps. The location not only defines the material resources available, but also the available craft skills and experience, which are passed on from generation to generation and are thus based on tried-and-tested construction methods. In this context, tools and production methods are an important cultural aspect of the various civilisations, and exert their own influence – from the first simple tools used for building shelters through to current, technologically advanced, computer-controlled production methods with a high degree of prefabrication. Another aspect that is closely linked with the location is the climate. Japanese timber architecture for example, the open spatial concept of which had a major impact on the development of the Moderne style in Europe and America, is as much the result of the available materials as it is a response to the prevailing climate. Because in humid/warm climate zones, houses raised on stilts allow for enhanced air circulation and hence natural air conditioning of the living space. At the same time, the void beneath the building also helps to protect its timber structure, owing to the constant flow of air. ↘ 1, 2

In the wooded agricultural regions of Europe – with their late Medieval aisled houses such as in Westphalia, Lower Saxony or central Switzerland – the traditional timber frame houses were an important precursor of modern timber skeleton frame construction. Stones collected from the fields when working the land were used to build

a solid stone plinth and to provide protection for the timber. It was used as a base for the timber frame, with the spaces between the studs being either filled with brick or, alternatively, with wattle and daub. Where hay was stored in the building, the facade was left open for ventilation purposes, as can be seen in the example at Saarnen in central Switzerland. ↘ 3, 4

These filigree timber structures contrast with the solid stone buildings in the high alpine valleys, for example in Corippo and in the Verzasca valley, which seem to present the opposite in terms of design and construction. ↘ 5, 6

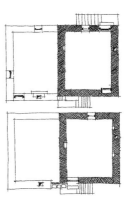

Today, owing to a large range of widely available building materials, efficient processing methods and almost ubiquitous good access, the decision regarding material and structure is largely independent of the local resources, unless ecological implications and the energy consumed in transport are taken into consideration. When these are taken into consideration – as is the case in some laudable examples – the building once again directly depends on local materials and the skills of local tradesmen, thus affecting the structural system and design. For example, the Vorarlberg building style fundamentally draws its inspiration from the centuries-old construction of timber buildings in Vorarlberg, and has developed into the leading architectural style of the region. Today, the architect Hermann Kaufmann is one of its representatives; he works on the innovative development of modern timber construction and thereby strengthens the cultural identity of the region.

An example is the conversion of an old stable in Alberschwende (2004) which was changed into a museum; this is a good illustration of how the historical timber frame structure can be complemented and modernised using modern timber board materials in an effort to enhance the historical continuity of the location. Other conceptual approaches exist. For the design of the Vals hotel and spa complex (1996), Peter Zumthor has drawn inspiration from the region's traditional, homogenous houses as well as the imposing, stone retaining structures on the mountainsides. The locality determines the poetic concept of the Bruder Klaus chapel in Mechernich (2006), where local stone is used in an unusual prototype application. ⟶ 7, 8 In Vrin, in the Swiss canton of Grisons, the architect Gion Caminada modifies the locality's impact on his designs by considering their social relevance. The changes affecting the alpine landscape and the migratory exodus of people from the higher locations of the alpine valleys impact on his concept, primarily affecting his decisions regarding materials and structure. Embedded in the wider, socio-economic context of Vrin, and with the aim of retaining the old farm architecture, he designed houses and farm buildings in the solid local style referred to as 'strickbau', which developed entirely from the place, its culture, architecture, social structure and economy, and above all from the skills base available at the location. ⟶ 9

1, 2   Katsura Imperial Villa, Kyoto, 1663. Japanese timber architecture, with its open spatial concept, had a significant impact on the Moderne movement in Europe and America.

3   Traditional stable building, Saarnen, central Switzerland.

4   A precursor of modern timber skeleton construction: north-German aisled house in timber-frame construction, Westphalia, 1686

5, 6   Stone houses in Corippo

7, 8   Prototypical development of a solid construction system: Bruder Klaus Chapel, Mechernich, 2006, Peter Zumthor. The chapel was built using rammed concrete, a method typical of the area. Inside the chapel, a fire was maintained for three weeks, which caused the tree trunks to dry out and become detached from the concrete so that they could easily be removed. Mouth-blown glass bungs close off the tie openings, which were needed to tie the outer and inner shuttering together when pouring the concrete.

9   Farm building in Vrin, Gion Caminada, in the regional 'strickbau' style

7

8

9

STRUCTURE AND TYPOLOGY

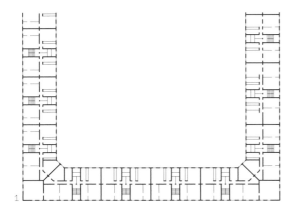

Even though the locality, material and skills resources and climate conditions have an impact on autochthonous buildings, nowadays typological and functional factors determine the complex requirements of structural systems and construction methods. Bearing these influences in mind, there is an obvious distinction between single and multi-storey buildings and, at the second level, between different kinds of use typology. Halls and tower blocks require different structures, as do residential buildings and those for administration, science or research.

For example, in housing, room sizes of approx. 3 × 4 m were commonly used as the base dimension for the structural system where it was not intended to deviate from the cellular layout, in order to create greater flexibility. For this reason and with very few exceptions, most apartment blocks through to the 20th century have been built using the cell structure traditional in solid construction. Outstanding examples are the apartment buildings in Copenhagen by the Danish architect Kay Fisker (1893–1965), who, with his projects in the so-called kilometre

style, provided high-quality, robust and sustainable living accommodation to satisfy the suddenly increased demand for housing in the 1920s. ⤳ 1, 2

Fisker divided the structure of the buildings into load-bearing longitudinal walls and non-loadbearing cross walls. When the structure of the cell-type layout is further analysed, it emerges that, for economic reasons, not only the longitudinal walls, but also the cross walls and wall combinations are used in a loadbearing capacity.
⤳ Chapter 2

It was only a few years later that Ludwig Mies van der Rohe made a significant contribution to the Weißenhofsiedlung in Stuttgart (1927) and, with his highly flexible design, produced a forerunner of his apartment buildings. He transferred the room typology of his spacious, freestanding housing concepts to the design of apartment blocks by combining this with the construction systems of his commercial buildings. A prerequisite for this was to 'press the construction into service for the spatial solution' (Schulze) using an optimised steel skeleton construction with brick panels. ⤳ 3, 4

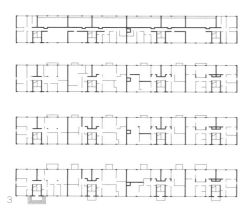

1, 2 Kay Fisker organised the structural layout of his residential developments – such as the Hornbaekhus in Copenhagen, 1923 – in loadbearing longitudinal and non-loadbearing transverse walls. Layout 1:1000

3, 4 With his contribution to the Weissenhofsiedlung, Stuttgart, 1927, Mies van der Rohe applied the spatial typology of his freestanding houses to apartment buildings, by combining it with the structural system of industrial buildings. Layout plans, 1:1000

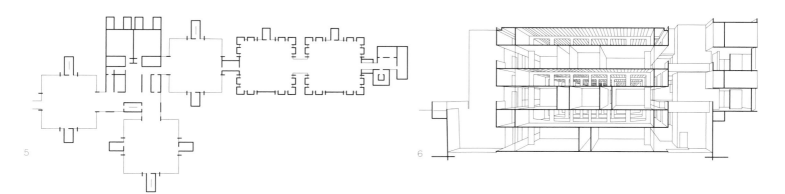

5

6

In multi-storey construction, the wall as loadbearing structure had reached its limit at a height of about 60 m, owing to the increasingly reduced thickness, and hence footprint, of the walls. The Monadnock Building in Chicago (1891, Daniel Burnham and John Wellborn Root) is exemplary for the limited height achievable with this structural system and material and, with its up to 1.8 m thick outer brick walls in the lower floors, is a marker in the transition from solid construction to skeleton frame systems, as represented by the Reliance Building by Daniel Burnham, which was created at the same time. The concentration of loads on optimised, loadbearing elements of the steel and reinforced concrete skeleton became the industry standard for high-rise housing and administration buildings. With this increase in height, the horizontal wind loads are significant, in addition to the vertical loads, and have to be absorbed with the help of suitable bracing elements: for example tubes, tube bundles, externally positioned frameworks, or core structures. ↘ Chapter 3 In addition to tower blocks, there were other new building projects that encouraged the introduction of new construction methods. These included both the railway stations of the 19th century and the airship and aircraft hangers of the 20th century, as well as various exhibition venues. As early as 1889, the Galerie des Machines in Paris by Victor Contamin and Ferdinand Dutert featured a clear span of 115 m using a three-point-arch structure. With their large open spaces on the ground floor, these buildings represent the typological counterpart to multi-storey construction. In this case, it is not the vertical elements of the structure that are the most critical design components, but instead the determining factor is the horizontal loadbearing element that has to resist deflection – usually the roof construction itself. Further improvements were achieved in the transport structures of early modern times. The experience gained with the wide spans of these cast iron constructions was to be made use of in bridge-building to obvious advantage. When this line of development is studied further one finally arrives at the highly efficient tensile and membrane structures used, for example, in the buildings by Günter Behnisch and Frei Otto for the 1972 Olympic Games in Munich, or the wide-spanning structures of the high-tech architecture of Norman Foster, Renzo Piano or Richard Rogers.

For a long period of time – almost 1,800 years – the Pantheon was the largest free-spanning dome structure with a span of 43.30 m. The fact that it was not overtaken until 1913, by the Century Hall in Breslau, demonstrates the restrictions applicable to wide-spanning structures throughout the centuries. The continuing development of materials in order to achieve better performance made it possible to increase the span to 65 m for the first time with this reinforced concrete ribbed cupola. However, reinforced concrete ribbed constructions had their limits. Structural systems in the form of folded plate or shell structures with 'paper-thin' wall thicknesses made even larger spans possible. In 1916, Freyssinnet designed an airship hangar in Orly with a folded plate structure which, with a thickness of just 9 cm, achieved spans of 75 m; this was soon bettered by Maillart's shell construction for the Cement Hall at the 1939 National Exhibition in Zurich.

The influence of specific typologies on structural, system-integrated design concepts can be demonstrated by comparing two projects by Louis Kahn. The Richards Medical Research Building in Philadelphia and the Salk Institute in La Jolla, two research and laboratory buildings, impress with their logical integration of structural system, construction, typology and shape. The extensive services installations required in these laboratory buildings and their allocation to the main service areas resulted in a strict zoning arrangement, which also impacted on the structural system. In the Richards Medical Research Building in Philadelphia it was the arrangement of vertical shafts outside the square laboratory areas which resulted in zoning of the layout into primary and secondary, loadbearing and non-loadbearing, servicing and serviced areas. In a similar fashion, albeit in the horizontal direction, the intermediate storeys of the Salk Institute were used for the services installations as well as the structural system. By using full storey-high Vierendeel trusses it was possible to keep the floor areas free from any vertical loadbearing elements: in other words, these are two solutions that are based on the design strategies of stacking and zoning, which demonstrate an integrative approach to the structural system, the services installations and the fitting out. ↘ 5, 6

STRUCTURAL SYSTEM, MATERIAL REFERENCE AND CONCEPTUAL QUALITY

Careful selection of the construction method and structural system is not only required for stability, durability and flexibility, but also offers a high potential for conceptual expression. Criteria for the assessment of the shape of a built structure can be particularly easily formulated when the structural system is the determining factor: in typical engineering structures such as towers or bridges. Although, for example with road bridges, other aspects such as surface sealing, drainage and the effect of contraction and expansion have to be taken into account, as well as static structural and dynamic loads, they are of comparatively secondary influence on the geometric design of the structural system. In this case the force vectors, the degree of transparency in space and the materials' own physical characteristics and manner of production are dominant influences on the geometric shape. In his analysis of reinforced concrete structures created by Robert Maillart (1872–1940), David Billington has defined the criteria of economy, efficiency and elegance as parameters for assessment. For Maillart, efficiency is synonymous with material efficiency. He wanted to keep the amount of material as small as possible in order to develop lightweight, slender loadbearing structures. Maillart achieved this through the integration of all parts of a structural system in a homogenous form, such as in an arch, a pillar and the road deck of a bridge.

For him, economy meant keeping the construction and maintenance costs as low as possible. In 1928, when together with building contractor Florian Prader, he won the competition for the bridge across the deep Salgina ravine, his success was based particularly on the economical production process of the arched hollow box section bridge. Maillart devised the wooden falsework for the Salginatobel bridge only for the first concreting section, the thin lower arch. Once this section had cured, it was capable of carrying the road deck supports, and the scaffolding structure was only used as reinforcement, not as support for the arch. ➘ 1, 2 The profile of the Salginatobel bridge in cross section illustrates its slender dimensions: the lower arch and the faces of the road deck supports both recede compared to the side face of the road deck and thus create narrow lines of shadow which visually separate the bridge's segments from each other. This is further emphasised by the flush-fitting detail at the crown of the bridge. Other characteristics are the shallow arch (which gives an idea as to the solidity of the flanking rock faces), the transparency of the wide openings in the outer quarters, the heavily tapered bearing ends of the arch, and finally the contrast between the bright concrete and the dark background of the shadowy mountain slopes.

1, 2   Robert Maillart devised the wooden falsework for the Salginatobel bridge near Schiers, 1928, only for the lower arch which, after it had cured, was capable of carrying the road deck supports on its own. The filigree appearance of the bridge is further enhanced by the profiling of its elements.

1

2

3 The approach cultivated by Kazuyo Sejima & Ryue Nishizawa (SANAA) involves the 'dematerialisation' of surfaces and the visualisation of pure form, as expressed at the Zollverein School in Essen, 2006.

4 For Mülimatt sports training centre in Brugg-Windisch, 2006, Studio Vacchini architects selected a shell structure in the form of a folded plate, which comprises prefabricated roof members and wall supports.

In the case of buildings, the multitude of influences on the overall geometry and shape is much more complex than with pure engineering structures. The degree to which the construction method and structural system determine the appearance and geometry of a building depends on the task and, above all, on the architect's approach. Simply put, this approach stretches from 'legibility' to abstraction and from 'materialisation' to 'dematerialisation' of the architectural form. In this context, Pierre von Meiss differentiates further between 'the emphasis, visual expression, falsification, subjugation and taming of technology'. A structural principle becomes apparent if the force flow can be perceived when a solid structural system is subdivided into its individual vectoral force elements. Both brickwork and 'strickbau' log construction and, in particular, skeleton frame construction fascinate through the syntax of elements and joints, of bearers, supports and nodes. These elements express the flow of vertical and horizontal forces. In steel skeleton frame construction, this led to designs which were modelled on mechanical engineering solutions of the 1920s. Typical examples are the 'machine urbaine' of the Pompidou Centre or the industrial buildings by Norman Foster.

In contrast to an expression of the structural elements, the approach here is one of abstraction, of emphasising the 'dematerialised' surface, the pure form; it is one of geometric clarity and reduction – as was promoted by the Bauhaus and 'De Stijl' movements – and which is expressed today in buildings by John Pawson or SANAA. ↘3 The extent to which structural systems find expression in the appearance of a building depends entirely on the individual architectural interpretation, as can be demonstrated by the example of the Mülimatt sports training centre by Studio Livio Vacchini. ↘4 In this case the designers opted for a folded plate structure rather than the skeleton construction that is the common structural solution for wide spans across sports halls. The construction consists essentially of in-situ concrete foundations and a small-scale plinth storey which gives support to a wide-spanning roof and wall structure. This was designed as a folded plate structure composed of prefabricated roof members and wall supports. Both the roof deck and vertical supports are prestressed and the joints are filled

3

4

with in-situ concrete. Thanks to the pre-tensioning, the roof elements have few cracks and also form the covering layer; the roof drains openly through the larger cross sections – resulting from the construction details – at the field centres, to the uprights. ↘ Examples p. 150 The integration of the structural and detailed design, the enclosure, and the manufacturing process allows the folded plate structure of the hall to reflect the elegance, economy and efficiency of Maillart's concrete structural systems. The degree to which efficiency will be understood in the future as energy and raw material efficiency is made clear in the following section.

OUTLOOK

As to new approaches to structural, detailed and material design, several aspects are highlighted: the significance of changeable, adaptive structures and materials; the influence of new materials (smart materials, biological constructions, bionics, cybernetics); the effect of new production conditions, especially in view of the expansion of digital process chains and degrees of prefabrication; the importance of life-cycles and the greater need for recycling; and finally, the trend towards greater energy efficiency in design and careful use of raw materials, in accordance with their ecological performance profiles. Adaptive designs can be modified as conditions change. An historic example is the turnable wooden scaffolding of the Pantheon: for the restoration of the dome in 1756, it was designed in a lattice frame construction which followed the circular profile of the dome while rotating around a vertical axis which had its anchor point in the central opening, the opaion.

Other more current examples of changeable structures that border on mechanical engineering are the structural systems of observatories, lifting gear and mobile cranes. Adaptive bridges, such as early drawbridges and the 'transporter bridges' of the 19th and 20th centuries through to turning, folding and sliding bridges, represent a wide spectrum of moving structures. Architectural examples involving adaptive principles can be found in the visionary projects designed by Future Systems in London, for example the Peanut House (1984).

Today, adaptive structures are used in all those situations where the function or efficiency requirements are expected to change. For example, modern stadium design not only has to deal with the structural concept, but also with issues such as how to open the roof and manage visitor risk in order to be able to accommodate different types of function, as well as changes in the weather. Dynamic structures such as those used in single and double-axis solar panels play an important role in optimising these renewable energy systems.

Adaptive constructions may also develop following the pattern of bionic and biometric systems. Centuries ago, Leonardo da Vinci studied examples from the field of biology in order to develop and transform analogous systems. The architect and engineer Curt Siegel (1911–2004) analysed the structural shape of bones – taking the flowing change in their properties as an example of functionally graded material – and shells; Frei Otto and the Institute for Lightweight Construction at Stuttgart University designed efficient shell and membrane structures taking soap bubbles as the guiding principle. ↘ 1

Bionic phenomena will continue to provide inspiration for the development of structures and materials. The development of digital process chains and construction robotics will have a large impact on design and production processes.

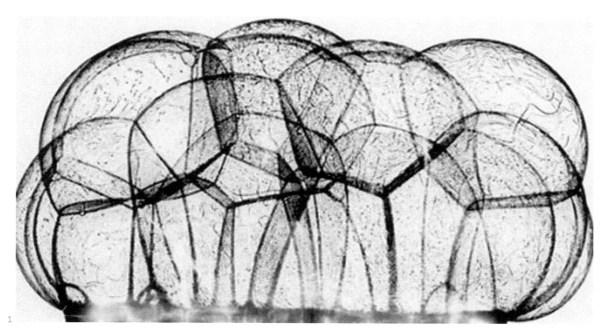

1 Soap sud experiments, Stuttgart, 1960s. Soap suds naturally form the smallest possible surface between any given edges. Based on his trials with soap bubbles, Frei Otto developed design principles which, compared to conventional building methods, only used a fraction of the materials.

2 Parametrically generated and produced wooden canopy, TU Munich, 2010, Stefan Kaufmann & Gerhard Schubert.

3 FlexBrick, ETH Zurich, 2008, Gramazio & Kohler. Construction robotics expands the spectrum of conceptual design options.

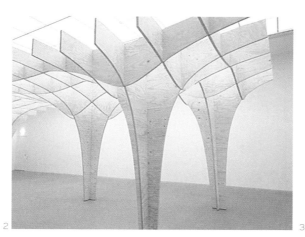

For example in timber construction, this development – together with new wood-based materials – contributes to marked process optimisation. Precise production, pre-assembly and a significant reduction in construction time are made possible without intermediate steps, from the computer-assisted design stage through to the fully computer-controlled timber cutting process. Examples such as the Chesa Futura in St. Moritz (2004) by Norman Foster – with its typical rib construction, curved in two directions and reminiscent of ship-building – illustrate that the move away from traditional artisan skills, local conditions and the specific aspects of material properties opens up the option of non-repetitive building components, and hence a new range of design patterns. Other examples are the irregular honeycomb roof structure of the works canteen in Ditzingen by Barkow and Leibinger ↘ p. 130 and the digital carving at the Monte Rosa chalet (2009) by Bearth and Deplazes Architects as an ornamental image of the integrative digital fabrication process. The effects produced and opportunities offered by digital design and production in respect of jointing principles are demonstrated by the parametrically generated wooden canopy (2010) by Kaufmann and Schubert. ↘ 2 The plywood rib structure is properly jointed with push-fit connections and is only fixed by concealed tensile metal straps. The impact of a high degree of prefabri-

cation on the design and construction process in modern timber construction is illustrated by the Alpenhotel Ammerwald project (2009) by Oskar Leo Kaufmann and Albert Rüf. By prefabricating the room units as modules, complete with installations, in a cellular construction, they achieved a high-quality workmanship, a short construction time and the best possible economic efficiency in equal measure. The use in masonry construction of construction robotics, with its digital control mechanisms, is resulting in surprising extensions of the usual tectonic spectrum, as can be seen from the expressive image textures of the masonry wall prototypes produced by Gramazio & Kohler. Some of these can also be produced on site using mobile fabrication facilities. ↘ 3 The phenomenon of adaptation to changing performance profiles also influences the development of materials which, as 'smart materials', feature adaptive performance profiles. Foremost examples in architectural construction are the outer building skins or envelopes, which can be adaptive and multi-layer, or consist of switchable glazing, offering the opportunity to bring about temporary change in the interior. With regard to the choice of materials, we will in future have to develop solutions that integrate energy and raw material efficiency, as well as life-cycle considerations suitable to the performance profile of the material, into the design process.

SUPPORT | MATERIALISE
STRUCTURE

STRUCTURE AND DETAILS

Following the introduction of historic, local, typological and conceptual aspects, we will now turn to the systemic relationships and definitions of structures, to the construction detail and material on the one hand and architectural concepts and space on the other hand. In his book Tragsysteme (2006) (Structural Systems), Heino Engel aptly describes the fundamental significance of structure beyond that of built construction: 'Of all components that contribute to the existence of solid material forms such as a house, machine, tree or living being, structure is the most important.'

As a general principle, a construction can be divided into three parts: the loadbearing structure, the elements that enclose the space and the services installations.
In short, the loadbearing structure is needed to transfer forces. In Frei Otto's definition, forces are transferred by material (building materials) or immaterial (magnet effect) constructions. In the case of the material constructions, the loadbearing function is carried out by the structural elements and systems, for example the uprights, beams and floor slabs in a skeleton structure or by transoms and mullions in a frame structure. These elements will transfer all vertical and horizontal loads to the ground, including the structure's own weight, imposed loads from furniture and fittings, people, machinery, and those resulting from earth and wind pressure, snow and ice.
The design loads to be allowed for are defined in DIN 1055, 'Design Loads for Buildings'. Supplementary definitions for temporary structures are contained in DIN 4112, and for road and pedestrian bridges, in DIN 1072. In addition to the outer forces, the structure is also affected by inner forces resulting from deformation due to thermal exposure, swelling, shrinkage, creep etc. Forces may result in point, line or area loads.

Space-forming construction refers to all construction systems that form and delimit space, e.g. protecting interior rooms against the effect of sound, cold, heat etc. The space-forming construction can be identical to the loadbearing structure, as is the case in solid or wall constructions, or it may constitute a secondary part, such as the envelope system in skeleton construction. Services installations are needed for the supply and discharge of services in the widest sense, as well as for air-conditioning the building. In certain circumstances, these installations can also be integrated in the loadbearing structure. This therefore makes it necessary, for the purpose of a comprehensive design approach, to consider the technical installations with both horizontal and vertical ducts and shafts, and the necessary voids, as part of the detailed design of a project. In this context, an important aspect is the utilisation of inher-

ent material properties for the purpose of heating or cooling. ⤳ p. 47

Fritz Haller (1924–2012), like Norman Foster, intensively studied the systemic integration of the three parts making up a construction and produced innovative concepts. For example, at the Swiss Federal Railways training centre in Murten (1982), Haller demonstrated the MIDI structural system for the first time which, in the form of a modular system, included the integration of technical services installations and therefore offered a high degree of user-flexibility. ⤳ 1
At the Sainsbury Centre in Norwich (1978), Norman Foster integrated the loadbearing, envelope and services systems in the service zone of the double U-shaped space enclosure.

1 Model of the MIDI structural system, which was designed as a modular system for buildings with a high degree of services installation, showing integrated structure and services. 1972, Fritz Haller.

1

The term 'construction' (con = together and struere = build) refers to the technical means of the implementation of an architectural task. It can be evaluated through the technical and aesthetic aspects of the individual parts and the way in which they are joined together.

The ordering and organising principle of a structure is determined by the relationship between the individual elements and the system, as well as the link between them. Construction links may be the result of joining structural elements or that of internal links of the elements produced during manufacture; they may refer to the bearings of a beam on a post in a skeleton system, or the connection of the head or base of a post to the beam or plate of a traditional timber frame construction.

A comparison of two projects by Ludwig Mies van der Rohe (1886–1969) and Angelo Mangiarotti (1921–2012) demonstrates how these construction links vary according to the system, for example in skeleton construction. While the steel structure by Mies van der Rohe clearly expresses the articulated joint and the rigid connection of the point bearing and the restrained, tapering upright, which consists of crossed T-profiles, Mangiarotti's reinforced concrete skeleton structure features an upright with a hammer-shaped head which, like a tongue, engages in the groove of the U-shaped beam and thereby transfers the forces with appropriate jointing details in a most obvious and elegant manner. ⟶ 2, 3

The geometric basis for the design of a structure is formed through arrangement systems and dimensional relationships in the form of tolerances, modular order, grids and dimensional patterns. These geometric patterns and modules are not self-serving, but are needed for sizing components and structures in a system with a uniform inner organisation which also reflects the properties of the respective materials.

2 New National Gallery, Berlin, 1967, Ludwig Mies van der Rohe. The columns with crossed T-profiles are fixed in the ground and hence restrained while those with point bearings are typical examples of hinged bearings.

3 Company headquarters, Turate/ Como, 1982, Angelo Mangiarotti. The hammer-shaped heads of the reinforced concrete columns engage like a tongue in the groove of the U-shaped beam and thereby elegantly mirror the force vector.

For example, in masonry wall construction – which has been the subject of one of the earliest standards in the construction industry – DIN 4172 'Modular Coordination in Building Construction' defines the relationship between the building block and the wall as a system. It takes into account the ergonomic conditions of the work process involved. It is interesting to note here that the dimensions of bricks were primarily determined with reference to the human hand. Economic efficiency and the use of bricks across and along in bonds led to the development of their proportions: twice the width of a brick + the width of the joint equals the length of the brick. On this basis a brick dimension of 125 mm was selected as the basic dimension of the octameter system and determined to be the basis for the sizing of building components and buildings in masonry construction. The standard has given rise to additional construction standards that provide a dimensional basis for the design and construction process.

However, particularly in view of the rather more complex geometric coordination needed in the development of prefabrication processes, a system using a base unit of a tenth of a meter proved to be more appropriate: DIN 18000 defines the decimetric system as a modular order. Starting from the base module M (100 mm), preferential dimensions called multi-modules of 3 M (300 mm), 6 M (600 mm), and 12 M (1200 mm) etc. are obtained through multiplication; sub-modules of M/10 (10 mm), M/5 (20 mm) etc. are obtained by dividing the base module.

Measuring systems and modular orders define a three-dimensional, geometrical coordinate system which defines the precise location of each component in space in terms of point, line, area or body. Using axial, areal and spatial grids, this modular system is built up from a base module and is divided into functional, structural and fit-out grids. ➔ 1

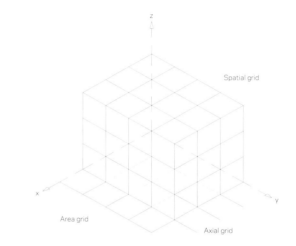

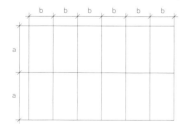

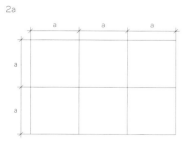

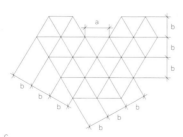

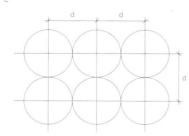

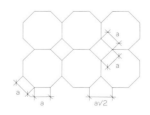

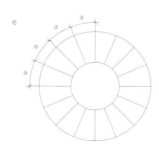

2a

b

c

d

e

f

1 A three-dimensional geometric coordinate system defines the precise position of each component in space as:

Axial grid   x
Area grid   x, y
Spatial grid   x, y, z

2 Grid geometries:
a Rectangular grid
b Square grid
c Triangular grid
d Circular grid
e Octagonal grid
f Circle segment grid

The geometric nature of the grid would initially suggest an orthogonal grid. In addition, triangular, octagonal, circular and segment grids are used. ⟋ 2

Within these systems a further differentiation is made between axial and modular grids. ⟋ 3

The axial coordinate defines the axes of components, with the components' dimensions not taken into account, while the boundary reference in the modular grid is based on the components' dimensions. The latter defines a geometrical ribbon, which can serve as a base for loadbearing or delimiting construction elements. As primary and secondary grid it also defines the hierarchy of the construction elements, such as the uprights in skeleton construction in the primary system and the envelope construction in the secondary system.

The Kimbell Art Museum (1972) by Louis Kahn demonstrates how the modular grid, in particular, integrates aspects of structure and typology while not failing to accommodate the requirements of construction detailing. The project is an outstanding example in which the grid is also used for the contextual design concept. The dialectic between rule and play finds expression in the compliance with the rules of the grid and at the same time in the freedom it allows for the formation of spaces. ⟋ 4, 5

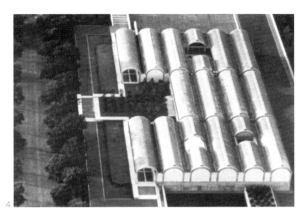

3 Grid types:
Axial grid, linear grid, combination of both grids (from top to bottom)

4, 5 The Kimbell Art Museum, Fort Worth, 1972, Louis Kahn, is an example of a design concept based on a grid. Floor plan 1:750

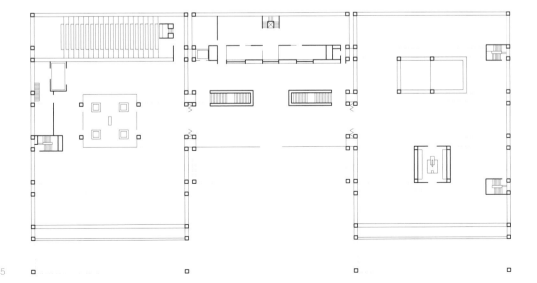

STRUCTURAL PATTERNS, ELEMENTS AND SYSTEMS

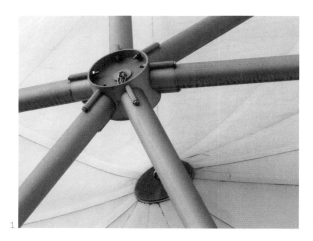

Generally speaking, elements are those parts that make up a greater whole and which, within this greater whole, cannot be divided any further. When these elements are joined with each other in accordance with the rules of a structure, they form a system. Consequently, the smallest units and parts of such a construction system, which cannot be divided any further without impairing their function, can be called construction elements.

In Buckminster Fuller's geodesic dome of 1954, the struts and nodes are the construction elements making up the 'space-frame structure' construction system (primary system) and the membranes are the construction elements making up the space-enclosing construction system (secondary system). ⟋ 1, 2

In room-forming skeleton systems, the space-enclosing construction consists of the following construction elements: outer weatherproof skin, thermal insulation, vapour barrier, internal lining.
Construction systems and construction elements form a hierarchy of systems and sub-systems. For example, the struts in a lattice girder that are exposed to normal forces are elements of that girder or construction system, which in turn is part of the larger construction system that makes up the roof structure, which in turn is part of the 'roof' system etc. ⟋ 3

1, 2   Geodesic dome, Detroit, Buckminster Fuller, 1978.
Struts and nodes are the structural elements (primary system), the membrane is the enclosing system (secondary system).

3   Hierarchy of systems

4   Overview of structural systems according to Engel, *Structure Systems*

3

2

GEOMETRY	LINEAR		NON-LINEAR	
	STRAIGHT	CURVED	FLAT	CURVED/FOLDED
LOAD TRANSFER	SINGLE-AXIS		DOUBLE-AXIS	TRIPLE-AXIS
Type of load NORMAL FORCE	Lattice girder determined by vector	Cable determined by form	Space frame grid determined by vector	Grid shell determined by form
	Lattice girder frame determined by vector	Arch determined by form		
Type of load BENDING AND SHEAR	Beam determined by mass	Shaped beam determined by mass	Slab, plate vertical/transverse determined by area/mass	Shell, with single- or double-axis curvature barrel vault/dome determined by area
	Frame determined by mass		Beam grid determined by mass	Folded shell structure determined by area
Type of load BENDING AND NORMAL FORCE hybrid	Beam with bottom tensioning determined by mass determined by vector		Space frame grid with bottom tensioning determined by mass determined by vector	

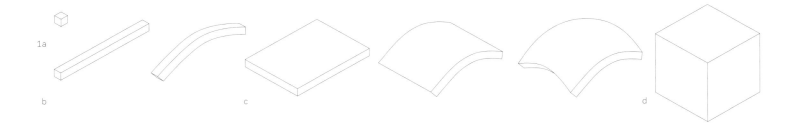

The construction elements are sub-divided and grouped together in accordance with their geometric form (point, line, area, space) and structural function. Linear and plane elements also occur in curved form.

1. Pointed elements ↘ **1a** refer to the smallest possible part of a structure. A typical example is the node in skeleton construction, as shown in the node of Buckminster Fuller's dome. ↘ **p. 28**

2. Structural elements that extend along one dimension ↘ **1b** are called struts, girders or beams. They are geometrically defined by their proportions: their length is much greater than their width and height. When such an element is drawn up as a linear structural element in systemic abstraction, only the structurally effective axis of the system is shown. Struts and girders are used in various shapes and guises such as single span and continuous girders, cantilever girders, solid, lattice and frame girders, as well as girders with additional tensile elements.
Curved girders are called arched girders.

3. Two-dimensionally functioning structural elements ↘ **1c** are typically used in shell structures and may consist of plates (force within the plane of the element) or slabs (force perpendicular to the plane of the element). They are geometrically defined by their proportions: both their length and width are many times greater than their height, or, in more general terms, two dimensions are significantly larger than the third one.

Plates and slabs can be installed as both vertical and horizontal structural elements. The defining factor is the direction in which the main force is acting on them. For example, a cellar wall that resists earth pressure, a facade that resists wind load, and a floor deck that supports an imposed load all function as slabs; on the other hand, a wall or roof bracing a structure functions as a plate.

Comparatively thin structures with large spans and curved shapes in one or two axes are referred to as shell structures. Horizontal structures that are made up of folded plates are referred to as folded plate structures. Shell structures tend to have very thin structural elements and therefore use material very efficiently, which is possible by the transfer of loads through normal (perpendicular) or longitudinal forces (diaphragm forces). These are forces without any bending moment, i.e. the only forces occurring result from compressive and tensile loads; this is equivalent to the system of a column that resists a compressive force, or a cable that resists tensile forces.
The structures are referred to as membrane shells and represent the ideal case of a curved, shell-type structure. However, where shells are also exposed to bending moments, their thickness dimension will be comparatively large and they will lose a great deal of their material efficiency, as well as some of their elegance and construction logic.

4. Three-dimensional elements ↘ **1d** form a particular class of structural element, which these days is only used in foundations or similar structures.

Such systems are rarely used in their pure form; instead, they are mostly combined with other forms. An outstanding example of this is Bagsvaerd church by Jørn Utzon (1976). ↘ **2-5**

The architect has limited himself to a specific material medium (reinforced concrete) and has combined structural systems in such a way that the resulting space follows the logic of its typology. Each area of the latticed typology, which accommodates different use functions in its layout, is assigned a specific type of reinforced concrete construction: examples are the prefabricated, additive skeleton structure of the linear access zones or the curved shell used for the sacral sections, which have been built as shell structures using in-situ concrete.

1 Construction elements:
a point structural element
b one-dimensional structural element
c two-dimensional structural element
d volumetric structural element

2–5 Bagsvaerd Church, Copenhagen, 1976, Jørn Utzon. The building comprises a combination of different structural systems. Each area of the lattice, which accommodates different uses in its layout, is assigned a specific type of reinforced concrete construction. For example: the linear access zones were constructed in a pre-fabricated skeleton structure; the sacral sections were built using a curved shell structure in reinforced concrete.

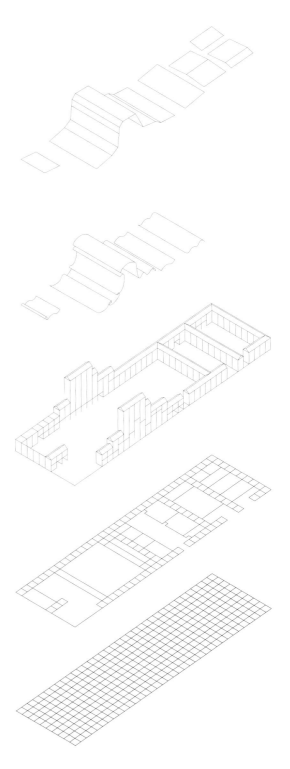

REQUIREMENTS AND FUNCTIONAL PRINCIPLES

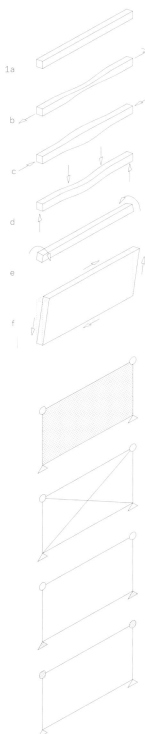

Generally speaking, structures are needed to ensure the structural integrity of buildings and their fitness for purpose. The structural integrity is at risk when the structural equilibrium is lost, when there is excessive deformation, material fatigue or sudden material failure. Structures are exposed to the forces of tension, compression, bending, torsion or shearing. ➔1

Often these forces act on the structure in combination, such as compression and bending. The construction material must be selected accordingly (for example, unreinforced concrete can only sustain 10 % of the pressure that reinforced concrete can resist).

Forces acting on the structure are also called loads. They occur as point, linear and area loads and are transferred along one, two or three axes. Loads can act on the structure horizontally, vertically or diagonally.
The different loads acting on the structure result from both external and internal forces. Changes of temperature, humidity and tension can lead to deformation. Such changes in form may be of an elastic or plastic nature.

– Elastic deformation is the result of exposure to tension or compression (negative distension under pressure) and to temperature changes (heating up will cause expansion; cooling down will cause contraction).

– In contrast to elastic deformation, plastic deformation is permanent and depends on the material. Examples are the shrinkage of timber, concrete and brickwork as a result of drying out, the plastic flow of steel and the creep of concrete, metals and plastics.

Damage resulting from deformation caused by shrinkage and creep will often not become evident until after a delay. In order to avoid the risk of cracking, for example as a result of restraint, the design of a structure has to make appropriate provision for absorbing these deformations, such as expansion joints, movement joints and false joints, or using low-shrinkage materials. Building materials of different physical properties should not be used in combination (example: gypsum plaster on concrete ceilings).

TRANSFER OF VERTICAL AND HORIZONTAL FORCES

Vertical forces can be transferred into the ground either directly or indirectly. As a general principle, the shortest way for transferring vertical loads is the most economical, for example a beam on two uprights. In the transfer of forces, long distances – such as in a suspension structure or wide cantilever – do not seem appropriate unless prompted by special requirements, such as a concentration of loads, contextual or typological requirements, for example floor areas without impeding upright supports, or maximum transparency, or a filigree appearance.

In the case of the Hongkong and Shanghai Bank (1985) by Norman Foster, it was the wish for maximum transparency and flexibility in the office floors which led to the design of a suspension structure, and hence an innovation in the tower block typology. The loads of the five storey sections with different heights, which are suspended over a free span of 40 m, are transferred to eight building-high frame structures. They are made up of four tubular supports each, which are connected with each other in each storey to form a rigid frame, and which thereby also absorb all horizontal forces. ➔2

1 Different forces acting on a
structure:
a Original form
b Tension
c Compression
d Bending
e Torsion
f Shear

2 With the Hong Kong and
Shanghai Bank, Hong Kong, 1985,
Norman Foster created a new
tower block typology in the form of
a suspended structure. The loads
from the five multi-storey structural
units are transferred via frames as
high as the building.

3 Horizontal load transfer

4 Structural systems:
a Solid construction
b Compartmental construction
c Skeleton construction

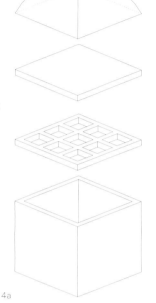
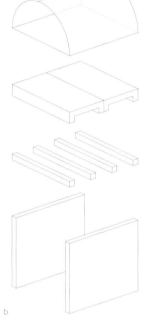
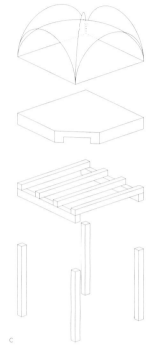

4a   b   c

Horizontal forces resulting from external loads (wind, earth pressure) can be transferred into the ground either via the moments in restrained uprights, plates or frames, or vectorally split constructions (triangular or bracing piers, frame constructions, diagonal crosses etc.). Either way, the construction method will determine the spatial transfer of forces. ↘ 3

Internal, horizontal forces resulting from a certain structural system, for example the rafter feet of a roof (without purlins), truss frames and tensioned or arched load-bearing structures, are transferred either on the inside through tensile cables or on the outside through appropriately heavy counterbearings.

The loads can be transferred into the ground either directly or indirectly. Loads are transferred directly when the geometric shape of the structure allows the continual direct transfer into the ground of all vertical and horizontal forces, be it in longitudinal or ring-shaped structures. Loads are transferred indirectly, for example, via walls as plates (continuous bearings: box, compart-

ment, plate), or via single-span floors (reinforced concrete slab, timber beam floor, element deck) or via the double-pitched or arched roof of a building – in each case with continuous support from walls acting as plates etc. When this is applied to the point-load situation in skeleton frame construction this may result in:

- a flat floor slab spanning crosswise in two directions with support at the corner points;
- a folded plate structure as a shell structure which transfers the loads via this structure in the lateral and longitudinal directions (the resulting tensile forces at the bearing points have to be taken into account);
- a dome with supports at the respective points.

The overview illustrates how horizontal and vertical structures depend on walls and slabs. ↘ 4
The following section illustrates how different structural systems and different construction methods affect the resulting spatial typology of a building.

SOLID AND SKELETON FRAME SYSTEMS

In his book *The Logic of the Art of Building*, Christian Norberg-Schulz differentiates between two major systems: solid and skeleton frame systems, which are defined by their space-forming and covering modes and by the relationship between support and enclosure. Both systems use different means to the same end: the construction of enclosing walls and the covering of the rooms created, using vertical and horizontal structural elements.

Solid systems are characterised by the fact that all structural elements of the system fulfil the same technical function, i.e. both supporting and enclosing. They typically consist of isotropic structures that are produced either by adding smaller elements, for example bricks, or by pouring a monolithic mass. While the enclosing solid system – which is primarily exposed to compressive forces – allows much freedom for the sizing of rooms, the covering part of the system – which is subject to bending and tensile forces – limits this freedom to a large extent. That is why solid space-forming structural systems are often combined with skeleton-type covering systems consisting of beams and girders. In addition to these combined solutions, there are purely solid systems that are homogeneous in using only compression elements in their construction, such as Roman cupola and vaulted constructions, or African clay huts. In contemporary architecture, the chapel in Oberrealta by Rudolf Fontana (1994) comes very close to this homogeneous solid system, both in terms of material and interior effect – although the roof structure, which is exposed to bending forces, does not strictly comply with the criteria of a solid system. ⟍1

In a solid system the shape and size of rooms and the dimensions of openings are limited. Prompted by these restrictions, efforts were made at an early stage to split the vectors of the solid system and create a skeleton frame system by gradually reducing the originally homogeneous walls to piers that became ever more slender. Typical examples are the Gothic cathedrals or temples on Malta: 'An effort was made to counteract the limitations of the solid systems by coming closer to a skeleton system' (Norberg-Schulz); this development from heavy to lightweight structures and to more open spaces progressed in the 20th century, not least due to the demands of modern building hygiene.

The homogeneous brick construction of the Grundtvigs church (1921–40) by Peder Jensen-Klint and Kaare Klint, with its significant synthesis of expressionistic and Gothic-style elements, is a good example of this approximation to the skeleton system by the reduction of the solid walls to loadbearing piers. ⟍2

1 St. Nepomuk Chapel, Oberrealta, 1994, Rudolf Fontana, is an example of contemporary architecture that resembles classic solid construction in its homogeneity and spatial effect.

2 Grundtvigs Church, Copenhagen, 1921–40, Peder Jensen-Klint and Kaare Klint, in which the solid walls give way to loadbearing piers, is an example of an approximation to the skeleton system.

3 Basis of skeleton construction:
the three-dimensional spatial grid

4 The skeleton system offers
maximum flexibility, transparency
and incependent structural and
enveloping elements, particularly
so in curtain-walled buildings such
as the VM House, Copenhagen,
2005, BIG Bjarke-Ingels-Group.

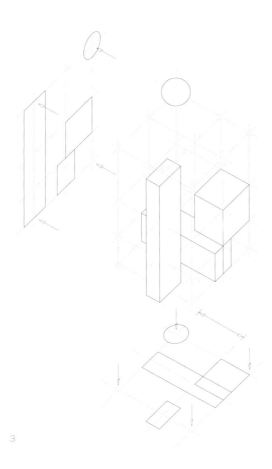

3

In contrast to solid systems, skeleton systems distinguish between room-forming and loadbearing parts of the construction. These are independent of each other. Rooms can be created 'with a higher degree of freedom' (Norberg-Schulz) in terms of size and shape and likewise, the openings also benefit from this reduction in limitation (cf. 'plan libre', Le Corbusier). The same applies to the covering elements. Wide-spanning, high-performance structures and three-dimensional shell structures drive the process of opening and freeing up.

The structural principle of skeleton construction is based on a three-dimensional grid ⌐ 3, which forms the basis for the precise arrangement and joining of primary (loadbearing) and secondary (room-forming) elements. It also gives rise to a distinct feature of skeleton construction, namely the repetition of identical parts, which creates the conditions for cost-efficient constructions. Ludwig Mies van der Rohe referred to this quality as an indicator of a 'clear construction'. The construction systems in skeleton construction can be distinguished by the size and scale of their elements. While, for example, the primary system as the loadbearing structure may have spans of 5–9 m, the secondary skeleton required in addition usually only needs a fraction of this span in order to transfer dead and wind loads and to allow an appropriate sub-division of the envelope areas into individual elements. The secondary skeleton fulfils the task of enclosing space and may be used independently or to fill in the spaces in the primary system, or often in combined application. The curtain wall facade is the best-known example of an enclosing system. ⌐ 4

Primary and secondary systems are defined geometrically using a primary and secondary grid, which also reflects a hierarchical order of support and enclosure. Designers use axial and modular grids and various grid superimpositions in order to coordinate the position of building components ⌐ p. 27. Similarly, the position of the facade is defined using the grid. As a general principle it may be located in front of, between or behind the outer structure. ⌐ p. 55

4

STRUCTURE AND SPACE:
VERTICAL AND HORIZONTAL STRUCTURAL ELEMENTS

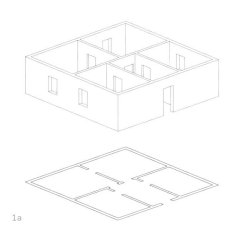 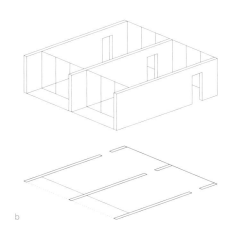 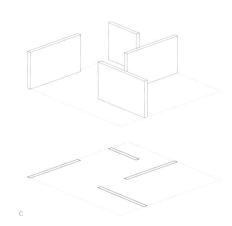

1a   b   c

Within the solid and skeleton construction systems there are further sub-divisions related to building style, function, space formation and openings.

When considering vertical structural elements, solid construction can be further sub-divided into the different building styles with the dominant design feature being box, compartment or plate; a secondary sub-division (primarily in multi-storey buildings) distinguishes between longitudinal and transverse walls and a combination of both. ↘ p. 38

The box design method ↘ 1a represents the traditional design method in solid construction, historically in brickwork, clay construction or, to an extent, also in timber-frame constructions and timber panel buildings. It is also conceivable in solid, timber or concrete constructions. The spatial characteristic of the box design method is the addition of rooms that are enclosed all round, with wall openings limited in size and appearing rather like holes. This method has little flexibility. Vertical and horizontal forces are transferred through the walls, which are connected, so that the box design method leads to enclosed, rather cube-like building volumes with characteristic solid corners. The advantage of the box design method is the uniform, linear load on the walls, particularly where concrete floors are used with a two-directional span. One-directional timber floors, which, in addition to vaulted floors, were the dominant floor construction up until the early 20th century, do not impose any loads on the flanking walls and therefore, from the structural point of view, are a less favourable solution.

The compartment design method ↘ 1b is characterised by series of transverse walls. It is therefore a typical solution for buildings with a regular addition of identical, independent units, while keeping the longitudinal sides as open as possible, such as in residential developments.

This system of loadbearing transverse walls is braced in the longitudinal direction by transferring longitudinal forces via the floor slabs into bracing longitudinal walls or core elements (stairwells, sanitary and ancillary rooms). The latter two cases represent a mixed-style construction involving both box and compartment design methods. An advantage is the quality of the rooms, which open out on the longitudinal flank and result in a fluid transition to the outside. The openness of the external walls, unrestricted by structural requirements, affords a maximum of light and an uninterrupted view from the interior. A special concern in compartment-based buildings is the sound insulation between individual units.

The plate design method ↘ 1c is the design method with the most flexible layout and the largest openings. It is characterised by a free arrangement of angled or linear wall plates, which allow rooms to be freely arranged in different sizes and directions – something that is hardly possible in the comparatively rigid systems of the box or compartment design methods. In this design method, the openings result from the distance between the different wall plates. Of special significance in these constructions are the horizontal structural members, i.e. floors/flat roofs, which have to fulfil complex bracing and load transfer functions (different spans, different bearing conditions, edge pressures at the contact faces etc.).

On the other hand, transfer of the horizontal loads is taken care of by the orthogonal position of the wall plates. As described above, these space and design typologies are often combined. This may be prompted by functional or layout considerations, for example a required polarity between greater privacy and more openness in housing, or by structural considerations such as in the combination of compartment and plate design methods, with box-shaped elements for the transfer of horizontal loads.

1 Construction methods:
a Box method
b Compartment method
c Plate method

2 Structural systems in skeleton construction:

3 Examples of simple structural systems

2

In the skeleton system ↘ **Chapter 3** the vertical load transfer takes place through uprights, posts and transoms using either rigid or flexible joints, depending on the construction details employed. Skeleton systems offer maximum flexibility, transparency and independent loadbearing and enveloping systems. They can be sub-divided into systems that build from the bottom up, are suspended from the top down, or which cantilever. ↘ 2

A number of different grid typologies are in common use and the horizontal slabs are structured in accordance with the design of the walls: longitudinally, transverse, in the form of a loadbearing grid, with point loads etc. In the case of single-storey constructions with a wide span, in which the covering structure is of particular significance, there is a wide range of different skeleton systems including linear types (single field, multiple field, frame, arched girders and grid systems, in the form of loadbearing walls, beams and lattice girders; tensile structures) and shell structure systems (including grids, shell structures and folded plate structures). ↘ 3

TIMBER	STEEL	CONCRETE
Timber joist floor/floor structure h = l/17 b = h/3-h/2 e = 0.7-1.0 m Flat roof structure h = l/16-l/24 b = h/3-h/2 e = 0.7-1.0 m	IPE steel beam Floor structure $h = \sqrt[3]{50 \cdot q \cdot l^2} - 2$ Bending around y-axis	Reinforced concrete upstand/downstand Floor structure Single span beam h = l/8-l/12 b = ≥24 cm
Single span glulam beam / shed structure h = l/17 l = 10-35 m e = 5-7.5 m Multiple span glulam beam h = l/20	Solid web girder, shed structure h = l/20-l/30 l = 3-20 m e = 5-7.5 m	Reinforced concrete floor, with point supports Floor structure h = l/25-l/20
Inverted bowstring glulam beam Shed structure h system = l/12-l/10 h = l/40 l = 5-20 m e = 5-7.5 m	Inverted bowstring steel beam Shed structure h system = l/12 h = ca. l/50-l/35 l = 6-60 m	Hollow prestressed concrete slab Floor structure h = l/35
Lattice girder Shed structure h = l/12-l/15 l = 7.5-60 m e = 4-10 m	Lattice girder Shed structure h = l/10-l/13 l = 8-75 m e = 5-7.5 m	Π-slabs Floor structure h = l/18-l/12 l = max 20 m h ≥ 10 cm Prestressed: h = l/24-l/18
Two-hinged glulam frame h = l/30 h2 = l/20 lk = 15-40 m e = 5-7.5 m	Solid steel frame Shed structure h = l/40-l/30 l = 5-45 m e = 5-7.5 m	Beam-and-slab floor Floor structure h = l/15-l/20 l = 6-14 m
Two-hinged lattice girder frame Shed structure h = l/12 l = 15-40 m e = 4-6 m	Lattice girder frame Shed structure h = l/20-l/10 l = 8-60 m e = 5-7.5 m	Ribbed slab floor Floor structure h = l/15-l/20 l = 6-12 m
Glulam beam grid Shed structure h = l/25-l/18 l = 10-25 m l max/l min = max 1:3	Solid web beam grid Shed structure h = l/35-l/25 l = 10-70 m l max/l min = max 1:3	Waffle slab floor Floor structure h = l/20 l max/l min = max 1:1

In solid construction all three typologies discussed can be combined with each of the four floor types (slab, vaulted, timber beam, proprietary element). Impacts and dependencies arise from the structural limitations and the room formation, and from the method in which rooms are added and laid out, i.e. in the form of vertical spatial arrangements and penetrations, such as arise from circulation and utility functions or spatial requirements. An appropriate floor structure for the box, with a square or slightly rectangular layout, is the two-directional slab with no preferential direction and with linear supports or – exceptionally – point bearings on piers.

With the seminar building (2004) as an extension of Villa Garbald in Castasegna, Miller and Maranta produced a significant example of a box-type design. In view of the orthogonal, polymorphous room layout, they opted for a reinforced concrete structure with a monolithic function comprising horizontal and vertical members.

The bedrooms are arranged around the central circulation core, creating a spiral-shaped room layout with rooms being accessed in sequence as they open out from the core zone. The design largely follows the direct vertical load transfer principle, and thermal heat transfer is reduced through the use of lightweight concrete and internal thermal delay strips. ⌐ 1, 2

By arranging the box-type basic module in an additive manner in one or two directions, it is possible to use the continuous span effect of the floor structure. Another optimisation has been achieved in the cantilever slab, for example.

The box design method is further differentiated by adding rooms in the horizontal and vertical directions. In multi-storey buildings the optimisation of functions, rooms and structures led to the three basic types: the longitudinal wall, transverse wall and cross wall types. ⌐ 3

3a

b

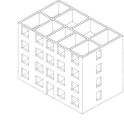

c

1, 2 Restoration and extension of Villa Garbald, Castasegna, 2004, Miller & Maranta, section 1:200

3 Typologies in multi-storey construction:
a Longitudinal wall
b Transverse wall
c Cross wall

1

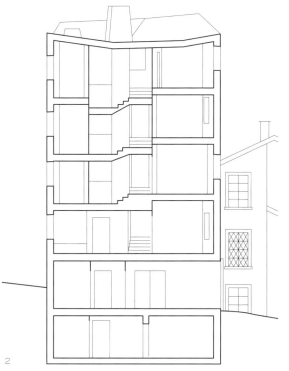

2

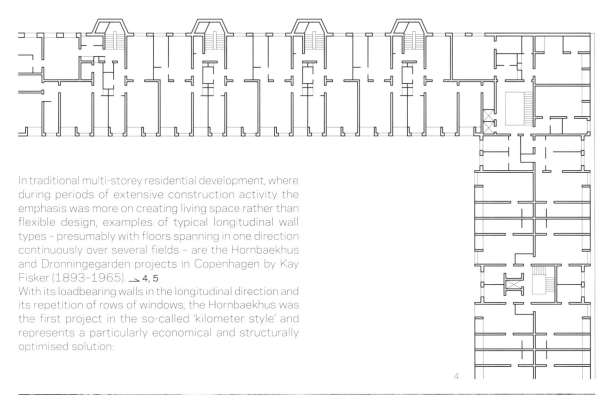

In traditional multi-storey residential development, where during periods of extensive construction activity the emphasis was more on creating living space rather than flexible design, examples of typical longitudinal wall types – presumably with floors spanning in one direction continuously over several fields – are the Hornbaekhus and Dronningegarden projects in Copenhagen by Kay Fisker (1893–1965). ⤳ 4, 5

With its loadbearing walls in the longitudinal direction and its repetition of rows of windows, the Hornbaekhus was the first project in the so-called 'kilometer style' and represents a particularly economical and structurally optimised solution:

4

4, 5 Dronningegarden apartment block, Copenhagen, 1946, Kay Fisker, layout 1:500

5

Due to their thickness, the loadbearing external walls of the longitudinal wall type also possess good physical performance characteristics.

The directional room layout is mirrored in the directional floor construction which spans continuously in one direction across several fields, using beam or proprietary element construction.
With their terraced housing project in Harlaching, Munich (2001), von Seidlein Architekten created a clear example of this structural and room layout concept. The basic structure of the vertical load transfer consists of in-situ concrete plates, without returns or directly connecting transverse walls on the ground floor, which are supplemented by prefabricated components in the terrace area. Horizontal loads in the structural system are transferred via the floor structure and one transverse wall plate which has been placed in the centre of the floor space near the central freestanding core on the ground floor and, respectively, as a connecting wall plate on the upper floor. ↘ 1, 2

In this plate-style construction the irregular arrangement of rooms in two axes results in comparatively complicated bearing geometries and load concentrations. For this reason, structures specifically designed for the different contact loads are more suitable than homogeneous wall constructions. This also applies to the floor constructions, which can be designed in the form of beam or element floors, but preferably would be built in the form of monolithic floor slabs. Reinforced concrete slabs are well suited to the different types of load as they are capable of transferring the various loads within the thickness of the floor when the reinforcement steel is arranged accordingly.

The multi-family dwelling by Christian Kerez at Forsterstraße in Zurich (2003) is a typical, albeit extreme, example of materials and structure being chosen to suit this type of internal layout. ↘ 3-6

1

2

1, 2 Terraced housing, Munich, 2001, von Seidlein Architects.
The clear design using in-situ concrete and prefabricated compartment walls determines the conservative style of the development. The industrial character of the construction method is reflected in the restrained appearance of the terraced houses.
Partial floor plan, 1:500.

4

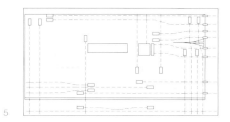

5

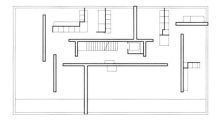

6

3-6 Private residence,
Forsterstrasse, Zurich, 2003,
Christian Kerez.
The design of this multi-unit residential building is unusual. The
'earth-bound' plate system has been
stacked in this case. The structure
is reminiscent of a house of cards
in which the wall plates and the
floor slabs combine to form a clev-
erly balanced system.

Systems with walls as plates are mostly suited to single-
storey applications, close to the ground, but in this case
it has been used over several floors with the wall plates
offset in the different storeys. A sophisticated and elab-
orate spatial and construction concept and an optimised
structural system were prerequisites for this solution,
which allows the transfer of vertical forces through the
available geometric cross sections and which relies on
the wall plates as an integral part of the structure for horizontal and vertical loads. This resulted in a multi-direc-
tional compound support structure consisting of slabs
and plates, which made it possible to use the lower level
for car parking, free of any intermediate uprights. On
close examination, it becomes apparent that this is a special case that does not fit within the categories outlined
above. On the one hand, one can see characteristics of
a monolithic solid construction in the homogeneity of the
materials used and the horizontal and vertical structural
elements; on the other hand, the separation of at least
the outer room envelope from the structure is a typical
characteristic of skeleton construction.

As mentioned above, the regular patterns resulting from
repetitive skeleton construction allow for a wide range
of floor structures. Examples of directional constructions
are either solid, beamed or element floors spanning between girders which can be combined with a directional
rectangular grid of uprights. Examples of non-directional
floors over non-directional square grids are two-direc-
tionally spanning slab floors, possibly in the form of mushroom construction. ➘ Floors p. 130

The freedom of the skeleton construction system allows all conceivable layouts with maximum flexibility ⟶ **1a**, such as in Le Corbusier's design of the Palais des Congrès building in Strasbourg (1964). The combination of vertical and horizontal structural elements is of special significance for the structural stability of a building, particularly so with regard to the transfer of horizontal loads. Together, the vertical and horizontal structures provide the necessary bracing, which is how horizontal forces from wind and other loads are transferred into the ground.

The necessary bracing can only be accomplished with vertical plates or a combination of vertical and horizontal plates. In the former case, vertical plates have to be provided in each storey and in each axis, transversally and longitudinally. In the latter case, the vertical plates can be reduced down to three per storey provided the floor slab is of rigid construction, and further provided that the effective axes of the vertical plates do not cross over at one point. ⟶ **p. 83** Plate- or slab-type structural elements can also be replaced by compound or frame structures, depending on the design concept and choice of material.

1 Layout design options:

a Sketch design illustrating Le Corbusier's plan libre, which offers maximum flexibility and freedom of layout design.

b Sketch design of a standardised skeleton construction which, owing to its repetitive properties, is highly cost-efficient.

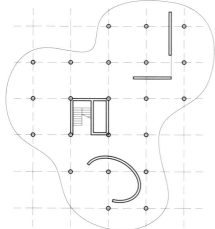

1a

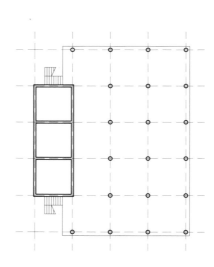

b

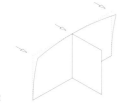    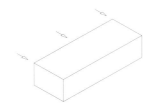

2

2 Acting forces and arrangement
of bracing components:
bracing achieved through the
formation of corners, transverse
walls and floor slabs

3 Bracing options:
a Core bracing in combination
with a floor slab
b Bracing using plates, the force
vectors of which must intersect
at more than one point since otherwise it is not possible to balance
torsion around this point.
c Bracing using bonds

4 Multi-storey bracing:
in higher buildings, bracing must
be provided in the form of rigid
floor slabs and also some rigid wall
plates with a transverse bracing
function. Where the floor slabs cannot perform a bracing function,
transverse walls have to be placed
at shorter intervals. A prerequisite
for maximum slenderness (ratio
between the thickness of a component and its surface) is a structurally effective joint between the wall
plates and floor slabs.

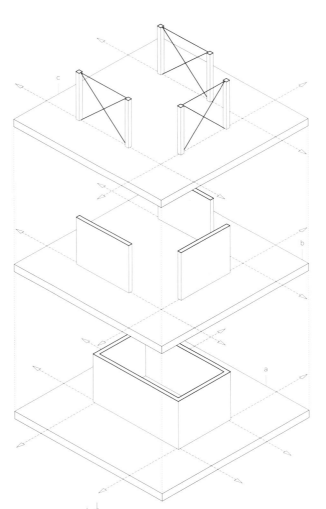

3

 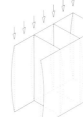  

4

PERFORMANCE PROFILES
AND ECOLOGICAL EFFICIENCY

1

2

3

Decisions as to the choice of material and structural concept are influenced by design considerations such as atmosphere, impression, texture and the tactile and acoustic qualities, as can be seen in the comparison of the different textures of concrete (homogeneous), brickwork (modular) and wood (linear) in terms of colour, depth and weathering/ageing. ↘ 1-3 In addition, the choice of materials and structural systems depends on physical characteristics, such as compressive and tensile strength, thermal conductivity, moisture absorption, sound insulation and fire protection.

In view of the threat of global destruction of the natural world, the increasing threat to the foundation of our lifestyle and, with a view to the context of nature, mankind and the environment, the performance profiles of materials and construction systems should be increasingly considered from the point of view of sustainability. Materials and construction systems should be examined to ascertain to what extent they are part of a natural cycle in respect of their production, transport, processing, use and ageing. It is also important to consider whether materials are available locally (i.e. the degree of transport involved) and whether they can be renewed naturally, as is the case with timber and clay. Before elaborating on the available combinations of materials for the purpose of detailed and structural design, we will consider how much the necessary ecological evaluation of a material affects the respective design decision.

Wood is known for its anisotropy, which results from the natural qualities of the material. Its cellular structure – with a bundled, linear organisation – results in a directional physical characteristic: for normal forces, solid timber is strongest in the direction of the fibres, which transfer compression and tension, while in the transverse direction it can only absorb a fraction of these forces. This mono-directional structural characteristic of solid timber and its differentiated deformation behaviour have led to the development of a multitude of wood-based materials, which are produced from shaved, sawn or chipped timber with the help of chemical or mechanical bonding. In terms of architectural expression and the formation of enclosed spaces, this structure reflects the development from linear to two-dimensional elements, and from skeleton to wall panel construction. In terms of ecology, timber has a positive performance profile: in its growing process timber binds CO_2, and it is eminently suitable for recycling due to reversible jointing methods.

1 Florist's kiosk, Malmö, 1969,
Sigurd Lewerentz

2 St. Peter, Klippan, 1963,
Sigurd Lewerentz

3 Kastrup Sea Bath, Copenhagen,
2005, White Arkitekter

4–6 Haus Rauch, Schlins, 2008,
Boltshauser Architekten, Martin
Rauch. The three-storey house
is built of rammed clay, which was
dug from the construction site.
Isometric 1:500

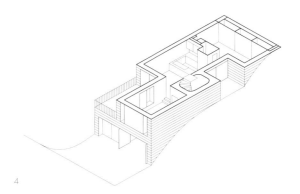

4

A good example is the Palais de l'Equilibre from the Swiss National Exposition in Neuenburg (Expo.02), by Hervé Dessimoz, which housed an exhibition on the subject of sustainable development. The choice of material for this project was a logical reflection of the aim of the exhibition. The choice of timber did not just demonstrate its importance as a renewable building material for the purpose of sustainable concepts. By using the Douglas fir boards from Peter Zumthor's Swiss pavilion for the 2000 World Expo in Hanover, it was possible to demonstrate the timber's quality as a re-usable material. Overall, solid timber and wood-based materials from Douglas fir, spruce and fir was used; the total amount of raw timber consumed (2,500 m³) grows back in the Swiss forest in less than three hours.

Clay building materials, being a mixture of clay, sand and silt, have an isotropic structure, which means that loads are transferred non-directionally. Generally speaking, clay is used as an infill material – as in traditional timber-frame construction – but is also used in combination with brickwork and concrete structures. Used as a homogeneous material in loadbearing walls, it is primarily limited to low-rise buildings. ⟶ 4-6

Compared to solid wall construction materials such as bricks or aerated concrete blocks, clay has excellent heat-storage and moisture-absorption properties. Due to its capillary action, clay provides good conditions for vapour diffusion with the result that it is not prone to dampness problems, even if condensate forms within the wall section. Clay has an excellent eco-balance: the raw material is available in sufficient quantity and it does not give off hazardous emissions during its collection, processing, transport and use. A special aspect of clay construction is the fact that it is suitable for DIY application, can be very easily recycled and is easy to maintain.

5

6

Steel is the most important construction metal; it has many uses, and in structural systems is often found in hot or cold-formed steel profiles and sheets, as well as reinforcement in combination with concrete, timber or brick constructions. It is also used in fittings and fasteners, for example in timber construction. In many applications, steel is indispensable owing to its outstanding structural strength. Structural systems based on steel are normally prefabricated to a large degree, do not involve any wet trades, are relatively lightweight compared to the building volume and allow a high degree of flexibility in the design of layouts and building envelopes. ⌐1
High thermal conductance is one of steel's notable physical properties. Steel needs to be protected against corrosion; this can be achieved with measures such as coating or hot-galvanising, or by adopting construction details at an early stage in the design process that inherently protect the material against corrosion. Structural steel components must be protected against the impact of excessive heat from fire: through coating, lining or encasing. In contrast to its outstanding structural performance characteristics, steel has a rather more problematic eco-balance: its mining, production and processing is associated with hazardous emissions and requires a high energy input.

Iron ore as the raw material for steel production is subject to ever more increasing geo-political competition for the natural deposits and is finite as a mineral resource. This means that the recycling of building components and semi-finished products is becoming increasingly important in both demolition and new construction: it is therefore necessary to consider the material's service life, recyclability and degree of prefabrication at an early stage in the design process.

The description of these three materials' properties as examples illustrates, in a general sense, which factors should be considered in the assessment of materials. Their technical characteristics have been included in a number of life cycle assessment models that indicate the respective performance profile: one of these establishes the PEI indicator for primary energy consumption, which takes into account the energy input required for mining, production, processing and transport, differentiated by renewable and non-renewable energy sources. Another model assesses the various impacts on climate and the environment, quantifying the contributions to the greenhouse effect, to the reduction in the ozone layer, to the increase in mining waste, to eutrophication (excess of fertiliser) and to summer smog. ⌐2

1 Contemporary steel structure: the Lausitzer Seenland landmark, Senftenberg, 2008, Stefan Giers

2 Table: Performance profile and eco-balance of walls according to Hegger et al., *Energy Manual*

3 Table: Data for floor slabs according to Hegger et al., *Construction Materials Manual*

4 Refurbishment of Liebfrauen Church, project, Duisburg, 2010, Hannes Hermanns and Susanne Klösges. Energy consultant: Günter Pfeifer. The dilapidated facade was replaced by an all-round air-collector facade made of polycarbonate sheeting. By collecting the solar radiation energy on all sides of the building, a warm 'airbag' is created. The existing reinforced concrete structure is used as storage mass.

1

Wall per m² Construction in layers	Primary energy content Primary energy not renewable [MJ]	Primary energy content Primary energy renewable [MJ]	Global warming potential Greenhouse gases [kg CO₂eq]	Durability [a]
Solid walls				
Reinforced concrete	650	83	45	70-100
Reinforced concrete C25/35				
2% steel content (FE 360 B), 200 mm				
Clay block	96	1.2	4.2	70-90
Clay block, air-dried, p=1.400kg/m³, 240 mm				
Clay mortar				
Aerated concrete block	410	14	65	70-90
Aerated concrete block (PPW 4-0.6 NuF), 240 mm				
Masonry mortar MG III				
Pumice light-weight block	247	5.1	26	80-90
Pumice light-weight block (VBL 2), 240 mm				
Masonry mortar MG III				
Calcium silicate brick	517	14	56	90-100
Calcium silicate brick (KSL 12/1.4), 240 mm				
Masonry mortar MG II				
Gypsum plank	186	25	8.9	90
Gypsum plank, 100 mm				
Gypsum mortar MG IV				

2

With regard to the sustainability of the materials selected, it is important to consider the energy consumption resulting from the choice of material not only at the construction stage, but throughout the life-cycle of the building. This means that the energy required for obtaining the raw materials and producing the construction materials should be balanced against the accumulated gain (thermal and sound insulation, energy storage) throughout the use phase of a building. In addition to the individual building materials used, it is also necessary to assess the building and its construction as a whole. Some building component catalogues provide an assessment of the compound effect of the various components in construction elements, for example the floor construction in a building. ⟶ 3

When taking into account the energy-related impact of the combination of materials to form building elements of several layers, two tendencies become apparent: firstly, that of integrating active components into the non-loadbearing building envelope and secondly, that of linking materials and construction details in a dynamic sense. An example is the cybernetic approach of Günter Pfeifer and Siegfried Delzer, who aim to provide documentary evidence of the optimisation of energy efficiency in their projects on the basis of experimental, dynamic models. ⟶ 4

As mentioned above, in addition to an assessment of the material and structural qualities, it is important to consider the whole life-cycle of a project. In respect of the durability of materials and their service life, it is necessary to investigate whether reversibility and certain methods of construction make disassembly and recycling possible, and to what extent the different life-cycles of the construction elements have to be taken into account.

Consequently, it is not only important to choose the right material, but also to consider how that material is used within the context of the overall construction. In an ideal case, one could envisage a closed biological material cycle, from mining via processing through to recycling, as an effective ecological process in the cradle-to-cradle sense (Michael Braungart).
In this necessarily sketchy discussion, a wide spectrum of possibilities emerges – in close connection with the design process – for developing sustainable solutions for structural systems which are based on the performance profiles of the materials used.

4

Floor construction system	Common height [mm]	Weight density [kg/m³]	Thermal transmission resistance [m²k/W]	Water vapour diffusion resistance [-]	Contribution to sound insulation	Common span, single span beam [m]	Directional	Non-directional	Cantilever option	Formwork required
Solid floors										
Reinforced concrete floor	120-180	290-440	0.05-0.08	80/130	80/130	6-9		•	two-directional	•
Trapezoidal sheet metal floor	120-320	270-375	0.05-0.08	≥100000	≥100000	2-5.8	•		one-directional	
Ribbed concrete floor	187.5-500	180-430	0.03-0.05	70/150	70/150	6-12	•		two-directional	•
Beam-and-slab floor	350-900	280-620	0.03-0.05	70/150	70/150	≤14	•			•
Hollow slab floor	120-400	210-580	0.67-0.77	5/10	5/10	8-11.5	•			
Hollow pot floor	90-290	125-470	0.13-0.36	5/10	5/10	≤6.5	•			
Timber floors										
Reinforced concrete floor	140-200	120-180	0.61-0.71	2	2	4-6.5	•		one-directional	
Trapezoidal sheet metal floor	120-216	85-155	0.71-1.18	90/220	90/220	≤6	•		one-directional	
Ribbed concrete floor	120-320	40-90	0.46-0.74	5	5	6-10	•		one-directional	

3

STRUCTURAL PRINCIPLES

Skeleton construction is a construction system that, although self-contained, is not found very often in contemporary architecture. Most buildings are built using combined construction methods with a fluent transition between wall and skeleton construction. Nevertheless, it is necessary to illustrate the principle of 'pure' structural systems in order to understand the different principles of the various construction methods.

Wide-spanning constructions, such as those used in hangar-type buildings or sports and leisure centres, are regarded as typical examples of skeleton construction to this day, as are large spaces without columns in industrial and commercial premises or places of assembly. Skeleton construction offers advantages particularly for high buildings with a limited footprint, as in the tower blocks owing to their small dead load and good flexibility in the layout design, while in residential construction with small floor spans, it is of less importance. The possibility of omitting internal partition walls entirely and of modifying entire floors to accommodate changes in user requirements at subsequent stages has led to the popularity of skeleton construction in office development.

Owing to its lightweight character, skeleton construction lacks the mass that is inherent in wall construction, and hence the heat storage capacity, which has to be re-introduced through additional layers in order to achieve a more favourable energy performance. Buildings designed in skeleton construction require a high degree of design discipline, as they involve complex systems that follow a strict logic. This means that the building will be determined by the details – more so than in wall construction. Skeleton construction forces the designer to think in terms of systems, orders and hierarchies. ↘1

The jointing methods typical of skeleton construction and the specific economic constraints of the use of materials led people to consider possible ways of reducing construction time and costs through prefabrication. This marks the beginning of prefabrication in skeleton construction, which today seems to be an irreplaceable part of commercial construction. For economic reasons and prompted by a complex design process, most new buildings today are built with a combination of skeleton and wall construction methods.

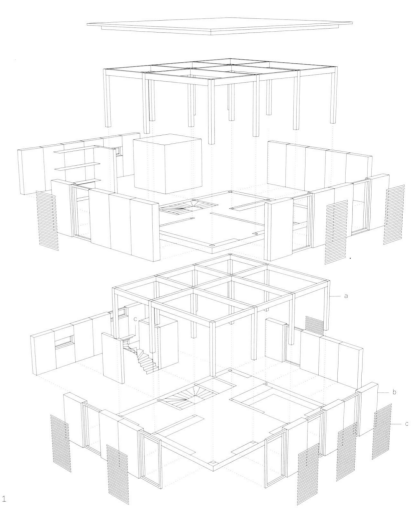

1

Skeleton construction employs a range of different structural systems. Buildings with a multi-cell room structure, usually over several floors, require different structural systems than do single-storey buildings with large open spans. While the latter often benefit from a simple horizontal structure with a wide span and are less constrained by requirements for sound insulation and fire safety, multi-storey buildings need upright supports at closer intervals in order to support the heavy weight of solid floor systems, which are required to provide the necessary separation between floors of office and residential buildings. What both systems have in common are the basic principles of separating the structure into individual elements and of separating the loadbearing structure from the building envelope. In multi-storey construction, a distinction is made between standing, suspended and cantilever systems.

1 Skeleton construction principle, separate primary system:

a Structure

and secondary systems:

b Envelope
c Fitting-out

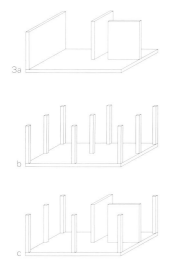

3a

b

c

4a

b

Most common are standing systems ⟶ 2a in which loads are transferred to the foundations via girders and uprights. In suspended systems ⟶ 2b the outer uprights of the standing system, which are mostly exposed to compression, are omitted and replaced by tensile members, the loads of which are transferred to the foundations via a solid core. Building a suspended structure is comparatively costly and only makes sense when it is intended to keep the ground floor zone free of uprights. In cantilever systems ⟶ 2c the floor beams are connected to the core in a rigid manner. The advantage of this is that there are no loadbearing elements in the facade. Because cantilever beams are subject to deformation, the facade connection details have to be flexible enough to allow for some movement.

All parts of a building are, in some form, part of the structural system and transfer loads and forces. A skeleton, which may consist of strut-like loadbearing elements, such as uprights and girders and superimposed roof or floor plates, not only has to transfer loads and forces in the vertical plane, but also has to keep the structure stable against the impact of horizontal forces.
For this reason, all forces and loads are initially collected in the horizontal plane using a system of beams (as a plate) and then concentrated in the vertical plane on individual struts (upright supports), which transfer the loads

to the foundations. In such a system, walls – or uprights linked in with such walls – are needed as non-loadbearing partition walls, facades or for bracing. The horizontal loadbearing members either consist of a hierarchically joined system of individual strut-like elements (beams) or of a solid plate (floor slab) which combines a number of different structural functions. This results in the distinction between the 'post-and-lintel' and 'column and slab' systems. ⟶ 4

The system can be further differentiated into longitudinal and transverse beam systems as well as into primary and secondary beam systems. Depending on the requirements, beams may span single or multiple fields; in the case of large-span buildings there are often frames that may be composed of individual elements, as in frame construction. Where a horizontal frame has a rigid connection with upright supports, these supports have to be able to withstand additional bending moments. In a so-called 'beam grid', longitudinal and transverse beams cross each other in the same plane. They are rigidly connected at the cross-over points and therefore transfer the loads in two directions. In these systems, the forces are transferred into the foundations at certain points, rather than (as in wall construction) along a line. This means that the uprights are particularly important as vertical loadbearing members in a skeleton construction.

2 Skeleton systems:
a Standing system
(Seagram Building, New York, 1958,
Ludwig Mies van der Rohe)
b Suspended system
(BMW tower, Munich, 1972,
Karl Schwanzer)
c Cantilevered system
(German pavilion, Brussels World
Fair 1958, Egon Eiermann,
Sep Ruf)

3 Skeleton construction typologies, without bracing elements:
a Plate construction method
(individual loadbearing wall plates)
b Pure skeleton construction
method (loadbearing columns)
c Combined skeleton construction
method (columns and wall plates)

4 Skeleton construction systems:
a Column-slab system
b Column-beam system

2a

b

c

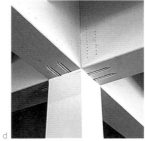

1a   b   c   d

1 The node detail reflects the order of the entire construction:
a Diagram of a node, independent of material
b Steel node, bolted
c In-situ concrete node, poured
d Timber node with steel metal plates

2 Structural systems:
a Directional structure
b Non-directional structure

The transition between a horizontal and vertical load-bearing member (i.e. the connection between beam and upright) is called the 'node'. The node identifies the place at which the floor loads are transferred into the uprights, from where they are then vertically transferred to the foundations. The grid of uprights determines the layout of the skeleton building. The node detail reflects the order of the entire construction.

The ideal diagram of a node consists of a three-dimensional structure of beams and uprights ⌐ 1a, the force vectors of which cross over or intersect.

Such nodes in the same plane are often associated with costly installation details, as can be illustrated by a comparison of the three materials: steel, reinforced concrete and wood ⌐ 1b-d. Only in in-situ concrete construction is it possible to achieve such a node, involving all components in the same plane, without additional costs. In steel construction, additional elements are needed, such as head and foot plates and welded fillets, in order to achieve satisfactory load transfer from the upper upright through the beam to the lower upright. Although it is possible to achieve nodes in timber that resemble intersections, these nodes are not capable of transferring moments without additional devices such as steel angles or bracing elements. On the other hand, the double joist system shown on ⌐ p. 74 is very suitable for timber construction and can also be employed with other materials. Nodes in two planes are easier to achieve in terms of detailing and, in their additive manner, suit the nature of prefabricated components and semi-finished products.

In this context, the foot of an upright – which is at the transition point of the structure to the foundation – is of special importance. The non-rigid foot of an upright is able to accommodate movement of the structure without transferring this into the foundations. By contrast, the fixed foot of an upright will transfer movement of the structure into the foundations. In order to understand the loadbearing principle of skeleton construction, one has to follow the force vectors, from the floors via the beams and uprights through to the foundations. Certain areas of the structure are designated as load fields, and loadbearing beams have to be distinguished as primary and secondary beams, edge and field beams. Some uprights will carry greater loads than others because their area of loading is greater. The deflection in one load field can be used to lessen the load in an adjoining field. The height of the joists or beams is largely determined by the size of the areas of loading they support.

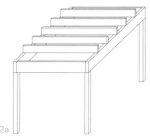

2a

Generally speaking, a distinction is made between directional and non-directional structures. However, this question is rarely raised in practice because with non-directional structures, connections are required in both loadbearing directions. This is significantly more costly than when the connections are required in just one loadbearing direction. The construction of identical facades on all sides and extensions in either direction is possible with a non-directional square grid. Space frame systems and loadbearing grids are usually non-directional structures. ⌐ 2a A directional structure is based on a rectangular grid and can only be extended on an uneven basis: the facades are different at the shorter and longer sides of the rectangle. Most buildings with a large span are constructed using a directional structure. ⌐ 2b

b

Skeleton buildings can be constructed with any material that is capable of absorbing both tensile and compressive forces at the same time. The most important of these building materials are timber, steel and reinforced concrete. Semi-finished products and prefabricated components are particularly suitable for skeleton construction because of the latter's additive structure. Compared to monolithic wall construction, the advantages of skeleton buildings based on steel and reinforced concrete mostly become apparent in multi-storey buildings.

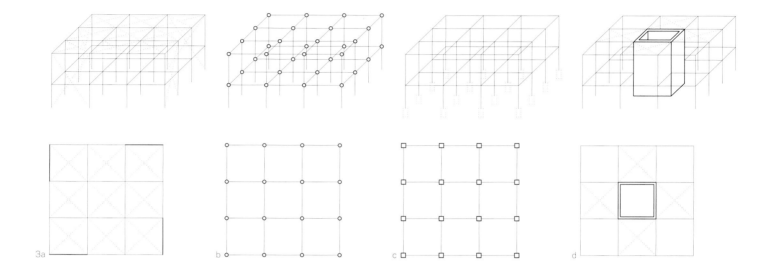

3 Bracing methods:
a Bracing with diagonal crosses
b Bracing with rigid nodes
c Bracing with restrained columns
d Bracing with a central solid
building core

The fact that the room-enclosing elements are independent of the structure affords greater flexibility in the layout, and hence also in later changes to the room layout. At the same time, a loadbearing structure that is reduced to point loads has much reduced own loads and construction volume, and can therefore support a greater number of floors. By comparison, timber as a construction material – which for centuries has dominated the structural system of most skeleton buildings – is of secondary importance in current housing construction. This is due to the natural limits of this organic material, particularly its absolute loadbearing capacity, form stability and durability. In regional construction methods, it is only recently that timber – as a sustainable material – has been able to demonstrate its structural potential for larger skeleton buildings through the development of modern wood-based materials. ⌐ **Timber Construction p. 116**

BRACING

In order to ensure that a building is stable under load, it is necessary that its structural system be suitably braced. The skeleton structure has to remain stable and retain its form when exposed to horizontal forces such as wind loads.

A number of systems are commonly applied, often in combination: cross-bracing in the facade ⌐ **3a**, for example building walls or floors in the form of a plate, rigid detailing of nodes ⌐ **3b** or the restraining or fixing of columns ⌐ **3c**, or the provision of a solid core to the building ⌐ **3d**. It is important to ensure that such a skeleton structure is braced in both horizontal directions, as well as vertically i.e. in three planes in total.

In order to achieve a sufficiently rigid skeleton construction without additional components, it is necessary either to restrain the uprights at their base or to construct rigid nodes. These two systems can be called a 'restrained or fixed upright' (with flexibly connected beam) and a 'frame' (with a rigid corner and flexible bearing). For commercial reasons – and also in order to avoid deformation problems – these systems are mostly limited to one and two-storey large-span buildings.

The rigidity of multi-storey buildings is mostly achieved through core structures such as stairwells, lift shafts, service ducts and sanitary zones. Solid floors can also be used for bracing purposes, absorbing horizontal forces and transferring these to the core. These floors may be cantilevering out from the building core and be vertically supported with flexible bearings at the periphery. In contrast to the other bracing systems, a core used as bracing also provides some of the space needed for the building's functions. Another option for bracing skeleton structures is to place wall plates outside, or within, the construction plane. These vertical plates can be constructed either in solid materials or as a frame (with diagonal bracing). The axes of vertical plates on plan must not cross over at one point, and all horizontal forces acting on the building must be securely transferred into these plates and from there into the foundations, without deformation of the overall structure. In practice, peripheral bracing requires floor plates and wind bracing in several planes. ⌐ **p. 27**

GRID SYSTEMS

Much more so than in wall construction, skeleton construction is determined by a grid measuring system. A distinction is made between those dimensions that define the different parts of a building and dimensions that are determined by the characteristics of the construction material or its transport or processing.

The grid is a virtual spatial/geometric coordinate system which fixes the position of points, lines, areas and volumes in space. A grid represents a uniform sequence of identical spacing: so-called 'intervals', which are based on a module dimension or its multiples. The basic module determines the visual and structural order of the building. A distinction is made between the construction grid and the fit-out grid, which is also called the use or installation grid. The geometric position of the vertical part of the structure, the uprights, is determined via intersections and construction axes. The fitting-out axes define the geometric locations at which the dividing walls within the building are to be placed. As such they also define the points where these dividing walls can be connected with the facade. Beyond that, the fitting-out grid defines the dimensions of the ceiling and lighting elements, services lines, air-conditioning systems and ventilation, through to furnishing details.

When several grids are superimposed, a distinction is made between the primary and secondary grids.

The construction grid is called the primary grid and the fitting-out grid, the secondary grid. By separating the grid systems it is possible to avoid complicated nodes and to create regular fitting-out dimensions for facade divisions. It is common practice for the construction grid to be a multiple of the fitting-out grid. The size of the grid, the distance between the axes, depends on the function of the building. In office buildings for example, the grid axes are determined by the width of a single office. For the geometric relationship between construction and fitting-out grids, three patterns have developed. When structural and fitting-out axes are identical – albeit with the structural grid spaced at a multiple of the fit-out grid – the upright is placed centrally on the construction axis. This means that the entire fit-out has to adjust to the shell construction with all its inadequacies and tolerances.

If one wants to be free from the dimensional restrictions of the shell, the construction and fitting-out axes have to be offset. This method has become the preferred solution for the industrial prefabrication of facades and fitting-out elements. The introduction of a modular grid, which assigns a dedicated 'strip' to the uprights, can result in interior rooms of different widths. The strip will become apparent in the interior, for example in the dimensions of a suspended ceiling, as well as in the facade.

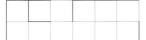

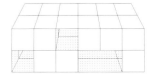

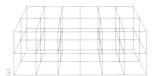

1–3 Working with a grid as a design
principle: Beroun House, 2003,
HSH Architects

4 Structure and envelope:
a Structure behind the facade
b Structure in the facade plane
c Structure in front of the facade

5 Historical example of a corner
conflict: corner detail of inner
courtyard at Palazzo Medici-
Riccardi, Florence, 1444,
Michelozzo di Bartolommeo

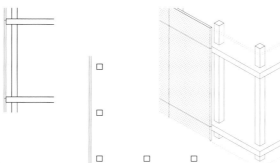

4a

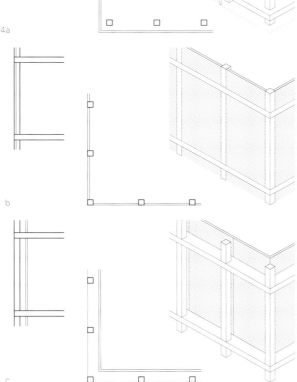

b

c

5

The geometry of a skeleton building is determined by the position of the uprights, which may be placed behind the facade, or within the plane of the facade, or in front of the facade.

Most frequently, the uprights are placed on the warm side, i.e. behind the facade ⌄ 4a. This ensures that there will be no undesirable cold bridges. The facade envelops the entire structure. The insulation is placed within the plane of the facade. By placing the uprights within the interior, the use of the interior space is restricted. This can be avoided if the uprights are positioned within the facade plane ⌄ 4b. In that case, different construction details have to be used for the connection points, and the building's physical performance characteristics are different. Structural components on the outside have to be encased in insulation, thereby losing their material appearance and usually their slender proportions. In addition, the joints at the connections between facade and upright must be able to accommodate the differential movement of the various components. If the upright is placed in front of the facade ⌄ 4c, the structural system becomes visible from the outside. Where structural members penetrate the facade it is possible that cold bridges are created which, like differential movement due to temperature fluctuations, are difficult to deal with. The material of the facade, the way in which it is used and how it relates to the loadbearing structure – all these factors give the building its unique appearance. However, it is not sufficient to perceive the outside wall – in its geometric relationship to the construction and fitting-out axes – as a linear edge. It is part of a three-dimensional structure with projections and recesses, and internal and external corners, and thus demands more comprehensive consideration.

Hitherto, geometric pattern systems were often based on the idealised notion that a building component is equivalent to a line. However, each building component has its own dimension. This becomes particularly apparent when considering the corner of a facade. From our discussion of the geometric restraints of the facade, it is clear that corners require specific attention. In terms of construction, a distinction has to be made between the internal and external corners of a building. Since only square grids allow identical connections in each direction and in practice rectangular grids are used much more frequently, the 'corner conflict' of grid buildings is a recurring theme in the history of buildings, from Doric temples through to classic Modernism. ⌄ 5

STEEL CONSTRUCTION

CHARACTERISTICS

Steel achieves extremely good performance with relatively little material. This results in the small dimensions and the material efficiency of steel constructions.

The word metal (from the Greek 'metallon' – mine) refers to the class of chemical elements whose atoms combine to form a crystalline structure with free electrodes. This particular combination results in physical properties such as high density and strength, electrical conductivity, magnetic behaviour and the high melting point. Depending on the composition, they occur as pure metals – consisting solely of the atoms of the chemical element – or alloys – mixtures of different elements. Even small proportions of different chemical substances change the material properties of alloys, which thus can be modified to meet a wide range of requirements.

A special aspect of metals is their plastic deformation under great stress, known as the 'yield effect'. When (brittle) raw iron is processed to make (elastic) steel, the carbon, silicon, phosphorus and manganese elements contained in the iron ore are oxidised. Therefore when iron ore is smelted in a blast furnace, its carbon content has to be reduced from 4 % to below 2 % in order to achieve the malleability of steel. This oxidation process is referred to as refining. Iron compounds with a proportion of more than 2 % carbon are classified as cast iron and cannot be forged. The term steel only refers to those types of iron which can be forged or rolled. Construction steel, for example, only contains about 0.2 % carbon, because its weldability would otherwise be negatively affected.

MANUFACTURING

In nature, iron only occurs as iron ore, so the extraction of raw iron starts with the processing of this iron ore. Beginning about 1500 BC – the start of the Iron Age – lumps of iron were extracted using charcoal fires in clay pits. In the late Middle Ages, people finally succeeded in melting raw iron from the iron ore using early blast furnaces and in processing it to forging-grade steel. The industrial production of steel began in England in 1742, with the crucible melting process. Initially the fuel used was charcoal, but this was gradually replaced by coal. In 1783, steel production was further developed with the puddling process, which is used to refine raw iron in blast furnaces, and finally, in the mid-nineteenth century, the development of large-scale industrial production processes began. From 1855, the Bessemer converter – a ventilated container used for refining raw iron low in phosphorus and sulphur – was used to produce steel free of carbon and sulphur, known as Bessemer steel. A few years later, the Siemens-Martin process was the first technical open-hearth refining process; it allowed the re-processing of scrap metal in a regenerative furnace using higher furnace temperatures. This was followed, in 1879, by the Gilchrist-Thomas process, a development of the acid-converter process, which could also be used to economically process raw iron containing phosphorus into steel. At the end of the nineteenth century, the rolling process for the manufacture of profiles was developed, which is still in use today. Finally, in the twentieth century, many blast furnaces were converted to electric arc or induction furnaces. With the development of oxygen metallurgy it was possible to further improve these processes. Although in a technological sense this new high-performance material is no longer a primary construction material – such as stone or wood – steel, as opposed to the reinforced concrete developed later, is still a homogeneous material used in construction.

1a   b   c   d

1 Production of steel profiles:

a Plate prior to rolling
b Cutting steel joists to length
c Process of hot-rolling an I-profile
d Steel joist after cutting

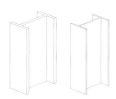

IPE PROFILES:
Owing to their rectangular cross section, IPE profiles are particularly suitable as beams; their narrow flanges indicate low buckling resistance.

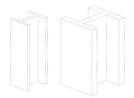

HE PROFILES:
The projection areas of HE profiles are square and, with their wide flanges, have a high buckling resistance in both directions; they are therefore particularly suitable for use as uprights.

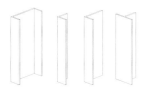

ANGLE PROFILES:
Angle profiles (U, L and T) are suitable for the construction of compound structural members.

HOLLOW PROFILES:
Hollow profiles have high buckling resistance but only limited loadbearing capacity. They are produced in various wall thicknesses; this means that, with the same outside diameter, it is possible to support different loads in a building.

SOLID PROFILES:
Solid profiles are suitable for transferring large vertical loads but, owing to their heavy weight and high price, they are used rather rarely. The fire resistance of these profiles is high.

STEEL GRADES AND PROFILES

In building construction, two main types of steel are used, which are referred to as general construction steels (S235 and S255) and weather-resistant steels.

In addition, there are high-strength, close-grained, construction steels and special steels for fasteners, cables and wires. Steel is available as typified elements in different forms, sizes and profiles. The individual elements are referred to as semi-finished products. These profiles – which are produced in rolling mills – facilitate precise and dimensionally correct processing. Modern skeleton construction started with the industrially standardised production of rolled profiles. Steel profiles are divided into section steel (I, U and Z), bar steel (T, L and solid), hollow (tubular) sections and steel sheeting. It is therefore the engineer's and architect's task – taking into account these serially produced semi-finished products and combinations thereof – to design a building structure; the link between contextual and detailed design will always be particularly apparent in steel construction.

Round steel bar

Square steel bar

Flat steel bar

U-channel

Leg angle, equal

Leg angle, unequal

T-bar

U-section: U80 to U400

I-section: IPE-80 to IPE 600

Wide flange (H) sections:
HE-A 100 to HE A 1000

HE-B 100 to HE-B 1000

HE-M 100 to HE-M 1000

Rectangular hollow section

Circular hollow section

CORROSION PROTECTION

The corrosion of steel is caused by moisture on the surface of building components. At a relative humidity of about 65%, which is about average inside buildings, corrosion is of minor importance; nevertheless, steel components should be protected. By contrast, it is imperative that externally used steel components are protected against corrosion. Contact corrosion can be a serious problem and occurs under the influence of electrolytes, such as water, where different kinds of metal are in contact. In such a case, the less precious metal will decompose; when non-ferrous metals are used, it is therefore important to take the potential of the electrochemical series into account. A distinction is made between active and passive corrosion protection, and there are five different corrosion protection classes. Active protection measures involve designs in which the component offers the minimum amount of surface area to corrosive attack, e.g. by placing the component in a protected position, or by purposefully sacrificing a less precious metal, which has been attached to the component in an electrically conducting manner. Passive measures are applied to the surfaces of the components. The simplest form of corrosion protection is the production of an alloy; in the case of steel, another element is added to refine the steel quality and thus make further protective measures unnecessary. Typical examples are non-rusting steels which are also known as stainless steels; they have a very dense molecular structure and form a protective layer which renews itself if damaged. ➔1

Typical fields of application are concealed structural elements, such as the wall ties used to tie face brickwork to the wall, or external railing constructions exposed to the weather. However, stainless steel is difficult to process and also more costly than normal steel; for these reasons its field of application is limited. There is also a special alloy amongst the group of special weather-resistant steels that creates its own corrosion protection: COR-TEN steel. ➔2 With this type of steel, a layer of rust forms on the surface which, after a few weeks, becomes a durable means of protection against corrosion. The most important group of passive corrosion protection systems are paint or plastic coatings. What they have in common is that they are all applied in several steps: depending on the corrosion protection class, one or several top coats are applied to the priming coat, which is designed to prevent the actual corrosion process. This coating must not be damaged by drilling or fasteners during the installation of the components; if this cannot be avoided, the damaged areas have to be re-treated. For the protection of steel components during storage, production and transport in the factory, it is common practice to apply an installation coating beforehand. Fire protection coatings are also suitable as corrosion protection. The best protection duration can be achieved with so-called Duplex systems, which consist of hot-galvanising with subsequently applied coatings.

1   Stainless steel facade:
Residence, Dornbirn, 2005,
Oskar Kaufmann.

2   COR-TEN steel facade:
Jakob-Kemenate, Brunswick,
2007, O. M. Architects.

3 Fire protection of steel profiles:
a Cladding with mesh and plaster
b Encasing with board material
c Cladding with prefabricated
components
d Encasing with concrete and
pumice

4 Cage elements are used to
thermally separate building
components and reduce thermal
bridging.

3a   b   c   d

4

FIRE PROTECTION

Like concrete, steel belongs to construction material class A1, which indicates that it is not combustible and does not propagate fire. However, at temperatures above 400 °C, steel loses its loadbearing strength and from about 500 °C, it also loses its form stability. For this reason, and as a precaution in the event of fire, it needs to be encased by another material. As a general principle, any loadbearing steel construction extending to more than one storey must be protected against the effect of fire. The heating up of steel components must be sufficiently delayed through suitable measures so that the temperature at which the structure fails is not reached until after the period defined as the fire-resistance duration has expired.

In the aesthetic assessment of steel skeleton structures, building fire protection plays an important role, because the slender appearance of steel profiles can only be retained when these components remain un-encased. Fire protection measures in steel construction are divided into encasing, lining and coating. Under certain conditions it is possible to omit direct fire protection at the component and to secure the structural stability of the building through appropriate extinguishing systems, such as a sprinkler system. Other common shielding measures for unprotected steel components are, for example, suitably constructed floors or walls, which prevent the steel from being exposed to the direct impact of heat. A suitable protection measure must be selected depending on the fire resistance class applicable to the respective steel component. Encasing can consist of spray plaster or spray concrete applied locally, often with mineral fibre additives. Linings consist of box or profile elements made of plasterboard or gypsum fibre board, as well as special

fire protection board made of composite materials. Both encasings and linings will completely conceal the members of the steel construction. Although it is possible to line a steel component with fire-protection board to replicate its shape – albeit in a larger form – the typical slenderness of the construction is lost. Coatings that form an insulation layer are considered to be most appropriate for steel constructions.

These coatings consist of brush applications or foils which – in the case of a fire at temperatures of around 200 to 300 °C – will foam up and prevent the direct exposure of the steel component to the flames. Coated steel components can be recognised by their unusually rough, markedly brushed surfaces.

THERMAL INSULATION

Like most metals, steel is a good thermal conductor, which is why unwanted thermal bridging is a common occurrence. On the one hand this leads to the loss of heat and, on the other hand, it is possible that the cold steel surface attracts condensation and in consequence suffers corrosion damage. Occasionally there are cases where, for example, a steel girder penetrates the facade and forms such a small proportion of the total building envelope that it appears negligible from the point of view of thermal insulation. In such a case it is important, however, to ensure the adequate ventilation of that component. It is also possible – similar to construction detailing for reinforced concrete – to install insulation strips as thermal breaks for the structural steel components that penetrate the external envelope. As a general principle, steel structures should – wherever possible – be located completely within the controlled environment, i.e. within the building envelope.

STEEL GIRDERS

Solid web girders
Consist of rolled profiles most commonly IPE and more rarely IPB, with parallel flanges (also as IPBl in lightweight and IPBv in reinforced version).

Cellular girders
With holes punched out of the web, have the advantage of reduced weight and make it possible to insert services installations in the plane of the girders.

Castellated girders
Are produced by welding together IPE or HE profiles with trapezoidal cut-outs.

Lattice girders
Can be composed of a number of different rolled or hollow profiles and are suitable for large spans. They can be built with large vertical girder dimensions with relatively little material and allow unimpeded services installations.

Inverted bowstring girders
Are suitable for large spans and reflect the shape of the force vectors. The relatively strong upper chord transfers compressive forces while the slender lower chord absorbs tensile forces and can also be constructed with a cable.

Vierendeel girders
Consist of series of square frames which are loadbearing solely owing to the rigidity of their chords and struts; as the openings can be very large, these girders can also be dimensioned at the full height of a storey.

1 Profiles of upright support
elements:
a Round column
b Square hollow section column
c Double-T column
d Composite angle column
e Cross-profile column made up
of angle sections
f Cross-profile column made up
of T-sections

2 Column bases:
a Hinged single-axis column base
b Hinged double-axis column base
c Restrained or fixed column with
anchors

3 Column base with load
distribution

1a   b   c   d   e   f

PILLARS

The preferred profiles of vertical stanchions in steel construction are HE profiles, as they not only provide good loadbearing strength, but also very good connection options for floor girders. Owing to their wide flanges, they have good buckling resistance in both directions. Hollow and tubular profiles can also support heavy loads, but do not offer any easy point of connection unless additional brackets or lugs are attached to them. They do have an advantage however, in that the different wall thicknesses of hollow profiles make it possible to accommodate reducing loads in the higher storeys of multi-storey constructions, without having to change their external dimensions. Large loads can be supported by joined box profiles or HE profiles enclosed with reinforcement plates.

Particular attention must be paid to the detailing of the base of uprights, since the much higher compressive force of the steel upright (approx. 140 N/mm²) has to be reduced to the much lower permissible compressive force of the reinforced concrete base (approx. 15 N/mm²). For this purpose, it is necessary to weld steel foot plates welded to the base of the upright which are reinforced with ribs and which distribute the load. These base plates have to be aligned and packed out, and the joint with the substrate filled with swelling mortar. The detailing needed for restraining the base of uprights is considerably more costly and necessitates sizable increases to the foundations.

As a rule, uprights are made up of several parts for transport and installation reasons. The detailing of the joint between the upright parts depends on the structural system; common joining methods are head plates or joining lugs. In the case of hinged uprights, these joints are often combined with those that join with the floor beams using plates welded into the web of those beams.

2a   b   c

3

JOINING

Fasteners are needed for joining individual structural elements to form a cohesive structure. They can also be used to join several individual profiles into one cross section, for example a lattice girder. A distinction is made between joints that can be separated, such as bolted joints, and joints that are permanent, such as those produced by welding or riveting.

The most common joining method is bolting. → 1 In this case, force is transferred through shear and friction. There are four different types of thread fastener, three strength classes and six types of thread fastener connection. A distinction is made as follows: thread fasteners with tolerance in the corresponding hole, which are used for the transfer of small point loads; fit bolts for the transfer of higher loads to the bearing of the hole, which also reliably prevent minimum shifting of the component; and high-tensile bolts (HT) made of special steel, which can be used for pre-tensioning and which allow load transfer via friction. Such slip-resistant joints require pre-treatment of the contact faces (for example, by sandblasting) and are capable of transferring more than twice the forces transferable through ordinary bolt connections. Nevertheless, the latter represent the most common jointing method in construction, not least because they allow small corrections and hence accommodate tolerances.

The most elegant, as well as the strongest, joints in steel construction are made by welding. The direct joining of individual semi-finished products without connecting parts results in a homogeneous construction without interruptions. There are quite a number of different welding methods, depending on the type of joint, the load to be transferred, the atmospheric conditions and the desired shape of the welded seam. In all welding methods, the two steel components to be joined are melted at their contact faces by the application of heat and are joined together into a single part using weld metal. In view of the risk involved in wrongly executed welded seams, loadbearing welded connections may only be carried out by qualified personnel.

While historic steel constructions feature many different visible types of riveted connection – notably at railway bridges → 2 which are still in use today – this jointing method is hardly used nowadays owing to the amount of noise generated by riveting, as well as the labour-intensive nature of the work. Nevertheless, riveting continues to play a certain role in the preservation of historic monuments. Rivets make connections that are permanent and they transfer point forces in a similar manner to bolt connections. Rivets are inserted in red-hot condition and the protruding shaft is formed into a head using a rivet hammer.

1 Bolt connection:
Corner of frame of multi-storey car park, Heilbronn, 1997, MGF Architects

2 Rivet connection:
Müngsten Bridge, Solingen, 1897, Anton von Rieppel

1

2

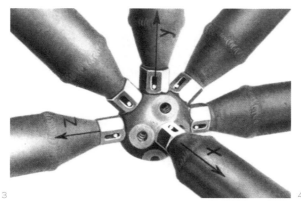

3

4

CONSTRUCTION SYSTEMS

In spite of the tradition of steel construction – which is closely associated with industrial development – it is nowadays much less systematised than timber construction, or construction using prefabricated reinforced concrete elements.

In Europe, steel construction systems were not developed until an effort was made to counteract the massive housing shortage of the 1920s, and were presented at construction exhibitions in Stuttgart (1927), Dresden and Breslau (1929). Numerous Bauhaus architects such as Walter Gropius, Marcel Breuer, Adolf Muche and Mies van der Rohe were leading proponents. However, early trials never went beyond the prototype stage since there was not enough time to resolve detailing and production problems conclusively. In the twentieth century, the first construction systems for housing developments that were advanced enough for serial production were finally developed by Jean Prouvé in France and Charles Eames in the United States in the 1940s. But here, too, customised solutions for particular applications were in the majority, which meant that the anticipated success of the systems initially remained elusive. By contrast, the MERO node developed by engineer Max Mengeringhausen as early as 1937 is still in use today. ➔ 3, 4 The Swiss engineer Fritz Haller who – based on designs for a modular furniture system – developed three different construction systems through to serial production stage, helped system construction in steel become more popular. The work of Konrad Wachsmann (1901–1980) and Buckminster Fuller (1895–1983) finally led to the industrial development of space frame structures, which could be used to span large spaces without columns.

As in timber construction, a distinction is also made in steel construction between skeleton, post-and-beam and modular construction.

In skeleton construction, the structure is reduced to beams and uprights and the skeleton normally remains visible. The floors are most often constructed using prefabricated reinforced concrete slabs which are supported by more closely spaced, light intermediate beams. In such a construction, the method of building the walls can be freely chosen and partition walls can be placed wherever they are needed. The post-and-beam construction method has been derived from the successful frame construction method used in timber construction. In this method, floors and walls are constructed using extremely lightweight, loadbearing cold-rolled profiles with a wall thickness of 1–2 mm. Similar to the drywall stud construction common in interior fitting out, metal studs are placed at a spacing of 40–80 cm and lined on both sides with timber or gypsum board material. The connection of the profiles with the planking creates a panel which acts in the manner of a plate and gives rigidity to the building. As in timber construction, it is possible to have separate frames for each storey (platform frames) or to have frames span several storeys (balloon frames).

Modular construction is based on a higher degree of prefabrication than post-and-beam construction. In contrast to the other prefabricated construction methods, this system results in room-sized modules which are produced at a factory, independently of weather conditions. The structure of a module consists of a three-dimensional frame system made of cold-rolled profiles and its size depends on the limitations imposed by the means of transport. Modules measuring 3 m in width, 4 m in height and up to 12 m in length can easily be transported to building sites by articulated lorries. This method is particularly suitable for temporary accommodation of a similar type which needs to be erected quickly, for example building site facilities or exhibitions. Modular construction is also increasingly used in experimental applications, such as for housing and cultural facilities.

CONCRETE AND REINFORCED CONCRETE CONSTRUCTION

CHARACTERISTICS

The building material that today is by far the most frequently used in skeleton construction – reinforced concrete – was not used until the middle of the nineteenth century, when it was discovered that steel in combination with concrete results in a compound material that combines the high tensile strength of steel with the high compressive strength, corrosion protection and non-flammability of concrete. Following this, reinforced concrete as a hybrid material became the most important material for the development of modern architecture. With the new building material it became possible to design structures which would have been unthinkable using just steel, wood or stone on their own. A basic condition for the combination of these two materials, steel and concrete, is that their expansion coefficients are nearly identical. Both materials react similarly to the impact of changes in temperature. Broadly speaking, both materials will expand by about 1 mm for each 10 m at a temperature differential of 10°. This expansion must be taken into account in the detailing of any building structure. One method of dealing with the resulting movement is to provide expansion joints. In addition to the above, concrete components are subject to shrinkage and creep as the water contained inside the material dries out.

Reinforced concrete is extremely well suited for use in skeleton construction. Components can either be cast on site ('in-situ'/'cast-in-place' concrete) or produced in a factory as prefabricated units. By relocating production to the factory, the production process is independent of the weather and can dispense with scaffolding and formwork. The results are more accurate and can be better controlled. However, the connection points of prefabricated units are often more costly, and the favourable effect of the continuous spanning of beams or floor slabs often cannot be made use of. For these reasons another production method – the semi-prefabricated construction method – has become popular in reinforced concrete construction, which combines the advantages of both methods. In this method the final component is made up of a prefabricated part and an in-situ part, which results in better load transfer and makes it possible to create homogeneous connection details.

The use of prefabricated parts is almost as old as reinforced concrete construction itself. As early as 1891, the French engineer Edmond Coignet used prefabricated concrete components in the construction of the casino in Biarritz. Ten years later, the Ingalls Building in Cincinnati was created (Elzner & Anderson), which is the world's first tower block using iron-concrete skeleton construction.

1

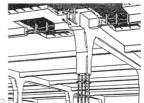

2

Although the exterior appearance of the early reinforced concrete buildings remained determined by the traditional pattern language of academy-trained architects, the method for detailing the structures developed by the French building contractor Hennebique – who used uprights with vaulted heads connected to beams and corrugated slabs – was very soon adopted. ⌐ 1, 2 This construction method, which was derived from the familiar timber skeleton but which was new in its monolithic manner of construction, was clearly commercially superior to the iron skeleton construction. In addition, the use of concrete solved the problem of fire safety. Milestones in this development were the private house of the Perret brothers in Paris (1903) and the Fagus factory in Alfeld by Walter Gropius (1914). Le Corbusier finally used the concrete skeleton construction system as an architectural means of expression (Domino House, 1915 ⌐ 3) and made the separation of structure and envelope the basis of his 'plan libre'.

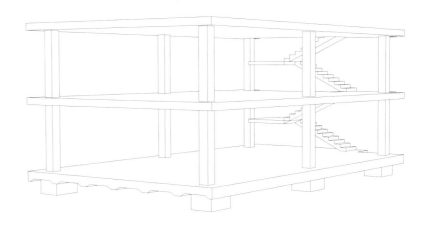

3

1 Patent drawing, Hennebique system, Paris, 1892, François Hennebique

2 Industrial building with Hennebique system (now ZKM – Zentrum für Kunst und Medientechnologie), Karlsruhe, 1915, Philipp Jacob Manz

3 'Domino' construction system for industrial fabrication of houses in reinforced concrete skeleton construction using prefabricated components. 1915, Le Corbusier, Max du Bois.

4 Mastic sealant joint in prefabricated component

5 Movement joint, faculty building, Oxford, 1998, Norman Foster.

6 Various joint profiles, 1:20

JOINING

Typical reinforced concrete cross sections have a relatively large compression area, owing to the compressive stress of concrete, which is low compared to the permissible tensile stress of the reinforcement steel. Compared to steel construction, reinforced concrete components are therefore often more substantial, particularly at the connection points.

The joints of reinforced concrete components are distinguished by their method of manufacture: with in-situ construction, the joints are usually monolithic – in other words they are formed by pouring the material – and are therefore rigid. In the prefabricated component construction method, the transitions between the different prefabricated elements (uprights, beams, floor slabs) can also be filled with liquid material – otherwise they can be joined rigidly or hinged with the help of steel installation hardware. Unless the respective components are subsequently lined, their method of jointing remains visible to the observer. With in-situ concrete construction it is possible for uprights, beams and floor slabs to penetrate each other geometrically owing to the possibility of installing the reinforcement and the entire node in the same level, and to concrete it in one process. This can be used to produce a slender and structurally optimised design of high aesthetic appeal. It follows that an in-situ concrete node comes closest to the ideal image of the node in skeleton construction. ⌐ p. 52

Prefabricated component systems often need more space in the intersection areas because the various elements have to be placed above or next to each other. As support for the beams at the uprights, these must be produced with suitable brackets. As a rule, reinforced concrete buildings are braced by wall and floor plates or solid cores. Access cores are often built on site, but can also be constructed with prefabricated components. Both walls and floors are often supplied to site as semi-finished components, known as 'filigree elements', and are fully finished on site to form a structural unit. In prefabricated component buildings with large spans, restrained uprights provide the necessary horizontal rigidity.

Concrete is subject to deformation due to changes in temperature and humidity, and also due to its own drying out process. These changes in length have to be accommodated with joints, otherwise damage can arise from cracks developing. Joints are unavoidable in prefabricated construction and have to be taken into consideration from the appearance point of view.

Depending on the structure, the individual components are firmly connected across the joints by steel components (e.g. cable loops or reinforcement). The width of the joint depends on the length and height of the building. The joint patterns have a significant impact on the external and internal appearance of prefabricated component buildings.

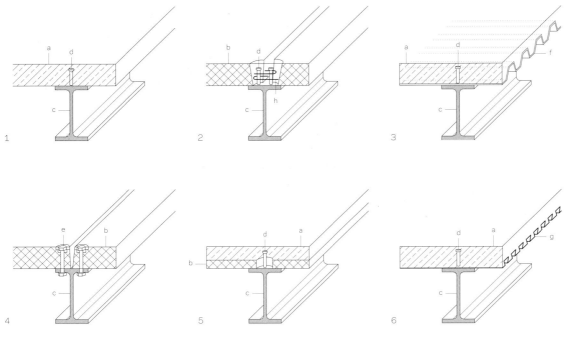

1–6 Types of compound beam, 1:20

1 In-situ concrete slab on steel beam
2 Prefabricated elements on steel beam with filled joint
3 In-situ concrete slab on trapezoidal steel sheet
4 Prefabricated slabs with friction bond
5 Prefabricated slabs with additional layer of in-situ concrete
6 In-situ concrete slab on structural dovetail sheet

a In-situ concrete
b Prefabricated slab
c Steel beam
d Headed shear studs
e HV bolts
f Trapezoid sheet
g Dovetail sheet
h Reinforcement loops

7 Composite columns (top to bottom):
a Hollow profile, filled with concrete
b Hollow profile, filled with reinforced concrete
c Steel profile encased in concrete
d Rolled or welded profile with concrete infill

COMPOUND CONSTRUCTIONS IN STEEL AND RE-INFORCED CONCRETE

In order to produce a bond between the different materials, the smooth surface of the steel has to be processed in such a way that concrete can adhere to it.

Steel components are provided with welded-on ribs or head bolts so that they can form a bond with concrete. This method is used to produce compound beams that consist of steel profiles which form a structural bond with the superimposed reinforced concrete floors on account of the welded-on head bolts. In this system the floor deck acts primarily as a compression slab and the beam is primarily exposed to tensile forces. Trapezoidal steel sheeting is often used as lost shuttering for compound steel and concrete floors. To this end specifically approved trapezoid sheets are used as shuttering for locally cast reinforced in-situ concrete, whereby the trapezoidal sheeting can be counted towards externally placed reinforcement. The sheeting also provides the finish on the underside of the floor. For heavy-duty components and also for commercial reasons, the advantages of steel construction are often combined with reinforced concrete building methods in compound constructions. When steel profiles are either filled or encased with concrete they become more rigid and also have much better fire resistance, and yet it is possible to install intersec-

tions and fixings through welding or bolting on site, resulting in both straightforward and economical installation. Conversely, the greater available strength of steel makes it possible to reduce the cross section dimensions while significantly increasing loadbearing capacity. Another aspect is that the concrete casing protects the steel from corrosion so that no additional anti-corrosion measures are necessary.

Steel profiles fully encased in concrete are distinct from profiles with the cavities filled with concrete, whereby the flanges and edges remain visible. While the latter are clearly classed as a form of steel construction from the point of view of appearance and jointing technology, the method of fully encasing profiles is more often considered to be a reinforced concrete construction method. Compound construction methods have increased in significance, primarily owing to the continually increasing requirements relating to fire safety. Filling the cavities within steel profiles with concrete also has fire safety advantages, even when the steel edges remain visible on the surface: although the external flanges of a hollow upright lose their loadbearing capacity in the event of a fire, the loads are transferred to the protected web and the reinforced concrete in the cavity, which in summary results in a significantly lengthened period of fire resistance.

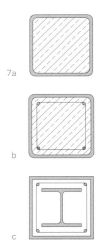

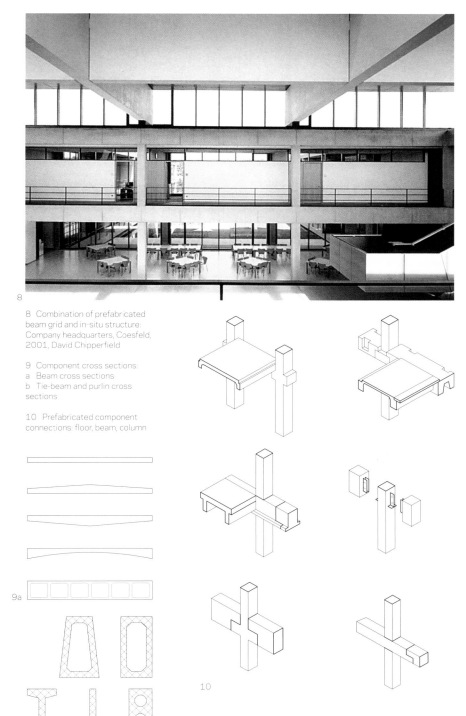

8   Combination of prefabricated
beam grid and in-situ structure:
Company headquarters, Coesfeld,
2001, David Chipperfield

9   Component cross sections:
a   Beam cross sections
b   Tie-beam and purlin cross
sections

10   Prefabricated component
connections: floor, beam, column

CONSTRUCTION METHODS

The advantage of the prefabricated reinforced concrete construction method is that components can be efficiently fabricated without exposure to the hazards of the building site and its weather conditions. This means that prefabricated components can be produced highly accurately and the time needed for installation on site is minimised. However, the need to transport and then install the components on site imposes numerous dimensional and weight restrictions.

Both production methods (in-situ concrete and the installation of prefabricated components) must be considered regarding their suitability. Prefabricated components that can be produced in serial production are ideally suited to structures for buildings with large spans, while in-situ concrete construction is the preferred method for smaller and more complex building developments. The question as to which of these two principles should be selected rarely arises in practice, since both construction methods are often combined for commercial reasons and to suit the requirements of both structural engineers and building contractors. Foundations, floor slabs, uprights and loadbearing beams can be built cost-efficiently using in-situ concrete; the upper floors are usually constructed using semi-finished products (filigree precast floor slabs, → p. 135) with an upper layer of in-situ concrete. The cellar/basement can be constructed with cavity walls, and the cavities filled with concrete, while the stairs can be inserted as prefabricated concrete elements. In summary, these methods involve a combination of prefabrication and in-situ work.

Fully prefabricated building methods were popular during the sixties and seventies of the last century, when they were used for large buildings such as universities and offices. The loadbearing skeleton – which consists of uprights with bearing brackets on which girders or beams are placed – is put together in the form of a modular system. Such structures can be braced in several ways: by restraining the uprights in bucket foundations, by placing solid floor decks and walls, or by means of a solid access core. As it is not possible to cover the joints between the components, these construction methods do not comply with the stricter thermal insulation requirements applicable today, except in the case of uninsulated buildings in industrial and commercial developments. The widest application of prefabricated building methods is in buildings with large open spaces and spans. → 8 With pre-stressing it is possible to achieve spans of over 40 m. Owing to the rapid construction sequence, the high performance of the structure and the robust installation method, reinforced concrete is often the most economical alternative for large building developments.

TIMBER CONSTRUCTION

Timber was the material used for the first framed buildings. In former times this material was almost universally available, offered sufficient stability and was easy to process. Even today timber is a cost-efficient building material in wooded geographical zones and, in addition, is perceived by many people as agreeable, warm and sensually pleasing. Timber construction methods have developed throughout all cultures and across all geographic boundaries, which demonstrates the many different applications of the material and, at the same time, many similarities.

In this way, timber construction in all its variations has become an important form of architectural expression. Many later forms of construction have taken their cue from timber frame construction. When we speak about 'timber frame' construction, it is the timber architecture of the late Middle Ages ⌐1 that first comes to mind, as can be found to this day in many European cities; however, the framing technology as such can also be applied to other materials.

In timber construction, a distinction can be made between methods using solid timber (e.g. log houses) and those that use timber for framing only, i.e. timber skeleton construction. The durability of timber structures depends – even more so than with other building materials – on the appropriate detailing of the material. This applies especially to the joints. Timber connections can be evaluated according to their structural function, how they are made and how they are put together. What types are there and how much load can they transfer? Are they produced manually or industrially, and are they permanent or can they be undone? Fasteners have to be capable of reliably transferring not only the bearing forces, but also the compressive, tensile and shear forces from one component to another.

With regard to the jointing methods in timber construction, a distinction is made between those made by carpenters and those industrially produced. Traditional timber constructions which cannot be exactly mathematically analysed and which – for structural integrity – rely on craftsmen's knowledge, are crafted without any additional load transferring fasteners, for example those made of steel. Timber pegs may be used to secure beams in their position. These systems are constructed primarily to transfer compressive forces. Of the large number of traditional timber joints ⌐2, only stepped joints, square splices and simple pegs are in use today (except for the purpose of preserving historic buildings). The reason is not just the amount of work associated with producing the more sophisticated joints, but also the fact that these traditional timber frames often involve significant

1

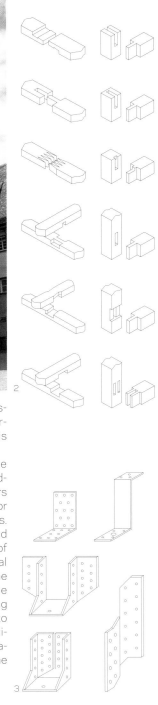

2

weakening of the timber sections and therefore necessitate an altogether higher timber consumption; furthermore, the complexity of these joints means that there is no mathematical proof of their structural capability.

Timber skeleton construction has developed from the historic timber framing method. A prerequisite for modern timber skeleton construction is the use of fasteners and fittings made of steel ⌐3 such as angles, straps, or joist hangers, as well as pegs, bolts, or thread fasteners. This means that the transfer of compressive, tensile and shear forces can be calculated. Special fittings made of steel sheeting make it possible to design horizontal nodes in which all timbers are positioned in the same plane. The use of joist hangers, anchor straps and angle straps has led to a significant simplification of jointing methods in skeleton construction; the same applies to the use of nail plates and metal gussets in timber engineering. Automated production methods are accompanied by a distinct impoverishment of the erstwhile 'fine art of jointing' in timber construction.

3

1   Town hall, Markgröningen,
    15th century, timber-frame
    construction

2   Traditional timber joints

3   Structural steel fixings

4   Joints in timber construction:
a   Open joints
b   Overlapping joints

Structural timber elements, which traditionally were placed rather closer together, are installed today at larger grid distances. Through separation of the loadbearing structure from the space-forming walls, it is possible to design layouts more freely and hence to achieve a more flexible division of interior rooms. The structure determines the design grid. Timber skeleton systems can be divided into those which have their loadbearing elements all in one plane and those in which the loadbearing elements are placed in different planes. The selection of a certain construction system depends on the loads arising. The architectural appearance of a timber skeleton building is largely determined by the selected structural system. For this reason it is necessary to familiarise oneself not only with the structural properties of the systems, but also with the conceptual effect of the different timber construction methods.

The separation of the structural system from the building envelope results in much functional and conceptual freedom. A distinction is made between structural systems that are integrated into the wall and those that are not - or else are only partially integrated. The choice of structural system also determines the position of the facade, which can be placed before, between, or behind the structure. In the case of an integrated structure, the loadbearing members are not open to view, while in partially integrated systems the wall surfaces are divided by the grid pattern of the uprights. In the case of non-integrated designs, the uprights protrude, thereby becoming a prominent feature in rooms. Owing to the exacting thermal insulation requirements of modern buildings, it is usually preferable to enclose the structural system fully and to position it on the warm side of the building envelope. Where the facade is located between structural members, thermal bridging occurs, which is hard to control.

Furthermore, it is possible that structural movement is transferred to the facade elements. The natural swelling and shrinkage properties of timber have a negative effect on joints, such that it is quite difficult to achieve airtight connections. The same applies when a structural system is located outside the building envelope. While such designs are aesthetically very pleasing, great care needs to be taken with the design of penetration points between the structure and building envelope in order to avoid physical performance problems.

JOINTS

Different connection details have to be created in a number of different planes between the loadbearing structure, on one hand, and the building envelope or fitting out elements on the other. Joints must be capable of accommodating tolerances in order to allow for variations in the hardware and in the installation process. In timber construction, joints ↘4 can vary between 5-20 mm. Depending on the arrangement, a distinction is made between: butt joints, which are used as a separation between the structural and fitting out system in a linear grid; sliding joints, which are concealed behind the loadbearing structure and which allow unrestricted expansion of the various fitting out elements; and single or double concealed joints which are used for separating fitting out elements from each other, for example in the case of timber linings. For the protection of timber through appropriate detailing, a correct joint design is important. Joints in facades must be closed to the penetration of vapour on the side facing the interior in order to prevent condensation. Where timber elements are used on the exterior, it is imperative that they can dry out again after they have become wet as a result of rain or snow. Suitable materials for joints in timber construction are primarily joint strips based on polysulphides or polyurethane, vinyl

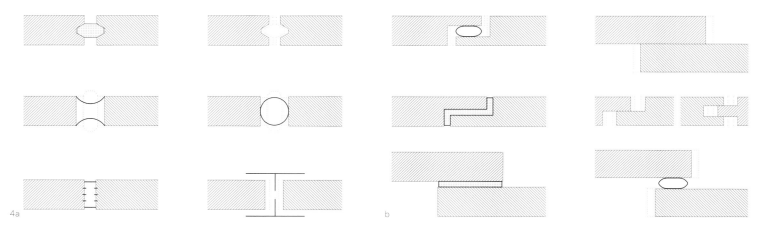

4a   b

1

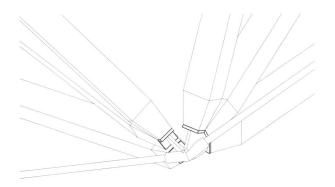

2

or mineral foam materials. Adhesive sealants are not considered permanent, owing to the tension occurring in
timber components. It is important to check the compatibility of the joint material with any prior coating and
timber preservation systems in each individual case.

HORIZONTAL MEMBERS
The design of horizontal members depends on the architectural design concept, as well as the required span and
the structural loads. In accordance with DIN 1052, the
permitted deflection of floor joists is limited to l/300 of
the span. While solid timber beams are commercially
viable for spans of up to 6 m length, larger distances can
be spanned and greater loads supported with laminated
beams, or composite structural systems. For example,
timber framing is composed of straight struts that are
joined in a triangular geometry. This means that the individual struts are only exposed to compressive or tensile
forces. In addition to nailed trusses, there are 'Greim' or
'Menig' trusses, which feature metal plates inserted into
a slot at the joint. In glued timber construction, we also
find lattice girders such as Trigonit girders ⮑ **3a** – in single or multiple parts – and triangulated girders ⮑ **3b**. Corrugated web beams ⮑ **3c** consist of veneer board that
has been formed into a sinus curve, then pressed and
glued into the matching grooves in an upper and lower
chord, thus preventing the beam from buckling. Plywood
web beams and box beams with chords made of laminated wood and webs made of wood-based material have
a high loadbearing capacity combined with low material
content. ⮑ **3d** Very slender beams are susceptible to tilting or buckling, and have to be secured with appropriate
bracing members. Inverted bowstring girders consist of
an upper chord subjected to bending, with compression
and tensile struts underneath to absorb tensile forces.
Laminated or glulam beams are produced in the form of

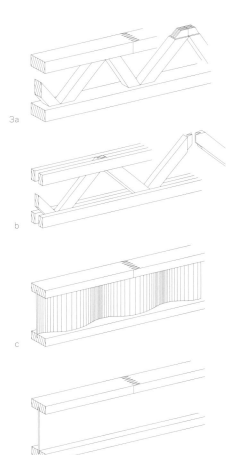

3a

b

c

d

1, 2   Inverted bowstring glulam
girders, indoor riding arena,
St. Gerold, 1997,
Hermann Kaufmann.

3   Selection of beam designs:
a   Trigonit girder
b   Triangulated girder
c   Corrugated web beam
d   Plywood web beam

parallel beams, monopitch and double-pitch roof beams as well as in angled and curved form. For spans of 10–30 m, framed girders have proven to be commercially viable. Framed girders of up to 15 m length are glued or nailed, whereas the struts of those for larger spans are jointed with dowels.

UPRIGHTS AND THEIR BASES

In modern timber skeleton construction, layout grids are usually developed on the base module of 62.5 cm, which means that the grids of uprights are often spaced at 250, 500, 750 or 1000 cm. The selection of a grid is primarily influenced by the spans of beams and floor decks. Owing to the longitudinal performance characteristics of timber, the loadbearing capacity of uprights is easy to calculate. They are often composed of two or more sections in order to achieve sufficient resistance to bending and buckling. A distinction is made between homogeneous and splayed cross sections. The latter are made up of separate sections which are only connected by intermediate struts at certain intervals. Owing to the length of tree trunks, uprights consisting of squared timber sections are usually limited to a length of about 8 m. The risk of cracking and twisting of the wood can be counteracted by machining grooves and by appropriate profiling of the sections. Nowadays, uprights with a large cross section are frequently produced using laminated timber.

Any timber posts that are exposed to the weather must be raised above the ground by at least 5 cm in order to prevent moisture from collecting between the lower edge of the timber and the ground, which would cause the timber to rot. The end grain of timber members must not be obstructed, so as to permit ventilation. Within buildings, posts can also be placed directly on to the floor slab using bitumen sheeting as separation. The transition to the foundations is often made via a steel base ⟶ 4, the metal parts of which are inserted into the post by drilling or slotting. Depending on the forces to be transferred, the base can either be detailed as a hinge, or the post can be restrained between appropriately dimensioned steel profiles. Where posts are located within the outer wall construction, they can be installed on a base plate. By contrast to traditional base plate design in timber frame construction, the post is anchored with steel elements through the plate to the foundations. In that case, the function of the timber base plate is reduced to that of an installation guy for placing the timber posts and it has to be protected against rising damp using bitumen sheeting.

4 Selection of columns/ column bases

5 Apartment building at Hebelstrasse, Basel, 1988, Herzog & de Meuron. The shape of the hinged solid-timber posts follows the line of force (entasis).

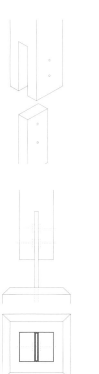

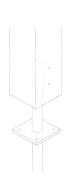

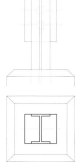

4

5

FRAMES

In buildings with wide spans of up to 50 m, structurally determined triangulated frames made of laminated timber have proven to be successful. The corners of the frames are designed to be rigid so that the moments from the cross bars can be transferred into the posts. The moment at the frame corner, which determines the size of the members, depends primarily on the form of the frame. The higher the ridge is in relation to the span, the less is the horizontal proportion of the bearing force. The largest bending moments are created at the frame corner, and the zero point of the moment is located at the hinged joint at the ridge.

A distinction can be made between glulam beams that combine the post and beam in one piece which, for spans of up to 20 m, can be transported to the building site, and structures consisting of a post and beam which are connected with dowels to form a rigid joint. Wedged joints between glulam posts and beams are constructed with a central joining piece in order to halve the angle between the force vector and the direction of the grain between the post and beam, and to increase the permissible stresses. Structurally indeterminate two-hinge frames are not used very often in timber construction.

1

1 Glulam timber beams at Hergatz Exhibition Hall, 1995, Baumschlager & Eberle

2 Frame construction:
a Post and transom with glued wedge, post base
b Single-part glulam timber frame member, post base
c Post and transom connected by dowel, post base
d Post with compression and tension members separated, post base

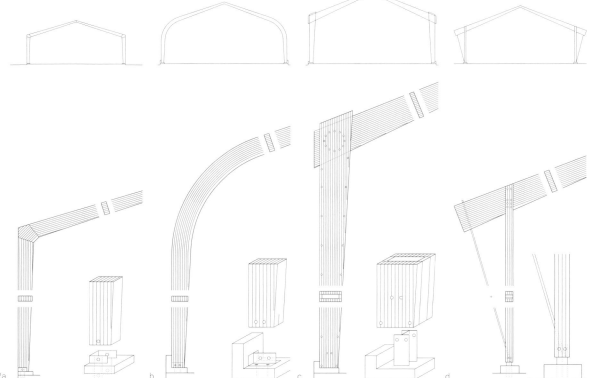

2a   b   c   d

TIMBER FRAME CONSTRUCTION

Timber frame construction refers to a method that uses individual elements for its vertical and horizontal members, which are called posts or studs and plates (head plate and foot plate). Diagonal braces between these components stabilise the walls in the longitudinal direction by transferring the wind forces directly into the foot plates and foundations. In modern timber frame construction, a grid dimension of 125 × 125 cm has become established; common cross sections for posts are 12/12 or 14/14 cm. This narrowly spaced construction grid determines the design of the facades. Windows are inserted directly into the fields between the posts. The floor joists are placed between the head plate of one storey and the foot plate of the next one above it, thereby providing the opportunity to allow a slight cantilever. The foot plate of the ground floor rests on a solid floor slab or on a layer of floor joists, which in turn are supported on strip foundations. In historic buildings the timber cross sections are relatively large, since they were sized not according to structural calculations, but based on tradesmen's experience of joining and construction. Forces are primarily transferred between timber members using pegs and stepped joints, which means that the strength of the cross sections is reduced and consequently has to be compensated for by choosing larger sections. The timber frame is a rigid structure consisting of many parts, and is built storey by storey one upon the other. Openings extending over two floors are not possible; apart for very few regional exceptions, timber frame construction consists of storey-high frames built upon each other. In traditional timber frame construction, the walls are built with stone, clay, or wood and they are left exposed both inside and outside. Modern timber frame construction uses engineering methods of joining and is therefore able to employ significantly reduced cross sections. The fields are filled with insulation and the structure is lined internally and externally; the appearance of the building is therefore no longer determined by the structure. The fasteners used, such as nail plates and angle straps, are concealed by the cladding on both sides. Today, timber frame construction is primarily used for single-storey utilitarian buildings and in the restoration of historical buildings.

3   Construction of a traditional
timber-frame building

4   Pegged connections, 1:20

5   Timber frame construction:
a   Threshold
b   Corner post
c   Window mullion
d   Door post
e   Bracing cross
f   Brace
g   Head plate
h   Floor joist
i   Transom
j   Transom over window

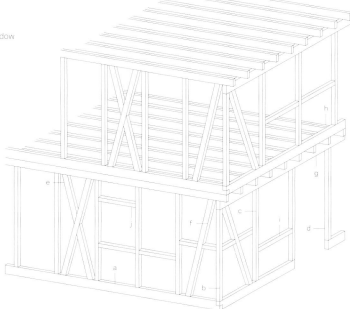

5

1

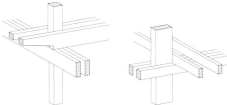

1 Beach facilities, Zug, 1999,
Alfred Krähenbühl

2 Double-beam post;
Elevation and cross section, 1:50:

a Foundations
b Double beam
c Post
d Lap siding
e Sub-structure
f Edge of metal roof
g Layer of gravel
h Roofing membrane
i Timber decking
j Floor covering

DOUBLE BEAM / POST
(DOUBLE JOIST) CONSTRUCTION

The hierarchically based construction principle of the double beam supported on a post is colloquially referred to as 'double joist construction'. The double joist construction shown here consists of single posts and a directional main beam system made up of pairs of continuous beams spanning several fields. The floor joists are supported on this primary structure, which results in a relatively large construction height of the floor decks between storeys. The main beams are connected to the posts using pegs, bolts, ring dowels or plate bearers, and the floor joists have to be braced against tilting using angle brackets. The base of the posts is detailed in the form of a hinged upright with a steel base on point foundations. Large loadbearing capacities and spans are possible because high beams can be used, and the span of the double joists is always longer than that of the floor joists.

The layout can be designed fairly independently of the upright grid. Since double joist systems are always open systems, the facade can be before, behind, or between the posts. From the point of view of building physics, the intersections of the construction with the facade must be carefully detailed. As the construction is directional, the connections can be made at different points and the openings given different dimensions; the structure lends itself to large glazed openings. If the facade is located in the plane of the posts, the posts will remain visible and the space between the floor joists is closed with filler pieces. If the facade is located behind the posts, it is fixed in the plane of the secondary joists. In that case, the connection between facade and double joists remains visible just like all other parts of the structure, including the bracing in front of the facade. Where the walls are placed in the plane of the outer of the double joists, the structure is concealed by the facade except for the protruding parts of the double joists. In this case, the bracing elements are fitted on the inside.

The posts can be used for attaching double joists at several levels, which means that it is easy to construct storeys with different floor levels. The option to allow floor joists to protrude beyond the beams on all sides is a typical design characteristic, but it does involve the need to level out the difference between main and secondary beams/joists. The protruding ends of the double joists – which are necessary owing to the dowel connections at the end points – are a typical feature of this construction method. These protrusions have to be protected through appropriate detailing, e.g. through a roof overhang, metal flashing or a weather-protection coating.

2

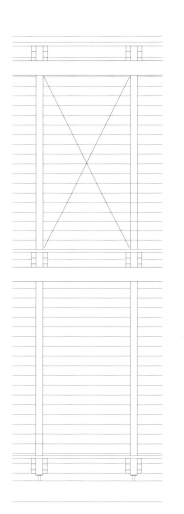

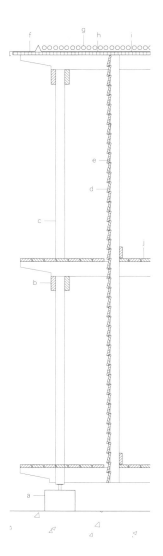

3 Youth village at Cieux, Limoges,
1985, Roland Schweitzer

4 Beam double post
Elevation and cross section, 1:50

a Foundations/base of post
b Double post
c Main beam
d Secondary beam
e Lap siding
f Sub-structure
g Glazing
h Infill board
i Edge of metal roof
j Layer of gravel
k Roofing membrane
l Timber decking
m Floor covering

3

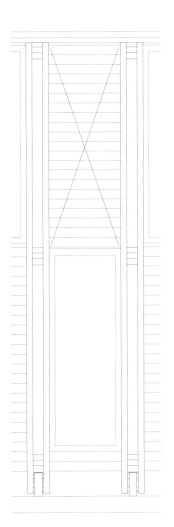

4

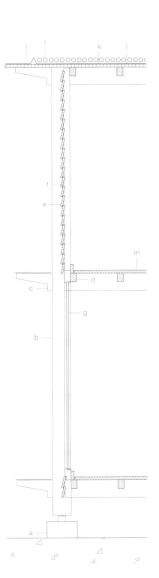

BEAM / DOUBLE POST
(DOUBLE POST) CONSTRUCTION

This system of construction also uses double members in parallel, but inverts the principle of the double joist: single beams or joists spanning several fields are held between pairs of posts. This allows economically feasible spans of up to about 7 m, and hence flexible layout and facade configurations. The structure is a directional one which, in contrast to the classic double joist construction method, provides even more options in terms of the conceptual design. Further variations include doubling up the pairs of posts, resulting in four upright members making up a post. Pairs of posts make it possible to arrange the main beams in one direction, whereas posts made up of four members can be used to fix beams in two directions. → 4

Where the posts are tall, the space between the members is packed out with filler pieces – either for particular stretches or at each storey – which can also be used as bearers for the main beams. It is possible to insert full length filler pieces in the gap between the upright members, although this will lead to the structure losing its filigree appearance. The main beam is attached to the pair of posts by mechanical steel fasteners, such as pegs, ring dowels or bolts, and the floor joists or secondary beams are connected with joist hangers or secured against tilting using simple metal straps. The base of the post must be restrained, and it rests on a point foundation, which means that the system can be adapted to different topographical conditions. Cantilevers are possible in one direction or in two directions with posts consisting of four members.

The facades can be placed in any location. A design with double joists is more economical than one using double posts. In addition, with the latter system it is more difficult to achieve the necessary fire protection because of the slender cross sections of the upright members. The system is therefore primarily suitable for skeleton buildings with large spans in which, for structural reasons, the dimensions of the cross sections of the posts have to be larger than average.

1 Martinszentrum nursery,
Bernburg, 2007, Weiss & Volkmann

2 Post-and-lintel;
Elevation and cross section, 1:50

a Foundations
b Post
c Main beam
d Secondary beam
e Internal cladding
f Insulation
g Additional insulation
h Counter battens
i Battens
j Vertical timber cladding
k Edge of metal roof
l Layer of gravel
m Roofing membrane
n Timber decking
o Ventilation/battens
p Underlayment
q Vapour check
r Floor covering
s Screed

TIMBER CONSTRUCTION BEAM ON POST (POST-AND-LINTEL CONSTRUCTION)

This system represents a simple directional construction, the main beams of which rest on the posts in one direction, as a rule spanning several fields. The secondary beams, or floor joists, are connected to the main beams in the same plane using angle brackets. Alternatively, they are placed on top of the main beams, which results in a greater floor depth. ⌐2 The posts are just one storey high and are also directional, thereby determining the loadbearing direction. The posts in the main bearing direction can be spaced as far apart as 8 m. At the base there are either main beams or base plates, which are attached to the foundations using anchors or fixing plates. Where there is a solid floor slab, the lower layer of floor joists can be omitted. Buildings of several storeys can be achieved by stacking this type of construction. The transfer of forces between the main beam and post takes place through the transverse pressure area of the beam and the end face of the post; the force transfer to the post beneath takes place via steel plates or brackets inserted into the main beam. If the bearing surfaces of the posts are not sufficient for the transfer of forces, they have to be enlarged by appropriate steel fittings.

In this construction it is important to remember that the posts are stressed along the grain, while the beams are stressed across the grain. The structure must be stabilised against wind forces using slotted and pegged connections, threaded bars or Simplex bolts. Cantilevers are only possible in the main loadbearing direction. Owing to the stacked construction method, horizontal offsets are not easy to achieve. The directional construction can produce a variety of facades, each of which requires specific details for the connection to the structure. Rigidity can be achieved with cross-bracing members or by using wall elements, provided these are sufficiently rigid in themselves. In single-storey construction, much larger spacing between posts is possible, provided the main horizontal support system is appropriately dimensioned, for example in the form of lattice girders. Here too, the length of the span depends to a large extent on the detailing of the bearings.

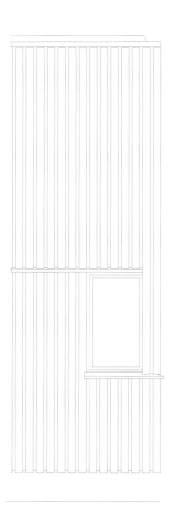

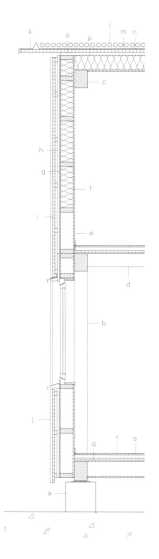

2

3 Residence, Appenzell, 2000,
Ecolo Architects

4 Post-and-beam;
Elevation and cross section, 1:50

a Foundations
b Post/insulation
c Beam
d Internal cladding
e Additional insulation
f Battens
g Shiplap siding
h Edge of metal roof
i Layer of gravel
j Roofing membrane
k Timber decking
l Back ventilation
m Underlayment
n Insulation
o Vapour check
p Floor covering
q Screed

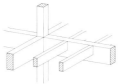

3

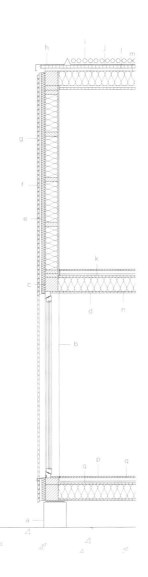

4

BEAM INTO SIDE OF POST
(POST-AND-BEAM CONSTRUCTION)

Post-and-beam construction is a non-directional system with its node geometry fully in the same plane. It consists of single continuous posts and main beams that are connected to the sides of these posts and which run in the same plane across only one span. The advantage of this classic node geometry is that the connection details are the same for all external and internal walls, at all levels and in every direction. The loads are transferred in equal measure via the beams to the posts. The secondary beams or floor joists run perpendicular to the main beams. Formerly, the relatively closely spaced post grid imposed considerable limitations on the layout design. However, with the timber qualities available today it is possible to achieve larger spans.

The beams can be connected to the posts using joist hangers, steel angles, steel dowels with Simplex screws or T-profiles with bolts. Concealed connection details can be produced with specially manufactured steel fittings. The secondary beams are connected to the main beams by angle brackets; the base of the post is held and fixed in a steel fitting.

The facade elements are located exactly between the posts and beams, which means that the structure can remain visible unless it is concealed with insulation material in order to improve thermal insulation. As with all timber structures, the designer has to weigh up whether to opt for a more substantial structure or better insulation, and consider how this affects the building's physical performance. Special attention needs to be paid to the detailing of all joints. The structure can be stiffened in the wall plane by inserting cross-bracing. Different interior levels can be achieved by raising the respective floor joists; cantilevers, however, are not possible. The relatively high cost of the node details has to be balanced against the simplification in fitting out, given the uniform floor levels and connection details. For this reason, post-and-beam constructions are particularly suitable for industrially produced construction systems that are manufactured in larger series.

STRUCTURAL PRINCIPLES

Buildings erected in wall construction are enclosed on all sides. As a rule, all loads are transferred by walls and floors in a typically linear fashion. The structure is formed by solid walls and floors which intersect with each other with firm connection details. While solid outer walls enclose the building, thinner walls divide the interior in a cellular manner. All loadbearing wall elements are used both as room-forming elements and for bracing purposes. The available materials are brickwork or masonry, concrete, clay, or solid timber. Wall construction is a popular building method for low or medium-rise buildings. In this system, walls and floors function together as loadbearing and bracing elements. Taller, multi-storey buildings are usually not braced via individual walls, but by walls that connect up to a core which can absorb torsional forces. Openings for windows and doors are cut out of the walls. Depending on the size of the openings, the load of the structure above may have to be supported by special elements such as lintels or beams. The size of the rooms depends on the loadbearing capabilities of the respective material and the type of floor construction used. In view of the fact that the loadbearing walls should be placed vertically above each other, it makes sense to as-

sign similar functions to the rooms above each other in the different levels, resulting in similar layouts. The structural and tectonic options in solid construction result primarily from the properties of the various construction elements and how they are joined together. In the classic configuration of wall construction, the same component performs the loadbearing and room enclosing functions. The loadbearing elements therefore take up more space within the available areas and volumes. Wall thickness is determined by the loads and the location of the wall within the building. Usually the thickness diminishes in the upper storeys.

The loadbearing elements used in solid construction also perform functions such as thermal insulation, sound insulation, fire protection, and protection against moisture and the weather. By comparison, the different members used in skeleton construction perform different functions. The exterior envelope and the room-forming elements are independent of the structural system, with each elements performing specific functions (thermal insulation, sound insulation, fire protection, protection against dampness, and structural support). ⤷ **Chapter 3**

1 Conversion and renovation of Bernhardskapelle community centre, Owen-Teck, 2001, Klumpp + Klumpp Architects

1

2 Single- and double-leaf wall
constructions:

a   Monolithic wall:
when built in brickwork or blockwork, usually plastered on both
sides. The solid wall construction
meets all requirements regarding
loadbearing capacity and building
physics. The thermal performance
can be enhanced by applying render on top of thermal insulation.
The outside (in this case the render
finish) protects the building against
moisture and the weather

b   Single-skin external wall
with sandwich insulation system:
the solid layer performs the loadbearing function, and the function
of protecting against fire, noise and
heat. The sandwich insulation system provides the required thermal
insulation and weather protection.

c   Single-skin external wall with
internal insulation:
the solid layer performs the loadbearing function and protects
against fire, noise, heat and the
weather. The inner skin takes care
of most of the thermal insulation.

d   Single-skin external wall with
external cladding:
fixing brackets are fitted to the
loadbearing wall and thermal insulation is placed in the gap. Back-
ventilation of the cavity is required
to allow evaporation of condensate.

e–h   Double-skin external wall:
made up of solid inner and outer
skins and, in many cases, a cavity
with thermal insulation (possible
with or without air gap). The outer
skin provides protection against
the weather while the inner skin is
the loadbearing element and transfers the structural loads. The cavity
is used for thermal insulation, back-
ventilation or as a barrier against
moisture. The vertical loads imposed by the external skin have to
be supported by the loadbearing
inner skin.

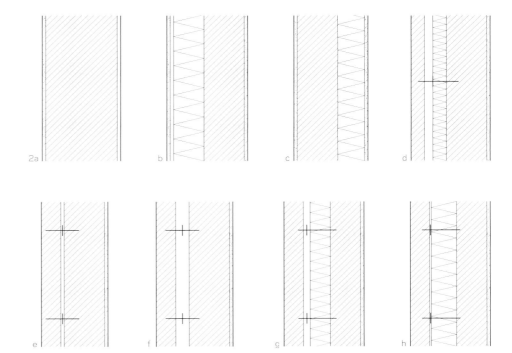

WALL CONSTRUCTION

Walls can be built monolithically or as several skins. In terms of the structure, a distinction is made between loadbearing, non-loadbearing and bracing walls.

Loadbearing walls absorb forces resulting from their own weight and from imposed loads, as well as loads from floors, roofs and wind. They function primarily as plates and can therefore be used for bracing purposes. Walls used for bracing essentially only carry their own weight, and possibly that of other bracing walls directly above. Their function is to transfer horizontal loads resulting from wind, earth pressure, or buckling.

Non-loadbearing walls do not have any loadbearing or bracing functions. They are not relevant in terms of the structural system.

EXTERNAL WALLS

In addition to conceptual aspects, external walls play an important role in providing thermal insulation and weather protection. Without additional thermal insulation, brick-built, monolithic external walls require typical thicknesses of 30 to 36.5 cm, using special thermally insulating blocks. On the other hand, it is also possible to separate the structural function from that of the external building envelope, and build external walls in several skins to meet the different requirements (loadbearing, thermal insula-tion, protection against moisture).

INTERNAL WALLS

Internal walls have to fulfil requirements relating to fire protection, sound insulation (particularly party walls), air-tightness, cooling in summer (as buffer storage), support-ing and bracing. Internal loadbearing walls are normally built as single-leaf walls. They must be able to support/ transfer their own weight as well as minor cantilever and point loads.

NON-LOADBEARING WALLS

Non-loadbearing internal and external walls have to sup-port their own weight and possibly also transfer wind loads. These loads must be transferred to loadbearing building components. Non-loadbearing walls must not be used for bracing the building or in an attempt to prevent loadbearing components from buckling.

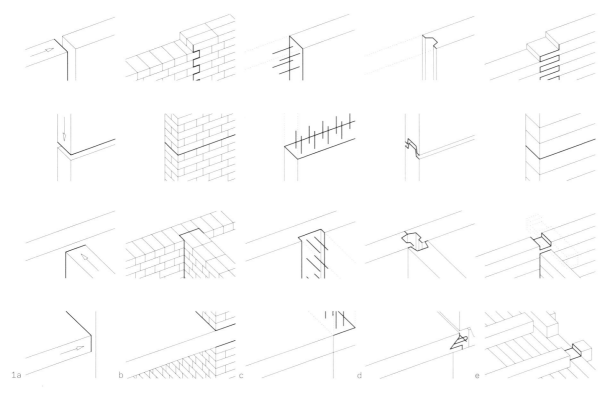

1   Wall construction systems:

a   System diagram
b   Brickwork
c   In-situ concrete
d   Prefabricated concrete
components
e   Solid timber

1a   b   c   d   e

LOAD TRANSFER AND JOINTING IN WALL CONSTRUCTION

Different use typologies require different methods of forming rooms. Different materials favour or prevent different construction methods owing to their structural capabilities, design potential and physical performance. In brick-built wall construction, the structural loads transferred are typically compressive forces, whereas tensile forces can only be absorbed to a limited extent. By deciding on a system, the designer also determines the choice of options relating to design, layout, lighting and future adaptability, because later on loadbearing and bracing components can only be modified or removed at high cost. In certain load scenarios, where the limits of a system are reached, it may be opportune to change between systems or materials. The structure of the system will be defined in cooperation with the structural engineer. In certain countries, the structural calculations are subject to examination by an external structural engineer. The construction systems can be distinguished by their typical geometry i.e. box, plate, or cross-wall construction. ➔ p. 36

When choosing a construction system, the capability of the material and construction method must be taken into account with respect to the selected system and the respective specific space qualities.

CONSTRUCTION AND INSTALLATION

When choosing between on-site construction and a prefabricated construction method, various project factors have to be taken into consideration, such as time management, cost, availability of material, the effect on the construction system and the appearance of the building. The construction period is considerably affected by weather conditions. When temperatures are low, especially below zero, it is not possible to carry out certain processes. The curing of mortar is delayed and the bond between bricks and mortar is not certain. By contrast, prefabrication is unaffected by weather conditions.

Producing buildings on site makes it possible to choose bespoke design features. Prefabrication is commercially attractive when buildings have many identical parts.

In that case, the installation of the prefabricated components does not take much time and no time is lost waiting for the building to become structurally stable. In certain circumstances, a possible compromise may be partial prefabrication, e.g. filigree precast floor slabs. With the latter floor construction, prefabricated components are complemented on site with in-situ concrete. This saves the cost of shuttering and reduces transport costs (owing to the reduced weight).

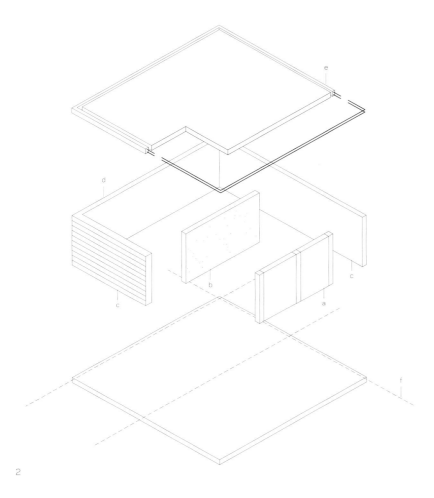

2

2 Retention of walls to be braced
in accordance with DIN 1053:

a Retained on one side
(only at base)
b Retained on two sides
(top and bottom)
c Retained on three sides
(top, bottom and one side)
d Retained on four sides
(top, bottom and both sides)
e Tie beam
f Force vectors
⤳ p. 84

BRACING

In wall construction, vertical forces (compressive stress) from the various loads are transferred via walls and piers. Walls held and braced on several sides by floors or cross walls are less prone to buckling, which means that they can be constructed higher with identical thickness. Buildings have to be braced against horizontal loads resulting from wind forces. Horizontal forces (tensile stress) are transferred via bracing elements or as imposed loads. A building will be sufficiently rigid when the floors between storeys are constructed as rigid plates, or with peripheral ring beams, and there are a sufficient number of longitudinal and transverse walls. This requires at least three vertical wall plates, the force vectors of which do not intersect at one point. If the three walls have the same point of intersection or the point of intersection lies at infinity, the system is not stable. Bracing walls are differentiated into those that provide rigidity to the whole building and those that provide rigidity only to building components. Walls that provide rigidity to the whole building are part of the overall system, and hence share the responsibility for the structural stability of the building. Walls that provide rigidity to building components only are typically those that brace long extended shear walls against any lateral movement (buckling, tipping) under compressive loads.

When designing bracing construction elements, one needs to determine the height, thickness and length of the bracing wall in relation to the length, thickness and weight of the wall to be braced, as well as the intervals between the bracing walls. ⤳ p. 90 In view of the deformation behaviour of the respective material, it is advisable to build the bracing walls from the same or a similar material as that of the wall to be braced, with connection details – possibly including reinforcement – to ensure adequate bonding to withstand tensile and compressive forces.

FLOOR SYSTEMS

Floors ⤳ p. 130 are the horizontal elements that enclose rooms and carry both the permanent loads of their own weight and the changeable imposed live loads. In addition, their important function as bracing, load-transferring and thrust-resistant plates means that they have to transfer any horizontal forces, for example those from wind or earth pressure, to the loadbearing and bracing walls. The floors used in wall construction systems are either one- or two-directional depending on the system, material and construction method. In the event of fire, floors must have adequate loadbearing capacity for at least the duration of the rescue work. In multi-storey buildings, impact sound insulation also plays an important role.

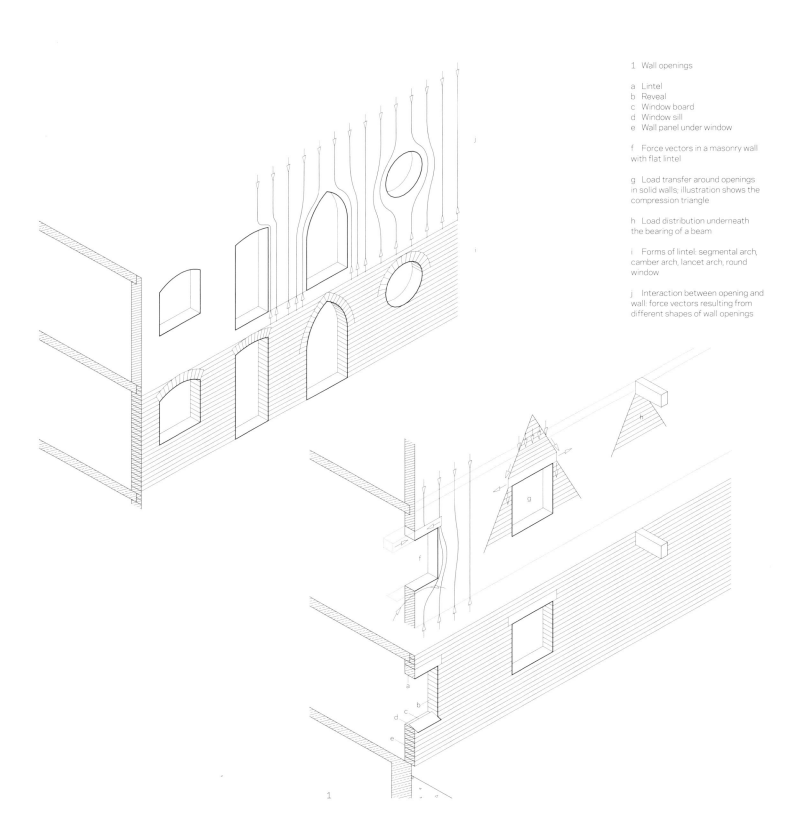

1   Wall openings

a   Lintel
b   Reveal
c   Window board
d   Window sill
e   Wall panel under window

f   Force vectors in a masonry wall with flat lintel

g   Load transfer around openings in solid walls; illustration shows the compression triangle

h   Load distribution underneath the bearing of a beam

i   Forms of lintel: segmental arch, camber arch, lancet arch, round window

j   Interaction between opening and wall: force vectors resulting from different shapes of wall openings

2 Temperature gradient for different masonry wall constructions:

a External insulation
b Internal insulation
c Core insulation

3 Thermal bridges in the construction of external corners; a smaller inside surface is opposite a larger outside surface that is losing heat:

a Layout
b Section

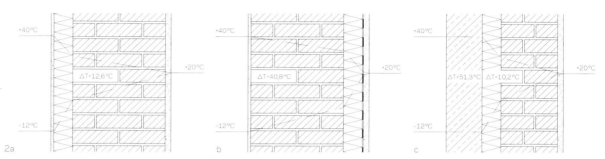

2a

WALL OPENINGS

Compared to skeleton construction buildings, those built using wall construction have smaller openings in relation to the overall wall surface. In order to facilitate the transfer of vertical loads, openings should be arranged at regular intervals and vertically above each other. Openings in wall plates necessitate the diversion of forces, which leads to the concentration of loads in certain areas. Large openings can be achieved using a mixture of piers and columns. However, this type of construction will inevitably increase the cost of the overall building. The size of openings is determined by the height of the storey, the beam above them and the height of the sill. The width of the opening and the height of the beam above is determined by the type of material and construction method. Whereas formerly it was customary to construct arches over openings, today the loads above are supported by steel lintels or reinforced concrete beams, which are easy to produce and install. The design of the openings themselves is determined by a number of different factors such as the amount of daylight required, the type of sill and the depth of the beam in combination with solar screening devices or roller shutters. The installation of domestic utilities requires apertures in both walls and floors.

Apertures and recesses in loadbearing walls are generally possible. Their number, size and position is determined by the requirements of the services installation and should be structurally checked. Horizontal slots weaken the wall cross section and are only possible to a limited degree. ➔ p. 91 During the detailed design stage, all the required installation slots and recesses are coordinated and appropriately documented. When completed, all services installations also have to comply with the requirements for fire safety and sound insulation. It is advisable to clarify beforehand who is responsible for closing apertures in floors or ceilings following the installation of services (coordination of construction sequence and clarification of costs).

BUILDING PHYSICS

When choosing a material for building walls, the different physical performance requirements relating to thermal insulation, thermal storage, strength, fire protection and sound insulation have to be balanced. This will influence the design of the cross section of the component, including its different layers. This requires close cooperation between the architect and the structural engineer, who will usually not only produce the structural calculations, but also provide the required evidence of fire protection, as well as acoustic and thermal insulation.

THERMAL INSULATION

Good thermal insulation creates the conditions for a hygienic and agreeable room climate and for avoiding the occurrence of condensation in the interior (DIN 4108). The type and location of the thermal insulation is an important aspect of the wall design. Owing to the different thermal insulating properties of solid construction materials, single-skin or double-skin constructions may be chosen, depending on the requirements and material. ➔ p. 81

When insulation is placed on the outside, it is possible to create an outer building envelope without gaps. Solid internal walls have a long heating up and cooling down time combined with high storage capacity and thereby generate a stable interior climate.

Insulation placed on the inside of the wall is more suitable for rooms with intermittent heating, because the heating-up time is relatively short. Furthermore, it is well suited to retro-fit installations (e.g. in existing buildings that are protected as historic monuments). A disadvantage is that the insulation layer is often interrupted by cross walls or floors; exact detailing is therefore required, particularly in order to avoid condensation. As the structural elements in this type of arrangement are on the outside, they are more exposed to the effects of the weather. The behaviour of an internally located insulation layer (e.g. core insulation) is similar to that of external insulation. The necessity for back ventilation must be checked in relation to the materials used for the wall and cladding, as well as their respective vapour diffusion resistance.

3a

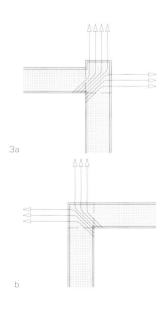

b

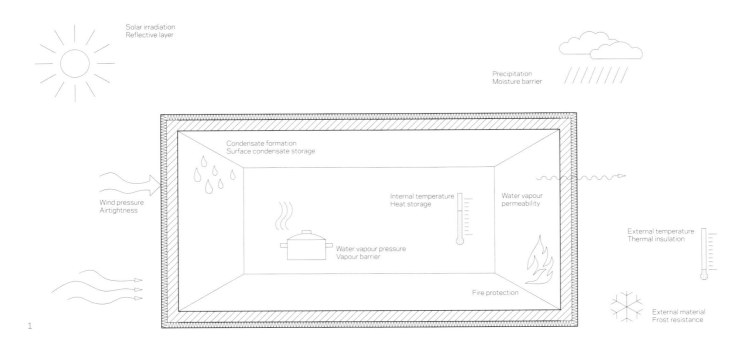

Solar irradiation
Reflective layer

Precipitation
Moisture barrier

Condensate formation
Surface condensate storage

Internal temperature
Heat storage

Water vapour
permeability

Wind pressure
Airtightness

Water vapour pressure
Vapour barrier

External temperature
Thermal insulation

Fire protection

External material
Frost resistance

1

HUMIDITY

Humidity contained in the ambient air will condense on component surfaces when the temperature of those components is below the temperature of the ambient air. This can also occur on the inside of components owing to water vapour diffusion. Moisture contained in the ground is the result of various sources of precipitation (infiltration) and is held there by the force of capillary action. A distinction is made between pressurised and non-pressurised water. Where structural components (basement walls, foundations) are in contact with non-pressurised water through contact with the ground, appropriate protection must be provided in accordance with DIN 18195-5. In the case of pressurised water and rising infiltration water, the construction of a waterproof concrete barrier is recommended.

AIR-TIGHTNESS

The increasing requirements of the Energy Conservation Directive (EnEV) are making air- and wind-tightness more and more important in order to achieve the guide values. Both joints and apertures must be finished airtight. Air leakages result in reduced sound insulation, increased moisture ingress into the construction, increased heat loss and reduced protection against overheating in summer. Masonry walls are considered airtight when they are finished with at least one wet plaster coat, usually the internal plaster. Documentary evidence can be provided via an air-tightness test (e.g. blower door test).

ROOM CLIMATE

Owing to the storage capacity of the material, solid brickwork, concrete, or clay walls are able to store heat, which they then emit over a period of time. On the other hand, the thermal insulation properties of this type of wall are not as good as that of lightweight materials. The ability to store heat is a positive factor in winter. Any solar radiation reaching the interior via the windows can be stored and given off again during the night.
Not least for this reason, the positioning of openings in a proposed building plays an important role. Conversely, the thermal storage capacity of wall materials can make a valuable contribution to buffering the effects of heat gain during summer, as they absorb heat during the day and emit it during the night (night cooling system).

1   Construction physics parameters

2 Movement joints:

a Movement joint with spray
gun-applied joint sealer
b Movement joint with
impregnated foam sealing strip

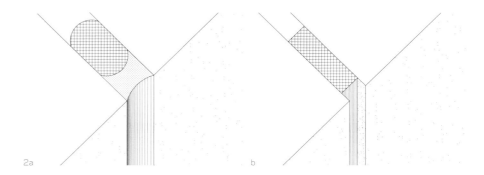

2a   b

FIRE PROTECTION

DIN 4102 part 2 specifies the dimensions required for fire walls. Fire walls are needed in various places: at the periphery of buildings, as separation between fire compartments within a building, or as party walls between terraced houses. Their function is to prevent the spread of fire to other buildings or building compartments. In order to prevent fire from spreading above roof level, fire walls normally have to extend 30 cm above the roof. During testing, fire walls have to resist exposure to fire for 90 minutes and still be able to withstand a standard impact test. For this reason their thickness is at least that of a full brick length. Loadbearing components have to retain their structural integrity for a specified period of time when exposed to fire. In addition to the materials of a wall (A for non-combustible materials, B for combustible materials), their position in the room or in the building, and their behaviour in the case of fire, have to be taken into account. A distinction is made between room-enclosing walls that separate the room from other units or rescue routes and which are only likely to suffer exposure to fire from one side, on the one hand, and non-room-enclosing walls on the other, which are located within a fire compartment and which are potentially exposed to fire from more than one side. Non-room-enclosing walls may therefore have to be thicker than room-enclosing walls.

SOUND INSULATION

Components with a large mass and two-leaf constructions achieve good airborne sound insulation. For this reason, the traditional masonry wall construction common in housing developments normally complies with the minimum sound insulation requirements. A solid, single-leaf wall with a weight per unit area of 350–400 kg/m² (this corresponds to a 24 cm thick calcium silicate brick wall with a specific gravity of 2.0 and approx. 1 cm thick plaster on both sides) achieves a weighted sound reduction index Rw of approx. 55 db. For stricter requirements, a two-leaf construction may be more appropriate. This may lead to additional cost as the walls have to be constructed with a separating joint without acoustic bridge, if necessary down to the basement floor.

DEFORMATION AND JOINTS

Different types of deformation such as deflection and/or changes in length may result from the respective material properties (thermal conductivity, thermal expansion, creep and shrinkage behaviour), the load (own weight or dead load, imposed loads, permanent loads), the direction of deformation (horizontal/vertical), and any external factors depending on orientation (north/south) and position (inside/outside).

In order to avoid damage such as cracks, it is necessary to allow for this deformation in the detailing of the construction. Suitable measures include expansion and movement joints. ⮌ 2 Joint widths of between 15 and 35 mm can be closed with sprayable elastic sealing compound. Smaller or larger joints can be sealed with joint sealing profiles. Parts of a building with different heights have to be separated with movement joints as these parts can be expected to be subject to differential settlement. The separation must be continuous i.e. through walls and floor slabs. The width and depth of expansion joints (DIN 18540) is determined on the basis of the movement and deformation to be expected, and the elastic compensation ability of the joint material also has to be taken into account. The choice of sealing material is determined by the strength and porosity of the substrate and by the compatibility of the substrate and sealing compound materials. The bonding between different materials can be improved with the application of a primer.

MASONRY CONSTRUCTION

1   Masonry as design element: this new IT training centre in Rwanda, with its distinctly archaic style, uses brick throughout – as a clear design concept – in walls, piers, as flooring, seating and in the ventilation openings. Nyanza, 2010, Dominikus Stark.

Masonry consists of inorganic, non-combustible masonry units and mortar. The structural and loadbearing effects are created by joining and interlinking the masonry units to form a so-called masonry bond. Basic construction components are piers and walls. The wall structure is created by laying masonry units to a certain bond. Masonry walls have to be interlocked if they join each other. The loadbearing capacity of masonry is limited. Modern masonry units have good performance characteristics and are economical owing to industrial mass production. They are also easy to use and they allow for individually tailored layout designs. By using large-format modular units, it is possible to achieve significant savings on the building site in terms of time and effort. In combination with different mortars, different kinds of masonry unit – with different formats, cross sections and other properties (compressive strength, specific gravity, thermal insulation and frost-resistance) – can be used for different wall constructions.

Today, masonry units are primarily designed for their load-bearing function rather than aesthetic aspects. The units have been optimised purely in respect of their structural and physical performance and, once laid, are generally plastered or clad. Monolithic systems are seldom used, owing to the thermal insulation required.

Where it is intended to feature brick in the appearance of a wall, it is usual to construct the wall in several leaves with specially developed weather-resistant face bricks on the outside, or alternatively to apply brick slips as a finish. As a design element ↘1, the material of masonry and its method of bonding determine its appearance. Variation of the composition of base material, the shape, the method of firing and the surface treatment means that the choice of different bricks is nearly unlimited. They normally have a very long service life and can even be returned to their original appearance through suitable refurbishment and cleaning methods.

2   A block bond and openings in
a wall:
a   Starter and corner block
b   Flat block lintel
c   Ceiling edge formwork element,
U-shaped or L-shaped brick
element
d   Offset block
e   Housing for shutter or roller blind
f   Reveal block
g   Reveal liner
h   Roller strap block
i   Insulation offset block
j   Non-standard block for lengths
of between 10 and 25 cm
k   Calibrated block element
l   Cut block
m Precast lintel
n   Vertical U- or L-shaped elements
for installation ducts or reinforced
concrete columns to support point
loads

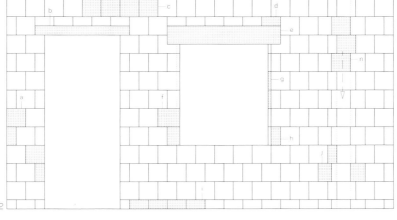
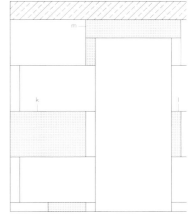

3   Types of load:
a   Imposed load/dead load
b   Wind suction
c   Wind pressure
d   Cantilever load
e   Impact load

4   Block/joint load conditions.
Different deformations at the point
of contact create stresses:
a   Compression
b   Failure of block
c   Tension
d   Compressive stress
e   Mortar deformation

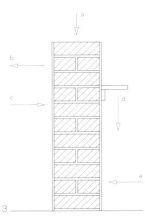

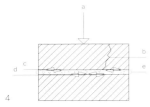

CONSTRUCTION PRINCIPLE

Masonry is primarily suitable for building elements exposed to compressive stress. Its compressive strength is significantly greater than its shear and tensile bending strength. Ideally, the transfer of loads is spread over a length or area. Load concentrations at points are not favourable. Tensile stress and bending (e.g. from wind or earth pressure) can only be absorbed to a limited extent. The following criteria have to be taken into account in the design as they affect the loadbearing properties:

–   provenance: natural stone or man-made blocks
–   type of block: bricks, calcium silicate, concrete or aerated concrete blocks
–   type of bonding: with or without mortar (dry-stone walling)
–   type of mortar: normal or lightweight, for normal or thin joints
–   thickness of joint: thin, medium or thick mortar beds
–   type of perpendicular joint: with or without mortar
–   method of bonding: clay block walling or bonded brickwork
–   surface finish: face brickwork or rendered
–   construction method: built on site or prefabricated
–   specific gravity (kg/dm³): for determining the loads and thermal insulation

The block, its bond and type of mortar joint determine the compressive strength of the wall. ➘ 4 This is highest with blocks laid in thin mortar joints. Thin-bed block walling is stronger than walls made of bonded masonry blockwork. Perforated blocks have less compressive strength than solid blocks. A masonry wall cannot develop its full loadbearing strength unless the blocks are bonded with each other so that they ensure full transfer of forces. The end result therefore depends on the quality of the mortar joints, i.e. thickness, correct horizontal and vertical detail, the entire joint being filled, and compliance with the required overlap resulting from the type of bond. ➘ p. 95 When blocks are placed or moved out of centre they will be exposed to bending stress, which can lead to breakage and ultimately to a reduction of loadbearing capacity.

Bonds ensure that block and mortar function together to optimum effect. In new types of construction method it is increasingly common that perpendicular joints are not filled with mortar as they do not influence the compressive strength of the bond.

Tie beams or reinforced masonry can increase the stability of a structure owing to increased tensile strength. The thickness of walls depends on their position. Basement walls will not only have to carry the loads from above but also the load resulting from earth pressure, and therefore have to be thicker than walls in the upper storeys.

BRACING

DIN 1053 distinguishes between walls that are restrained on two sides (top and bottom by floors), on three sides (one free vertical edge) and on four sides. ➚ p. 83 The minimum dimension of bracing walls is a length of $1/5$ of the wall height; where there are openings, $1/5$ of the clear height of the opening and a wall thickness of $1/3$ of the thickness of the wall to be braced; however, not less than a brick width. ➚ 1 Freestanding walls can be given structural stability by fixing them in the ground or at their base. Alternatively, structural stability can be attained by incorporating uprights that are fixed at their base (steel, concrete). ➚ 2

TIE BEAMS AND RING BEAMS

Tie beams are horizontal components at the top of the wall. They stabilise shear walls that transfer horizontal loads (tensile forces) and they are constructed around the periphery of the structure concerned without interruption.

Ring beams are horizontal beams within the plane of the wall which absorb tensile forces, bending moments and compression forces. They are required where the floor does not act as a bracing plate (e.g. a timber joist floor). Tie beams are required in a variety of situations: for buildings of more than two full storeys or a length of more than 18 m; for walls with many or large openings (width of openings >60% of the wall length or width of windows $>2/3$ of the storey height); under sliding joints and for loadbearing components that on their own are not sufficiently shear-resistant (e.g. brickwork). They may also be required as a result of the properties of the soil, or where the floors do not function as bracing. They are usually constructed at the edge of the floor as reinforcement within the depth of the floor. The minimum reinforcement for tie beams is two continuous reinforcement bars with a minimum diameter of 10 mm. Tie beams are constructed in reinforced concrete, steel or reinforced masonry.

It is important to note that, at the top floor level, there are no imposed loads from walls above. This means that the forces resulting from deformation of the floor cannot be transferred into the walls to the same degree as is possible in the other floors of the building. For this reason the top floor in the building is placed on a sliding bearing unless different details have been selected. Since in this case wind loads acting on the wall are not transferred into the roof slab via friction, it is imperative to insert a tie beam beneath the sliding bearings.

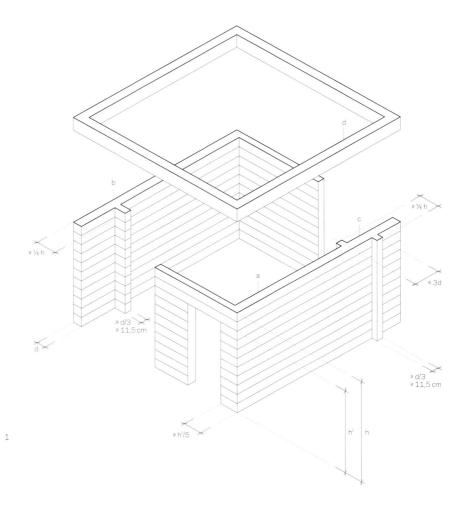

1

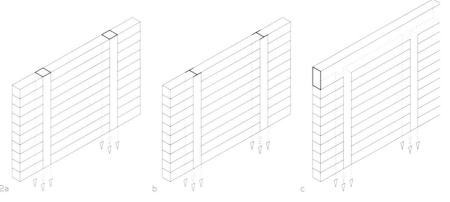

2a   b   c

1 Minimum dimension
of transverse bracing walls:
a   Wall to be braced
b   One-sided bracing
c   Two-sided bracing
d   Tie beam

h   Clear room height
h¹ Clear height of opening

2 Free-standing walls to
DIN 1053:
a   Bracing with reinforced
concrete piers
b   Bracing with steel profiles
c   Bracing with spreader beam

3 Horizontal and vertical slots
permitted without structural
calculation:
a   Slot of unlimited length
b   Flat block lintel
c   Temporary support;
required when clear
width (w) ⩾ 1.25 m

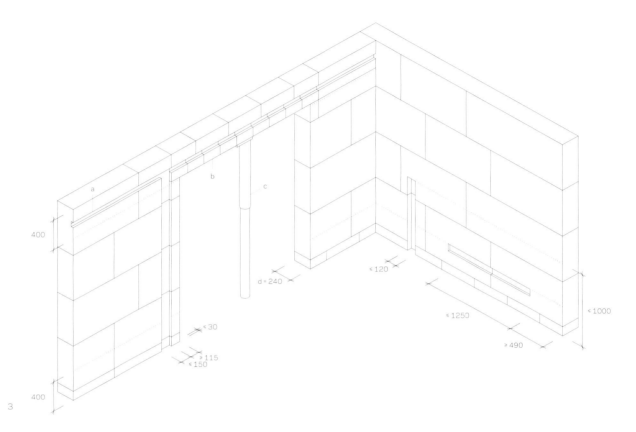

3

OPENINGS

Originally, the horizontal member above an opening for a door or a window in brickwork consisted of bricks. Today it is common to use prefabricated lintels (as single-span beams). Depending on the design, such lintels may have a tensile chord (e.g. prefabricated system lintel) and a compression zone (the brickwork or blockwork above the lintel). When reinforced form blocks are used and filled with concrete, it is possible to achieve a homogeneous wall surface. This offers the advantage of a uniform substrate for the render or plaster finish with equal deformation properties (avoidance of cracks). Where prefabricated system lintels are topped with brickwork or blockwork, it is imperative that the perpendicular joints are filled with mortar in order to create a cohesive compression zone. The lateral bearing depth is usually the width of a brick. Prefabricated system lintels can be used for spans of up to 3 m. Prefabricated lintels are made in lengths of up to 2 m, so the maximum clear opening can be that dimension less a full brick length.

In the case of face brickwork or blockwork, the dimension and position of openings should be selected in accordance with the intended masonry bond. Many masonry block manufacturers also produce prefabricated lintels to suit their system. Where it is intended to finish masonry with plaster or render, it is usual to cut the masonry blocks on site. For reasons of efficiency, opening sizes are best determined in accordance with the measurements of the chosen masonry block system.

RECESSES

Chases or slots (usually inserted for the installation of pipes or cables) result in a lessening of the loadbearing capacity. Rules for cutting and positioning chases are specified in DIN 1053-1. Where the rules of this DIN standard are followed, the result is deemed to satisfy and so no structural calculations have to be provided. The standard depth of chases is between 10 and 30 mm, i.e. the masonry is cut back to that depth. Horizontal chases are structurally less favourable than vertical ones.

MINIMUM SIZE

The definition in DIN 1053-1 says that loadbearing masonry walls are plate-type building components that are primarily exposed to compression and which support vertical loads from floors as well as horizontal loads, such as those resulting from wind. Since these walls have no tensile strength, any forces transmitted away from the centre can lead to a splitting of the wall, and hence ultimately to buckling. For this reason, the loads on masonry walls should be placed in the centre.

The simplified design method can be applied to buildings <20 m in height(table in DIN 1053-100). The specification for minimum dimensions will depend on whether a component is intended to perform loadbearing or bracing functions. The definition distinguishes between walls, piers and columns. Short walls, wall sections, or piers with a loadbearing function and a cross sectional area of <1000 cm² should be constructed of whole blocks. Cross sections of <400 cm² are not permitted as loadbearing components. The minimum thickness of loadbearing walls starts with the width of a brick for internal walls. The minimum thickness of external walls with a height of <2.75 m is 17.5 cm. The minimum thickness of basement walls with a height of <2.60 m is the length of a brick. Loadbearing piers must be at least one length of brick wide (possible formats {continental}: 11.5 × 36.5 cm, 17.5 × 24 cm or 17.5 × 36.5 cm). Bracing walls with a minimum thickness of 11.5 cm must have a weight per area of >200 kg/m². Recesses and chases in masonry walls do not require structural calculation if the wall thickness is greater than one length of brick. Apertures measuring <625 cm² with a proportion of width to height exceeding 1:1.5 and which do not weaken the wall by more than 15% are permitted without structural calculation.

AIR-TIGHTNESS

The air-tightness of masonry walls is achieved with the help of internal plaster. However, with vertically perforated bricks it is possible that air movement takes place within the brickwork. Open flanks (e.g. at window reveals) must be covered with special mortar layers.

FIRE PROTECTION

Fire protection is primarily affected by the block dimension, joint details and surface finish. Blocks and mortar made of mineral (non-organic) material are not combustible and do not constitute a fire load. Solid masonry walls in conventional construction in combination with solid floors therefore usually comply with the fire safety requirements.

SOUND, ACOUSTICS

The weighted sound reduction index (R'_w) of single-leaf walls with plaster finish on both sides depends on the specific gravity of the blocks and the thickness of the wall, i.e. the weight per unit area. Double-leaf constructions can improve the sound insulation values compared to a single-leaf construction with the same weight because the wall and cavity act as a mass-spring-mass vibration system, although it is also important to consider the frequencies in question. Likewise, the size of the cavity plays a role in determining the degree of sound insulation. There must be no connections between the two skins of the wall; the cavity should be filled with insulation.

THERMAL INSULATION

Thermal insulation in masonry walls depends on the construction (single or double-leaf system), the type of blocks used and the insulation material. A recent development is that of thermal insulation blocks, which have thermal insulation integrated in their cavities. Thermal bridges in masonry construction typically occur at the external corners of buildings → 2, the bearings of floors in external walls, lofts, cantilevering floors or balcony slabs. These can be avoided through thermal separation or additional thermal insulation layers. The mortar joints also represent thermal bridges, but these have already been allowed for in the calculated thermal conductivity of the masonry.

Wall thickness 70 mm
Specific weight class 2.0
thin plaster finish on both sides
R'ᵥ 40 dB

Wall thickness 240 mm
Specific weight class 2.0
R'ᵥ 55 dB

Wall thickness 2 × 115 mm
Cavity >60 mm
Specific weight class 2.0
R'ᵥ 67 dB

1

1   Sound insulation values of different wall thicknesses in calcium silicate blocks

2   Thermal bridges, 1:20:
a less than ideal solution with thermal insulation extended downwards
b effective insulation with the help of an insulating offset block

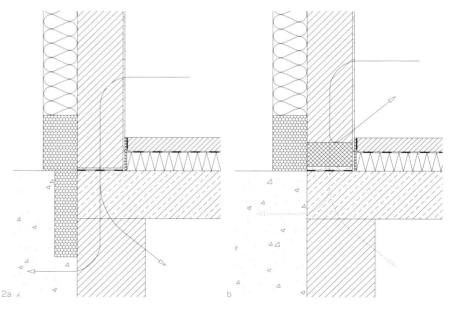

2a   b

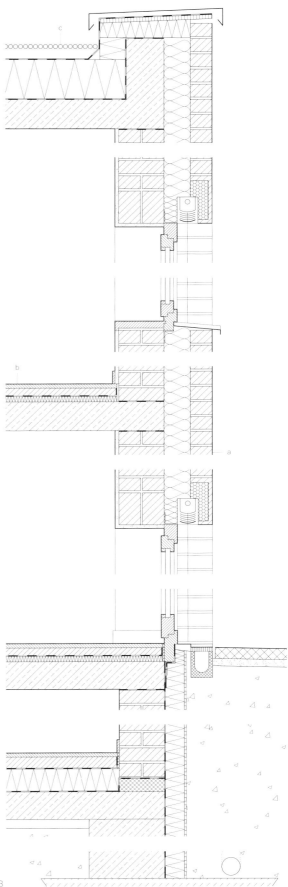

3 Masonry wall section, 1:20

a Wall construction:
outer skin consisting of
face brick 115 mm,
thermal insulation 140 mm,
loadbearing skin 240 mm,
internal plaster 20 mm

b Floor structure,
ground floor/upper floor:
solid floorboards 23 mm,
floating screed 40 mm,
separating layer,
impact sound insulation 30 mm,
reinforced concrete slab 150 mm,
underside plastered

c Roof structure:
extensive greening of roof,
root barrier,
sloping insulation 200 to 300 mm,
bituminous vapour barrier,
reinforced concrete slab 160 mm,
underside plastered

CONSTRUCTION OF EXTERNAL WALLS

Large-format blocks, new construction methods, new processing and installation aids, and perpendicular joints without mortar all help to make construction more efficient and cost-effective. When using thin bed masonry blocks it is an advantage to produce course layout plans in order to ensure a swift building process. By cutting blocks to suit any non-standard gaps, precise bonds can be achieved. A disadvantage of assembly on the building site is fluctuation in the weather. At low temperatures and particularly with frost, mortar sets more slowly and the bonding between block and mortar can no longer be guaranteed.

Many manufacturers of masonry blocks provide entire wall systems, including special fittings and prefabricated parts such as lintels, roller shutter boxes, specially shaped blocks for connections, and U-shaped formwork for constructing tie beams. There are also manufacturers who produce entire walls at the factory.

The size, format and weight of blocks determine the bricklayer's output. The traditional method for constructing a wall is by laying blocks manually. Depending on the weight and size, a distinction is made between one-handed blocks (6 to 7.5 kg suitable for handling with one hand) and two-handed blocks (7.5 to 25 kg). Above a processing weight of >25 kg, special equipment is used for laying (mini-crane), which can be used to lay large-format blocks individually or in groups simultaneously on a mortar bed. In that case it is advantageous to produce a process schedule for the sequence of the walls to be constructed. It is standard practice to execute regulation masonry work. In special cases, the construction of walls is subject to special testing (e.g. for highly stressed components) and has to be specially supervised during execution.

Where the outside walls of basements are built in masonry, they have to be sealed with bonded polymer bitumen sheeting or a self-adhesive bitumen layer. In housing, more economical thick plastic-modified bitumen coating is usually the preferred option. The horizontal sealing layer must be closely jointed with the vertical damp course. The plinth area must be protected up to 30 cm above land level against water splash using a water-resistant render. Openings (doors) must be at least 15 cm above ground level. Any precipitation water that penetrates the outer leaf must be drained back to the outside without causing damage. In many double-leaf constructions, the sealing layer is applied to the outside of the inner skin.

DIMENSIONAL SYSTEMS AND FORMATS

The dimensions for the structure and layout design, as well as for openings and the building envelope, are based on the size of the masonry block. Different formats are in existence, which allows an individual design of the building. By choosing the format and surface finish of the masonry block, an important decision is made with respect to the appearance and structure of the building; a uniform dimensional system is a prerequisite for efficient, cost-effective construction of the shell building. It is important to remember that the length of building blocks can be adjusted, whereas there is no variation in the delivered height of blocks. This means that the height of a brick wall is determined by the number of courses times the course height (block + joint). The basic dimensional unit is derived from dividing one metre by eight (12.5 cm); in the UK and other countries, this unit is based on dividing one yard by eight (4.5 inches or 11.25 cm). Some manufacturers also supply non-standard block thicknesses for use in the first layer so that the vertical bond can start level with the top of the floor deck. The design of a masonry wall should be based on the standard block unit size in order to minimise cutting and material waste. When putting up new buildings it is now common practice to use thin-bed masonry blocks with a thickness to suit the required wall thickness.

Thin-format bricks (approx. 50 mm high) are almost exclusively used for face brickwork. Even the normal brick format is less common these days, as large-format masonry blocks (thin-bed elements) require less time to lay and therefore result in a more cost-efficient construction. Thin-bed elements are available in different materials such as clay, calcium silicate, or cement-based materials and are designed with a tongue-and-groove system. These blocks have precisely ground bearing surfaces and are preferably laid in thin horizontal mortar beds (approx. 2 mm joint) with a dry perpendicular butt joint. Most manufacturers supply complete block systems including corner, half and accessory blocks. The formats are specified not as a multiple of the basic system unit, but as the actual dimension of the blocks. Nevertheless, the block systems are designed on the assumption that the sizes of wall openings, such as for doors and windows, are still based on the basic dimensional unit (continental: 12.5 cm; imperial: 4.5 inches). The blocks in the newer systems are manufactured slightly bigger to compensate for thinner joints, so that the overall dimensional system can still be maintained. Solid wall blocks must not have more than max. 15 % perforations perpendicular to the bearing surface. Vertically perforated blocks feature a number of small vertical perforations (15 % to 50 % of the bearing surface). Hollow core blocks are large-format blocks with one or several cavities.

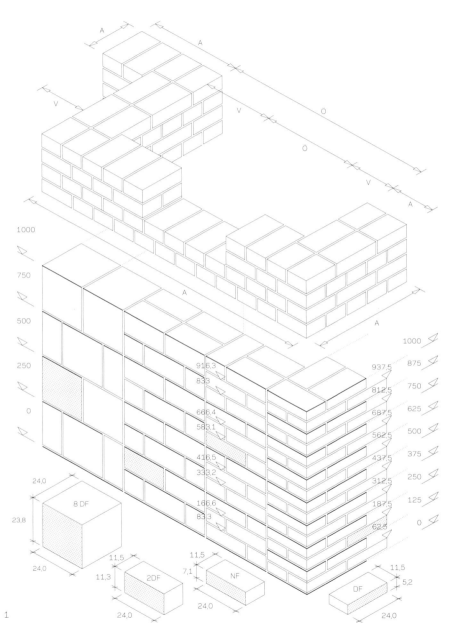

1

1 Dimensional system for blockwork and various block formats.

External wall dimension = × times 12.5 (modular dimension) or rather × times 12.5–1 (nominal dimension)

Dimension of openings = × times 12.5 (modular dimension) or rather × times 12.5 + 1 (nominal dimension)

Dimension of projection = × times 12.5 (modular dimension) or × times 12.5 (nominal dimension)

Course heights are calculated accordingly: × times 12.5 (modular dimension) and × times 12.5–1.2 (nominal dimension).

2 Masonry wall bonds:
a Stretcher bond
All courses consist of stretchers with alternate courses offset either by 1/2 brick length (standard stretcher bond) or by 1/3 or 1/4 brick length (raking stretcher bond). The stretcher bond provides the best strength and is common in 11.5 cm thick walls laid in small-format blocks Other common wall thicknesses are 24, 30, 36.5 cm using small and medium-sized formats.
b Header bond
All courses consist of headers with courses being offset by 1/2 brick width. Due to the small overlap, the loadbearing capacity of header bonds is less than that of stretcher bonds; however, this is not normally taken into account in structural calculations for masonry walls. This bond is often used for large-format blocks.
c English bond
In this bond, headers and stretchers are placed in alternate courses. The perpendicular joints of all stretcher courses are vertically above each other. The idea of this bond is to increase the loadbearing strength of the wall construction.
d Flemish bond
In this bond, header and stretcher courses alternate. Four courses are required. The perpendicular joints in every other stretcher course are offset by 1/2 brick length. This bond is used to increase the loadbearing strength of the wall construction.

3 Apartment building with exposed brickwork, Pécs, 2006, Ferenc Cságoly and Ferenc Keller

4 Offset in masonry block bond

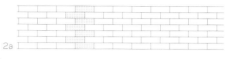

2a

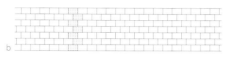

b

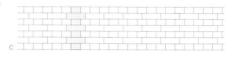

c

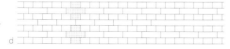

d

3

BONDS

The loadbearing characteristics and the loadbearing effect of masonry walls depend on the slenderness of the units and the selected bond. The general principle is that masonry blocks are laid to a bond. Transverse and longitudinal perpendicular joints of the different courses in a blockwork bond must be offset against each other by a minimum overlap dimension. This dimension is at least 0.4 times the height of the block for blocks >11.3 cm high, and at least 4.5 cm for blocks <11.3 cm high. ➘ 4 There are stretcher and header courses. Stretchers are placed along the direction of the wall whereas headers are placed across. In general, courses should be laid alternately and be vertically aligned with each other. Thin-bed masonry blocks take up the whole wall thickness in each course. The thickness of the wall results from the transverse or longitudinal direction of the block. Bonded masonry work consists of two or more regularly repeating block courses in every other or every second course. The minimum overlap dimension must be maintained in both the longitudinal and transverse directions. Large-format masonry blocks, which in the main are manufactured industrially, are normally laid in simple stretcher bond. In the case of face brickwork, the main criteria are appearance and production cost.

WALL CONNECTIONS

Walls that brace, adjoin, or form a corner with another wall must be constructed with a connecting bond. Sometimes it is more cost-effective not to build adjoining walls at the same time as the main wall (simpler and more time-efficient). In contrast, party walls between housing units should not be connected for acoustic reasons; instead they should penetrate the external wall. Where walls are connected via toothing, it is important that the courses of the two joining walls are at the same level, since different or mixed course heights would result in differential deformation characteristics. This can have a negative effect on the loadbearing ability. In the case of a butt joint, the cross wall will simply butt up against the longitudinal wall and a bond between the two walls is created by inserting flat stainless steel ties in every, or every other, horizontal joint, depending on the loading. The butt joints must be fully filled with mortar.
In the case of face blockwork, the appearance of the wall is primarily determined by the material and the pattern of the joints. Special effects can be achieved with special bond patterns.

4

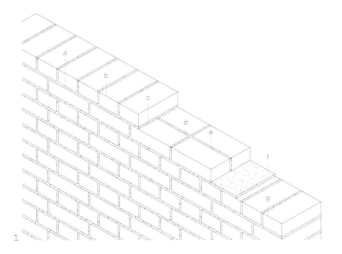

1

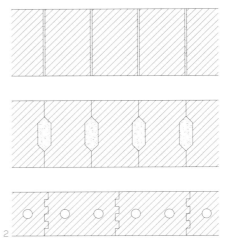

2

1 Position of blocks in masonry;
   terminology:
a Stretcher
b Header
c Bed joint
d Perpendicular joint (perpend)
e Longitudinal joint (middle joint)
f Mortar bed
g Face of block (head)

2 Perpendicular joint versions:
a fully filled
b with grip slot (filled)
c dry

3 Options for finishing joints in
   masonry wall construction:
a pointed
b pointed with rounded finish
c pointed flush
d recessed joint
e V-joint
f joint with weather cut
g full joint
f joint with undercut
i raked-out joint

JOINTS

Mortar joints can be horizontal or perpendicular joints. Perpendicular joints are the vertical joints between the masonry blocks in a course. In some systems, perpendicular joints are filled with mortar, but not in others. The horizontal joints are the joints between the block courses. Their thickness depends on the type of block used and the type of mortar. It is the design and material of the horizontal joint that influences the transfer of vertical and horizontal forces. The adhesion or friction between block and mortar is what permits horizontal forces to be transferred. Horizontal joints ensure that the building blocks make full contact with the course below. An additional function of the joint is to compensate for dimensional tolerances both in the size of the blocks and in the laying process. Thicker joints are required for irregular block surfaces, whereas blocks with precisely machined surfaces can be laid on thinner joints.

The material properties of masonry work differ according to direction: namely, perpendicular and parallel to the horizontal joint (orthotropic material behaviour). Perpendicular to the horizontal joint, the wall will have high compressive strength whereas only very low tensile stresses can be absorbed. Tensile forces must be absorbed not only in order to secure the structural integrity of the building, but also in order to avoid cracks which would impair the suitability for purpose (e.g. ingress of precipitation moisture). The tensile strength of a masonry wall can be increased by inserting reinforcement mesh into horizontal joints; this is rarely done however.

Joints have a relatively high thermal conductivity. For this reason the proportion of joints and joint material is an important factor in determining the thermal insulation property of a masonry bond. Usually the mortar element is already included in the technical data of masonry blocks. Depending on the material and bond, the mortar component in a masonry wall can be between 1 % and 20 %. In accordance with the DIN 4172 dimensional system, the standard height of a horizontal joint is 12 mm. The nominal thickness of joints refers to the finished condition of the masonry work. The nominal thickness of horizontal joints is 12 mm for normal and lightweight mortar, 1 to 3 mm for thin-bed mortar and 6 mm for medium-bed mortar.

The width of perpendicular joints is 10 mm in the case of normal mortar and 1 to 3 mm for thin-bed mortar. In certain masonry block systems the vertical joint is not filled with mortar. This saves time and material: no transverse bond has to be executed, and the transfer of forces in the masonry work is improved. The inner and outer leaves of cavity walls, and walls butt-jointed with a main wall, can be bonded using stainless steel wire wall ties, which are placed into the horizontal joints. In order to prevent moisture from penetrating the thermal insulation layers it may be necessary to fit drip discs or clips to these ties.

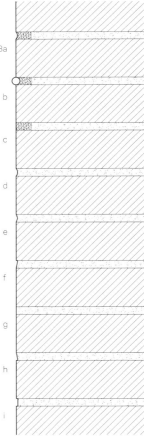

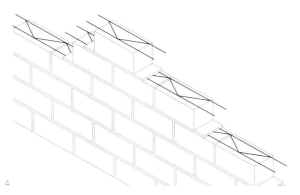

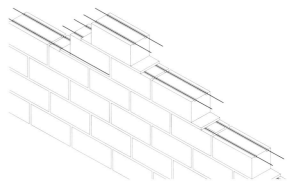

4

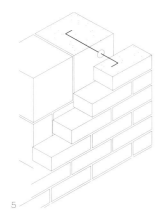

5

MORTAR

The main requirements for mortar laid in joints concern compressive strength and the bond between mortar and block (adhesive shear strength), as the properties of the mortar affect the loadbearing capacity of the wall (DIN 1053).

There are different groups of mortar, which are classed by their compressive strength; the mortar group must be selected to suit the chosen masonry block and the structural requirements. Depending on the location of the building project, mortar may also have to be weather- and frost-resistant, or open to diffusion.

Mortar is a mixture of sand, binding agent (cement, lime, gypsum, anhydrite, magnesite, clay, organic binders or plastics) and water. The property of mortar may also be modified by additives that are added at the factory. Depending on the binding agent used, mortars may be referred to as lime, cement, lime cement and gypsum mortar. The curing process depends on the type of binder; it can be the result of drying or of hydraulic reaction (chemical process between lime and cement which is triggered by adding water and leads to crystallisation). Hydraulic mortars cure faster and are more weather-resistant. Loadbearing parts of the building should only be finished with lime or cement render, possibly with added binder. Mortars are categorised by their respective uses, i.e. for brickwork, render or screed. For the construction of fire compartments there are special fire-resistant mortars, which are subject to approval. The aggregate used in mortar is usually sand. Alternatively, sharp sand, grit or woodchips may also be used. The grain size is 4 mm maximum. The trade also distinguishes between mortar according to how and where it is made, i.e. mixed on site, or delivered to site ready to use (factory-mixed dry mortar, pre-mixed dry mortar, ready-mix mortar, dry silo mortar). Today, pre-mixed mortars are the preferred choice because of their more consistent quality and modern construction site organisation. When the product is delivered to site as ready-mix mortar it remains workable for 36 hours. Where pre-mixed dry mortar is delivered to site, or stored on site in a silo, it only needs the addition of water to be ready for use. Owing to the fluctuations in quality and the more expensive process, mortar is only mixed on site in exceptional circumstances. During particularly dry weather, or when using masonry blocks with strong suction, it helps to pre-wet the substrate in order to ensure that water is not withdrawn from the mortar too rapidly. Mortar must be protected against unfavourable weather conditions. The colour of joints is determined by the mortar used. When repointing facing masonry, the colour of the mortar can be adjusted to match existing joints. Coloured mortars are available for this purpose. When used with face brickwork or blockwork, mortar is subject to more exacting requirements with respect to surface, processing quality and joint pattern. Likewise, the colour of the mortar in the joints is important. Contrast with the brick or block colour emphasises the joint pattern, whereas a similar colour reinforces the impression of a uniform surface.

In recent years a wide range of industrially produced blocks and accessories has been developed. Depending on the product, they meet different requirements with respect to compressive, tensile and shear strength. Even with today's exacting energy efficiency requirements, it is possible to use the monolithic wall construction method. Aerated concrete blocks have low specific weight and thermal conductivity and are therefore well suited for use in low-energy construction. In recent years, lightweight concrete blocks have become even more lightweight, and hence more insulating, through changes in additives and additional perforations. Calcium silicate blocks on the other hand are heavier but have a higher loadbearing capacity and good sound-insulating properties. By increasing the degree of perforation it has been possible to reduce the weight for easier handling. However, when it is intended to use calcium silicate blocks in external walls where thermal insulation is required, a multi-leaf wall structure is required. Generally speaking all masonry block materials are constantly undergoing technical development with respect to improved thermal insulation, greater air-tightness and a more efficient construction method.

CALCIUM SILICATE BLOCKS

Calcium silicate blocks are solid blocks which are produced in a range of different specific weights. Their advantages are their high loadbearing capacity, good sound insulation and fire resistance. They also have a high storage mass, which helps to prevent overheating in summer. Thermal insulation during the winter can only be achieved through additional thermal insulation layers. Calcium silicate thin-bed blocks are usually laid with special equipment, owing to their heavy weight. A number of different formats are available, including blocks with a hand slot, hollow-core blocks, standard-sized blocks and thin-bed blocks and elements. Facing and veneer bricks are produced in different strength classes, with veneer brick being suitable for more exacting conditions.

BRICKS

The development of bricks is moving from solid units that can be handled with one hand to lightweight vertically perforated units (thermal insulation bricks) with a perforation proportion of up to 60% and low thermal conductivity of 0.08 W/(mK). In combination with thin-bed processes, these units can be employed for monolithic wall construction without additional thermal insulation. Typical examples are monolithic external walls with thicknesses of between 30 and 50 cm. Thin-bed bricks with improved thermal insulation properties have a thermal conductivity of as little as 0.09 W/(mK). Filled thin-bed bricks can be used where higher sound-insulation prop-

erties are required. In this case the cavities in the bricks are filled with material such as concrete, poured in one go once they have been laid up to one storey high. These bricks are suitable as party walls between residential units or, with thermal insulation, for external walls. During manufacture the bricks are subjected to a sintering process whereby less air is enclosed in the material. The specific weight of these bricks is therefore high, which means that they have high compressive strength and are frost-resistant. For improved thermal insulation it is possible to add porous material with a lower specific weight such as sawdust or polystyrene beads. This material will burn during the firing process without leaving any residue.

a

GRANULATED SLAG BRICKS

These are artificial bricks made from recycled material without firing. Their base material is granulated furnace slag which is processed together with lime, ground slag or cement, and water. These bricks are compressed under high pressure and cure in the open air with the help of steam, or exhaust gas containing carbon dioxide. Granulated slag bricks can be used in many applications. They have high compressive strength, fire-resistance, good sound insulation, low risk of cracking, are dimensionally stable and resistant to frost.

b

AERATED CONCRETE BLOCKS

Aerated concrete blocks are solid blocks, owing to their manufacturing process. Their specific weight is very low, however, which means that the weight per block is low. The proportion of pores may be of up to 90% of the volume. Nevertheless, aerated concrete blocks combine good thermal insulation properties with high strength; furthermore, they can easily be cut to size by sawing. Large-format blocks come in sizes of up to 62.5 × W × 62.5 cm; cost-efficient solutions can also be obtained with wall panels or storey-high partition wall elements. For example, these systems are available with a height of 2.60 m and widths of up to 3 m. Thicknesses can vary between 15 and 36.5 cm. Both blocks and elements are very dimensionally stable and are laid using the thin-bed method and butt jointing. Aerated concrete blocks can be used to build monolithic, single-skin walls without the need for additional thermal insulation layers. Owing to their high air content, these blocks are open to diffusion and are not frost-resistant, which is why they need to be protected by cladding or external render.

c

d

e

f

g

h

i

Types of masonry block:

a Calibrated calcium silicate block
b Solid hollow-centred block
c Vertically perforated block
   with insulation infill
d Granulated slag block
e Aerated concrete block
f Lightweight concrete block
   without insulation
g Lightweight concrete block
   with insulation
h Natural stone
i Adobe

LIGHTWEIGHT CONCRETE BLOCKS

The basic material consists of lightweight mineral substances (such as expanded slag, pumice, expanded slate, expanded clay, coal slag, or brick chippings) with the addition of sand. The binding agent is cement. Through the curing process of the hydraulic binding agent, blocks can be produced in strength classes of between 2 and 12. Their specific weight is determined by the composition of the material. Improved thermal insulation properties can be achieved by adding thermal insulation material into the cavities, or by laying the blocks with lightweight mortar, or by using the thin-bed process. Depending on the material, walls using lightweight concrete blocks can be constructed monolithically or with insulation. The material is not frost-resistant and must be protected against the effects of the weather. Lightweight concrete blocks in solid construction can be used for loadbearing applications of up to four storeys high, with wall thicknesses of between 20 and 36.5 cm. Lightweight concrete blocks provide a good key for the render finish and the large formats are quick and cost-efficient to process. Elements are butted, connected using dowels, and the joints are filled with concrete.

CONCRETE BLOCKS

The basic material of these blocks is standard concrete (cement, sand, gravel or crushed rock, and water). Concrete blocks are produced in factories. Designations: hollow core blocks, solid blocks in varying formats and densities. They have a high specific weight and high thermal conductivity, and are therefore suitable in applications where thermal storage mass is required. Concrete blocks have high compressive strength and are frost-resistant.

NATURAL STONE

Unlike man-made blocks, natural stone cannot be deliberately varied in its properties but is determined by its material. Where natural stone is used in external applications, the material must be frost-resistant. The main types of stone used in building construction are limestone, travertine, volcanic tuff, sandstone, dolomite, basalt lava, granite, diorite and diabase.

RAMMED CLAY

In rammed clay construction, the walls are built monolithically. Typical rammed clay construction has its own specific appearance, which is aesthetically appealing. The colour of the material is determined by the type of clay and rock material, varying from pale yellow to brown, red and even grey. Loadbearing walls are designed and sized according to guidelines on rammed clay construction issued by national umbrella organisations. Rammed clay walls are produced by filling suitably robust shuttering with damp clay in layers of 10 to 15 cm depth; the layers have to be compacted either by hand or using machinery. On average, a freshly filled 15 cm layer is compacted to 9 cm (approx. $^2/_3$). Depending on the structural requirements it is possible to insert horizontal reinforcement. Lintels are inserted in the form of timber, prefabricated concrete, steel, or reinforced in-situ concrete. It is usual to insert a tie-beam at the top of walls to provide a bearing for floors. The drying-out period can be quite long, depending on the wall thickness, time of year and weather, but must be observed. If frost occurs during this phase it is possible that the loadbearing capacity is significantly impaired. Any further treatment (e.g. plaster finish) must not be applied until the walls have dried out. Rammed clay is made up of construction clay and stone aggregate of various sizes (e.g. grain 0 to 16 mm, with oversized grains up to 22 mm). Its specific weight in the dry state is approx. 2300 kg/m³. The thermal conductance is 1.5 W/(mK) and the compressive strength 2.0 N/mm². Shrinkage of the material must be taken into account.

ADOBE BRICKS

Adobe bricks (also called mud bricks, or cob) and lightweight adobe bricks are produced without firing and hence with low energy input. Lightweight bricks have better thermal insulation, whereas heavier bricks are capable of better thermal storage. Today it is rare to see a building that is completely constructed with adobe bricks. In spite of the fact that the bricks are suitable for loadbearing building elements, they are primarily used for non-loadbearing internal walls or as infill between the studs of timber frame walls. Adobe bricks are grouped into the I and II application classes, depending on duty and functional purpose. With respect to the room climate, the bricks have excellent thermal storage properties and are also capable of storing and giving off humidity. During processing it is important that the bricks do not swell as the result of excessive moisture absorption. A special clay mortar is used. Both horizontal and perpendicular joints should not be wider than 1 to 1.5 cm and the drying time of the mortar needs to be taken into account. It is a specific feature of clay mortar that it does not cure like cement mortar, but achieves its strength just by drying. Lintels above windows and doors are usually of timber.

CONCRETE AND REINFORCED CONCRETE CONSTRUCTION

1 Spiral structure in fairfaced concrete, part of a sequence of sculptural service facilities along the "routa peregrino" pilgrim route in northern Mexico. Guadalajara, 2009, HHF Architects.

Since ancient times, concrete has been known as a man-made construction material, but it was not until the twentieth century that it became one of the most widely used materials, in combination with steel reinforcement. Its specific properties make it suitable for different conceptual, structural and building physics requirements. Furthermore, its plasticity means that it can be used to create not only vertical, horizontal or slanting building components, but in fact any shape required. Thanks to numerous innovations in concrete technology affecting both the composition and processing of the material, concrete can now be used for a wide range of constructions and designs.

Concrete is produced from three components: cement, water and aggregate (stone fragments in different sizes). Depending on its composition, cured concrete achieves different strengths (grouped into strength classes). These days, highly refined concrete products with specific characteristics are produced by supplementation with various additives, compounds, or air. Concrete can be used in constructions that are covered (with plaster or cladding) or as face material. The type and design of the shuttering determines the appearance to a large extent. A range of different surface textures can be achieved by using shuttering panels with different surfaces or by inserting matrix material into the shuttering, or with caustic treatment processes. ➔ p. 108

CONSTRUCTION PRINCIPLES FOR WALLS

Concrete is used for the construction of walls where the conceptual design and structural system of a building calls for this material. Concrete and reinforced concrete are suitable building materials where large structural loads or other structural forces are expected. For example, it is possible to construct wall plates in order to bridge large openings, to form bracing elements or to withstand pressure from earth or water. With the appropriate detailing, concrete is even able to withstand explosions or the impact of heavy loads. Its use is limited primarily by its own weight.

Concrete is non-combustible and highly fire-resistant which, combined with a range of different construction methods (e.g. prestressed concrete), makes it a suitable material for both high-rise and filigree building constructions. Typical reinforced concrete construction elements are building components such as walls and slabs/decks, or elements such as retaining walls and bridge piers (which use mass concrete only). Reinforced concrete walls can be constructed to different concrete classes with steel reinforcement in accordance with structural requirements. External wall constructions may consist of single, double or multiple skins. Alternatively, it is possible to use prefabricated or partly prefabricated components (e.g. filigree floors). ➔ p. 102

LOADBEARING CAPACITY

Concrete on its own has high compressive strength (up to 40 N/mm²) but can only absorb low tensile forces (max. 4 N/mm²). It is the combination with steel reinforcement that turns the material into a high-performance compound construction material, in which the compressive force is primarily absorbed by the concrete and the tensile force by the steel. Although non-reinforced concrete is able to withstand high compressive loads, its suitability for components exposed to tensile stresses is very limited. Owing to its brittleness, it will fail quite suddenly without the formation of cracks that could provide a warning. It is therefore usual to use concrete as a compound material, generally referred to as reinforced concrete. Steel is inserted as so-called 'non-prestressed reinforcement' in the form of round reinforcement bars, mesh or cages. This gives the material the capacity to support large distributed or point loads. The strength of the reinforcement is a decisive factor in the tensile strength of the material. The compressive strength of the concrete is determined by the concrete quality. In order to establish the loadbearing strength of the material, a positive connection between the surface of the reinforcement and the concrete has to be achieved. This is possible owing to the nearly identical expansion characteristics of the two materials, with no significant tensions in the compound material. The steel is protected against corrosion by the alkaline concrete, provided it is encased in a sufficiently thick layer. As a rule, concrete should not be exposed to a full load until after 28 days of curing. During the curing period, the concrete is referred to as 'uncured concrete'. After 6 months it can reach up to 130 % of its originally measured compressive strength. In reinforced concrete construction it is possible to achieve thin wall thicknesses owing to the compound properties of the material. In the case of higher loads and more filigree construction, prestressed concrete is used (DIN 4227). Here the reinforcement (prestressing cable ⌐ 2) is prestressed in the direction of the load. This causes compressive tension in the concrete which leads to increased loadbearing capacity with the same diameter of steel reinforcements. This means that any given cross section is capable of spanning larger widths, which leads to a reduction in material and weight. A comparatively new development is that of textile-reinforced concrete. In this case, the concrete is reinforced with a glass-fibre textile. ⌐ 3 Glass-fibre reinforcement does not require as much concrete cover as steel reinforcement does, because it is not affected by corrosion. Its structural performance is comparable to that of steel reinforced concrete, but the overall construction is extremely lightweight owing to the slender profiles. In textile-reinforced concrete, the reinforcement mesh near the surface takes care of the tensile forces. The material also offers a wide range of design possibilities owing to the ease with which it can be shaped. Another type of reinforcement can be created by adding steel, glass or plastic fibres. ⌐ 4 Owing to the nature of the material, it is also possible in these cases to reduce the concrete cover of the reinforcement.

Unreinforced concrete is rarely used for structurally relevant building components. It is primarily used in situations where no significant tensile stress is expected, for example in foundations, floor/base slabs, blocks, or prefabricated components such as facade cladding elements. On the basis of a newly developed structural calculation method, it is now also possible to construct unreinforced walls with very slender cross sections using ready-mix concrete.

2 Prestressed concrete with prestressing steel cable

3 Textile-reinforced concrete with glass-fibre layer

4 Reinforcement with steel fibres

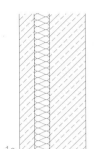

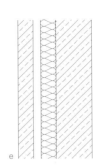

1a   b   c   d   e

1 Elements of concrete wall structure, 1:20:

a core insulation
b external insulation
c internal insulation
d single-leaf wall
e back-ventilated facing skin

2 Prefabricated component constructions:
a small-panel construction (element approx. 2 tonnes)
b large-panel construction (element approx. 10 tonnes)
c room cells (approx. 20 tonnes)

3 Prefabricated concrete elements

3

WALL CONSTRUCTION DETAILS

The thermal conductivity of standard concrete is not favourable; for this reason, single-leaf construction is primarily suitable for interior loadbearing walls. For exterior building components it is normal to use multi-leaf construction. The simplest method is to directly enclose woodwool slab panels in the shuttering, with or without foam insulation core. The slabs are inserted butt-jointed in the shuttering (they bond with the concrete through material adhesion and sometimes via additional anchors). In the case of fairfaced concrete construction, in which both sides are built as face concrete, it is usually a double-leaf construction with internal polystyrene or polyurethane insulation. It is preferable that the insulation layer be located near the outside of the building. In this construction (and with conventional use of the building) a vapour barrier is not required, owing to the density of the concrete. When the thermal insulation is placed on the inside, a vapour barrier has to be inserted on the inside of the concrete (between the insulation and the inner concrete face) in order to prevent condensation within the wall structure. It is advisable to carry out a dewpoint calculation. Loadbearing structures should be on the warm side of the thermal insulation, because in this way they will be less exposed to changes in the weather and less subject to thermal movement. In recent years, research has increasingly focused on monolithic concrete structures with thermally insulating concrete.

PREFABRICATED CONCRETE

When using modern formwork systems, in-situ concrete walls are an economical construction method. Construction with prefabricated concrete components tends to be more economical in larger projects, owing to shorter construction periods, production that is independent of the weather, and installation-ready delivery. The elements can be adapted to individual designs and detailed specifications; they may have very high surface quality and can be produced to highly accurate dimensions. Typical prefabricated components are produced as multiple sandwich slabs, sandwich elements (internal thermal insulation) or compound elements. In panel construction, loadbearing and bracing floors and wall panels are put together to form structurally stable rooms. These panels are joined together with appropriate connection elements or in-situ concrete components. Adequate tolerances should be included in the design. ↘ 2, 3

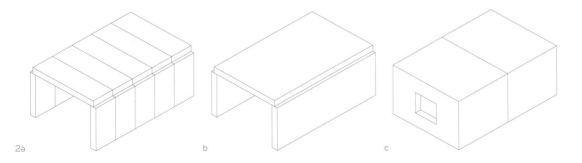

2a   b   c

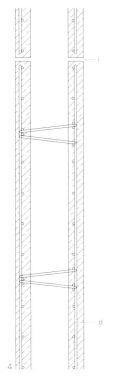

4, 5 Element wall, section 1:10, isometric 1:20:

a reinforced concrete skins
b in-situ concrete
c lattice girder and reinforcement
d minimum reinforcement to transfer the formwork pressure
e slab edge formwork
f electrical installations
g element ceiling with underside ready for decoration
h cavity wall with surface ready for decoration
i butt joint

6 Insulated formwork blocks: The outer layer consists of an insulating material and the cavities are filled with in-situ concrete.

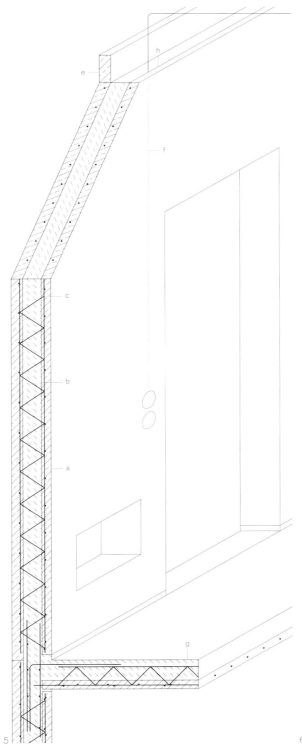

FILIGREE WALLS, HOLLOW WALLS

These reinforced double-wall elements are produced using standardised lattice girders. The items are cut to size to suit the respective project. The required main and transverse reinforcement is installed at the works, as are the openings for doors, windows, electrical switches (including conduit and boxes) and apertures. This means that the designer has to supply exact details for the production and connection of the individual parts. These semi-prefabricated walls represent a mixture of prefabrication and in-situ concrete, combining the advantages of both. The shells are installed on the building site as 'lost shuttering' and are then filled with in-situ concrete. This means that costly shuttering work can be omitted. Compared to fully prefabricated components, these elements have a low transport weight, but they have to be sufficiently strong to sustain transportation and must be capable of sustaining the pressure during concreting. The surface is smooth and free of any anchor holes. There is only limited space available for the reinforcement. ⌐ 4, 5

INSULATED CONCRETE FORMWORK

Insulated concrete formwork is another method of producing multi-layered concrete walls and is primarily used in smaller buildings. It can however also be used for walls up to 8 m high and it achieves good thermal and sound insulation values. The outer layer consists of an insulation material (e.g. cement-bonded woodwool slabs, expanded clay concrete) which is supplied in the form of large-format building blocks. These are loosely stacked in brickwork fashion, without mortar in the joints, using the tongue-and-groove connections. This represents a kind of lost shuttering and is also suitable as a plaster and render substrate. The insulation layer is very suitable for installing service lines and fixtures. It is also possible to apply an additional thermal insulation layer on the inside. The cavity is filled with concrete on site and forms the loadbearing core of the wall. ⌐ 6

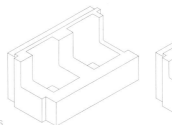
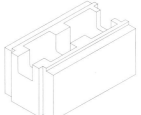

MINIMUM SIZES

The minimum thickness of loadbearing concrete walls is specified in DIN 1045 – *Concrete, reinforced and pre-stressed concrete structures* – for the different types of floor construction (continuous or not) and concrete quality. For in-situ reinforced concrete walls it is 10 to 12 cm, for prefabricated reinforced concrete components it is 8 to 10 cm and for unreinforced in-situ concrete walls it is 12 to 20 cm, and for unreinforced prefabricated components it is between 10 to 12 cm.

For continuous floor slabs a minimum bearing width is specified, which means that the wall thickness has to be between 14 and 20 cm. In order to meet the sound insulation requirements for internal walls, a thickness of approx. 14 cm is required, which is also sufficient to provide the necessary fire resistance. The more slender a component, the more reinforcement is required. For this reason, squat or moderately slender cross sections are more economical. The thickness of lightweight concrete external walls is assumed to be < 25 cm and that of loadbearing internal walls, 20 cm – or 15 cm if these walls also have a bracing function with a height of < 3.50 m. For non-loadbearing walls with a bracing function, a thickness of 12 cm is sufficient. Any reduction in cross section as a result of slots must be checked by structural calculation.

Since many standard dimensions of interior fitting-out components are aligned with standard brick dimensions, it is an advantage to opt for wall thicknesses such as a full brick, or a brick-and-a-half. In mixed construction this makes it easier to manage different kinds of connection.

BRACING IN CONCRETE CONSTRUCTION

In multi-storey buildings the same bracing rules apply to the overall system as in masonry construction. ↘ p. 90 Bracing is normally achieved through the stairwell cores or enclosing shear walls. The structural strength of components exposed to bracing pressure is increased by the placing of reinforcement, which gives the component greater resistance to buckling.

RECESSES, SLOTS

For the installation of cables and other services, it is necessary to provide openings and conduits in walls and beams (e.g. by inserting foam spacers on the inside of the shuttering). Cutting slots after concreting the walls is costly and time consuming. Openings can be placed in areas where transverse forces are low – usually in the middle of the field – without weakening the structure too much. Near the bearings the transverse forces are high, which is why openings in these areas have to be exactly designed to suit the force vectors in the building component. Often, the preferred method for inserting small openings is by subsequent core drilling, in order to save the effort of coordination.

OPENINGS

Openings for windows and doors can be produced in a wide range of shapes and sizes. The wall thickness, reinforcement and method of shuttering must be designed in accordance with the respective requirements. ↘ 1

1 Formwork for a wall opening before building the outer skin.

2 Trimming reinforcement around an opening.

3   The exposure classes determine the resistance of concrete to chemical and physical influences depending on its location and purpose; these influences are not taken into account as loads in the structural calculations; the example here is of a house:

a   reinforced foundations (XC1), XC2 , WF
b   foundation, blinding layer (unreinforced, rust-free) X0, WF
c   frost-free ground slab (XC1), XC2, WF
d   cellar wall (highly water-resistant concrete) XC4, XF1, WF
e   external wall with insulation XC1, WO
f   external wall without insulation XC4, XF1, WF
g   reinforced internal wall XC1, WO
h   reinforced floor XC1, WO
i   flat roof XC4, XF1, WF
j   pier (internal) XC3, XF1, WO
k   car port XC4, XF1, WF

4   Minimum dimension for reinforced concrete cross sections in accordance with fire resistance classes:
a   columns
b   walls

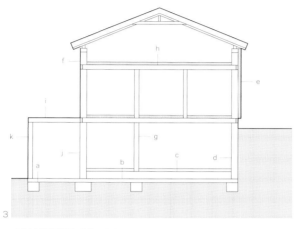

3

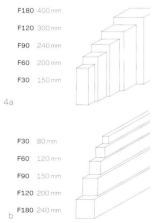

F180 400 mm
F120 300 mm
F90 240 mm
F60 200 mm
F30 150 mm

4a

F30 80 mm
F60 120 mm
F90 150 mm
F120 200 mm
F180 240 mm

b

CONCRETE COVER

Concrete cover refers to the amount of concrete between the reinforcement steel and the outside concrete surface. It is necessary in order to ensure an adequate bond between steel and concrete for the transfer of forces and to protect the steel adequately against corrosion and the effect of fire. The concrete cover is also determined by environmental conditions (exposure classes in accordance with DIN 1045-1). ⌐3 The depth of concrete cover should be at least the same as the diameter of the reinforcement steel, but not <15 mm. Usual dimensions are between 20 and 50 mm.

The concrete cover is created by means of spacers and support blocks (made of bent reinforcement steel) or cages (of plastic or concrete). Insufficient concrete cover usually leads to corrosion of the reinforcement steel and hence to damage of the concrete component. Such damage may occur in the form of simple discolouration (rust stains) through to spalling of the concrete. As additional protection against corrosion, it is possible to hot-galvanise reinforcement steel or to cover it with an epoxy resin layer. Alternatively, it is also possible to use stainless steel or glass-fibre reinforced plastic bars. In this context it is important to comply with building control approvals.

THERMAL INSULATION

Conventional concrete has poor thermal insulation properties. Standard concrete typically has a thermal conductivity of 2.1 W/mK and therefore normally requires additional thermal insulation. The thermal conductivity depends to a large extent on the additives. By choosing certain additives it is possible to produce thermally insulating concrete.

ROOM CLIMATE

Owing to its high storage capacity, concrete is slow to absorb and to emit heat. For this reason, ambient temperature fluctuations only have a slow effect on rooms with unclad concrete walls; the interior climate is balanced. Owing to the specific construction method of concrete walls, it is possible to install wall heating systems similar to underfloor heating systems in floors. In the same manner it is possible to integrate ventilation ducts or other technical apparatus within loadbearing floor slabs. However, concrete cannot absorb much humidity from the air, i.e. it cannot very easily balance fluctuations in relative humidity, which can be compensated for by a plaster finish.

SOUND

Owing to its high specific weight, concrete is an excellent insulator for air-borne sound but has poor impact sound insulation properties. In homogeneous building construction, particularly owing to the fixed connection between floor and wall, it is therefore necessary to insert a separating element between the building components. A common solution is to lay a floating screed as a floor finish. In addition to the direct transfer of sound it is important to consider secondary (or flank) transfer of sound.

FIRE PROTECTION

Concrete has very good fire-resistance properties. It falls into building material class A and, in itself, does not constitute a fire load. When exposed to fire, concrete remains largely intact; it does not spread the fire and it releases neither gas nor smoke. With reinforced concrete, it is the steel reinforcement that determines structural integrity in the event of fire. Adequate fire protection is achieved when the minimum dimensions for cross sections ⌐4, reinforcement and concrete cover are adhered to in accordance with DIN 4102. By increasing the amount of concrete cover it is possible to increase fire resistance. Concrete retains its fire resistance up to a temperature of 250 °C. Reinforced concrete will fail at about 500 °C.

MOISTURE INGRESS FROM OUTSIDE

Concrete provides good protection against dampness and it is also possible to produce waterproof concrete. Solid concrete basement walls can be constructed together with the floor slab as a watertight system. With facade elements, it is important to ensure that all surfaces are sufficiently sloping so that water can drain off. Projections and water drips should be arranged in such a way that water cannot run across the adjoining surfaces and cause unsightly staining.

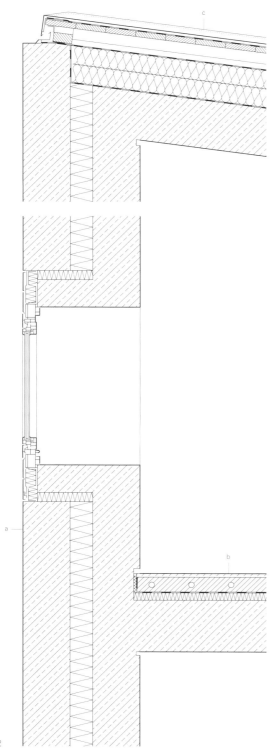

CONSTRUCTION OF EXTERNAL WALLS

Alternatively to prefabricated concrete components, concrete can be cast at the building site: 'in-situ' or 'cast-in-place' concrete. To produce this type of concrete it is necessary to provide shuttering and support material on site, and to install the reinforcement on site. Both shuttering and the installation of reinforcement are costly and time-consuming. It is therefore common, as an alternative, to opt for prefabricated components which are assembled on site. Although prefabricated components are more economical to produce, the cost of transport and assembly must be considered. In terms of the conceptual design, prefabricated components may impose limitations, since similar element sizes must be used in order to benefit from economical production methods. An advantage of the prefabricated construction method is the reduced construction time, since it is not necessary to wait until the concrete components reach their full loadbearing capacity. Construction with sprayed concrete is a special solution. In this method the concrete is pumped through a hose system and sprayed on to the building components. The spraying process itself ensures adequate compaction. → p. 111

1 School building, Paspels, 1999, Valerio Olgiati

2 Detailed section through the fairfaced concrete wall with core insulation, 1:20. School building, Paspels, 1999, Valerio Olgiati.

a Wall construction:
reinforced concrete/
in-situ concrete 250 mm,
thermal insulation 120 mm,
reinforced concrete/
in-situ concrete 250 mm

b Floor construction:
granolithic concrete 20 mm,
cement screed with
underfloor heating 80 mm,
bituminous sealing layer,
impact sound insulation 40 mm,
fairfaced concrete slab 280 mm

c Roof construction:
copper sheeting dressed over battens,
bituminous sealing layer,
solid timber boarding 30 mm,
battens/ventilation gap 100 mm,
underlay continuously bonded,
thermal insulation 200 mm,
vapour barrier,
reinforced concrete slab 260 mm

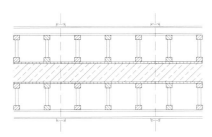

3 Plan, elevation and section,
1:50 of girder formwork system
for large wall construction:

a girder
b bracing strut
c hook strap
d scaffolding gantry
e outrigger bracket,
adjustable head

4 Conventional wall formwork
in section, 1:50:

a girders
b alignment/bracing struts
c support system/anchors
d release agent on surface
of formwork
e in-situ concrete

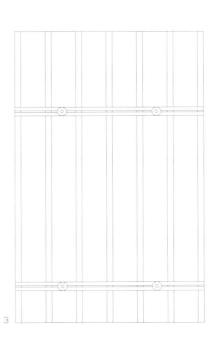

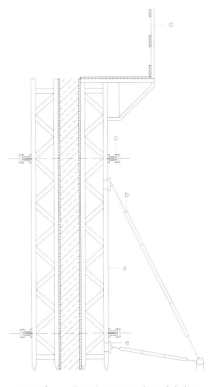

3

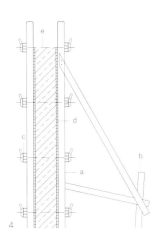

4

SHUTTERING

Shuttering is necessary for the production of any type of concrete component as it retains the concrete while it is being cast and while it cures. The cost of shuttering is relatively high and the material may be used once or several times, depending on the type. Common systems today include industrially produced large and small-format shuttering elements with plastic-coated surfaces (to prevent suction). In former times, timber board shuttering was common, but it is rarely used today owing to the extensive manual input required and the limited re-usability of the material. A porous surface of the shuttering material results in a darker, slightly porous surface of the concrete. As the porosity of the shuttering decreases with re-use over time, the resulting concrete surface becomes lighter.

The type of shuttering used depends on the dimensions required, the speed of concreting, the desired appearance of the concrete surface, the available lifting gear, and its re-usability. When shuttering is completed, it must contain the concrete without leakage.

Common systems include frame and girder formwork, wall, floor and space formwork, formwork scaffolding and formwork skin, as well as lost shuttering and insulated form blocks, which remain as part of the building structure. The striking time of concrete reduces with better cement quality. The striking time for walls is between 1 and 4 days and for floors between 3 and 10 days. With fairfaced concrete it is important to ensure that the striking time of all elements is the same, as this affects the colour of the concrete. Before the shuttering or formwork for floors can be fitted, the wall shuttering has to be removed.

It is possible to reduce the striking time by heating the shuttering. Floors from which the shuttering has been removed may require additional support until they reach their full loadbearing capacity.

RELEASE AGENT

In order to achieve a smooth concrete surface that is free of discolouration and to prevent the newly produced concrete components from adhering to the formwork, it is common practice to treat the shuttering material on the side facing the concrete with a release agent (shuttering/formwork oil) prior to installation of the reinforcement. The separating film prevents immediate contact between the surface of the shuttering and the fresh concrete. The treated shuttering elements should be protected against weathering through precipitation until concreting has taken place. Incorrect use of shuttering oil or separating agent can lead to defects in the concrete surface, as can their residues. For this reason, it is recommended to carry out a test beforehand.

FAIRFACED CONCRETE SURFACES

As a rule, concrete surfaces are very resistant to wear, weathering and chemical attack. A choice must be made between fairfaced concrete and concrete surfaces intended for subsequent plastering or cladding.

The appearance of fairfaced concrete is determined by its texture, proportion of pores, smoothness and colour. Important factors influencing the quality of fairfaced concrete surfaces are temperature (weather, material), installation method (technology), compaction and concrete quality. Additional factors are the condition of the formwork skin, the density and rigidity of the formwork, soiling or damage to the formwork, the spacers, edge details and the separating agent used. Criteria for assessing the quality of fairfaced concrete are smoothness, texture, porosity, air voids, gravel pockets, surface patterns, colour and colour consistency. Defects can include air voids, pores and gravel pockets, unevenness, untidy joints in the formwork skin, bleeding (separating) of the fresh concrete, evidence of corrosion of the reinforcement, lime effervescence, differences in colour shade and damaged edges.

There are many ways of designing the appearance of fairfaced concrete surfaces. The construction method using formwork means that the surface of concrete components is shaped as a negative of the surface texture of the formwork skin. The selection and arrangement of formwork and joints can result in different patterns and grids and should be considered in the conceptual design. Particularly noticeable is the imprint left by the anchor points of ties. They can be used as a means of achieving a particular design pattern or structure. ⟍ 3

Depending on the type of formwork (smooth, rough, textured), the surface of the concrete adopts the equivalent finish. Early methods of achieving a specific surface effect included rough-sawn boarding ⟍ 4 and steel shuttering for very smooth surfaces. By inserting pattern sheets into the formwork it is possible to produce relief-type patterns and textured surfaces. ⟍ 5 In the so-called photoengraving process, selected images can be reproduced on the surface of a pattern sheet. ⟍ 6 Another photographic method works with a curing delay agent which is applied in a screenprinting process.

1 Hotel at Cerro Paranal in the Atacama desert, Chile, 2002, Auer & Weber. The building was entirely constructed of fairfaced concrete in the colour shades of the desert.

2 Extension of the History Museum, Bern, 2009, :mlzd. Pixel-type recesses of varying depths were formed in the smooth in-situ concrete facade with its soft, plaster-like texture and yellowish colouring.

The formwork must be removed from the concrete between 16 and 24 hours after pouring it and the surface washed with water at low pressure. This produces areas of different degrees of roughness and tone (light, dark). Alternatively, there are numerous ways in which the surface can be technically treated subsequently (blasting, treating with acid, flame treatment, sandblasting, washing); manual masonry methods include nidging, chiselling, scabbling, bossing, sawing, grinding and polishing.

When designing buildings with fairfaced concrete surfaces it is imperative to make provision for services installations at the design stage, since subsequent cutting of channels is not really possible. In this case conduits are inserted into the formwork during the construction of walls and floors. In that situation it is difficult to check any water pipes for leaks. Another fact to consider is that the concrete cover for fairfaced concrete has to be thicker than that specified for lined or plastered concrete surfaces.

COLOURS

The colour of concrete can be modified through the addition of different types of stone aggregate, cement, or additive. Blast-furnace cement is light grey, Portland cement is medium grey and, with a high sulphate content, dark grey. In addition there are white cement and Portland slate cement, which has a reddish brown colour.

As an alternative to applying a surface coating to finished concrete (paint or stain) it is possible to colour freshly mixed concrete. By adding coloured aggregate or pigment (e.g. iron oxide, cobalt blue) a wide spectrum of colouring is possible. When this is used in combination with white cement, the resulting colours are brighter. When using metallic pigment it is important to ensure that any steel formwork is demagnetised.

3 Visible tie points as a design element

4 Red-coloured concrete with the pattern of the timber formwork

5 Moulded stud texture

6 Surface created by photoengraving process

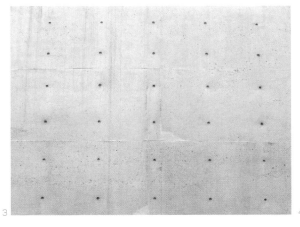

CONCRETE TYPES AND CLASSIFICATION

Concrete is classified by its compressive strength. For normal and heavy concrete there are the strength classes from C 8/10 to C 100/115 and for lightweight concrete, from LC 8/9 to LC 80/88.

Furthermore, a distinction is made between three concrete groups (DIN EN 206-1): concrete by properties, concrete by composition and standard concrete. The dry specific weight of standard concrete is between 2000–2600 kg/m³. Concrete that is heavier than this is called heavy concrete, and concrete that is lighter is called lightweight concrete.

CONCRETE BY PROPERTIES

The concrete manufacturer produces the concrete to meet a performance specification describing the required properties. With respect to the composition of the concrete, the manufacturer is free to make his own choice and thus bears responsibility for the quality of the concrete.

CONCRETE BY COMPOSITION

In this case the purchaser supplies a detailed specification of the composition of the concrete and is therefore responsible for the resulting properties.

STANDARD CONCRETE

Standard concrete is a material of relatively low strength (up to C16/20) which may only be used in certain applications within the exposure classes (X0, XC1, XC2) →p. 105 as standard concrete for unreinforced and reinforced concrete components. This type of concrete is supplemented only with natural stone aggregate. →p. 112 Other additives or agents are not permitted.

NORMAL CONCRETE (C)

Normal concrete (C 8/10 to C 100/115) →2a has a dry specific weight of 2000–2600 kg/m³. Unless the structural specification contains special requirements, normal concrete is used.

HEAVY CONCRETE

Heavy concrete (C 8/10 to C 100/115) has a dry specific weight of between 2600 and 5000 kg/m³. It is produced with particularly heavy grades of aggregate (barite, iron ore, steel granulate or similar) and is usually used for the purpose of radiation protection (medicine, research, nuclear power stations) or in the case of special sound insulation requirements.

1

HIGH-STRENGTH AND ULTRA-HIGH-PERFORMANCE CONCRETE

High-strength concrete (C 55/67 to C 100/115 and LC 55/60 to LC 80/88) is produced with cements of high compressive strength, high-performance liquifiers and extremely fine additives (e.g. silicate dust). This type of concrete is suitable for slender concrete components and is used primarily in bridge and high-rise construction.

LIGHTWEIGHT CONCRETE (LC)

One of the earliest, preserved buildings made of lightweight concrete is the Pantheon in Rome (Roman concrete with a specific weight of between 1750 and 1350 kg/m³, with the weight reducing towards the top). →1 Today lightweight concrete is not only used where the intention is to save weight (this can be an important consideration in high-rise and bridge construction), but also where thermal insulation is needed. As a rule, lightweight concrete →2b (DIN 4232, DIN 1045 with a specific weight of between 800 and 2000 kg/m³) is made using porous, lightweight, thermally insulating materials as additives, such as perlite, pumice, expanded clay or expanded slate. Depending on the aggregate and quality of the cement paste, lightweight concrete can achieve similar strength to normal concrete. Lightweight concrete can also be produced in fairfaced applications, as self-compacting or as prestressed concrete. Lightweight concrete in the form of aerated concrete is usually only used for prefabricated concrete components. Rather than using lightweight aggregate, aerated concrete is produced using compounds that produce air bubbles.

1 The Pantheon in Rome, completed in 120 AD, is considered to be one of the first buildings in lightweight concrete.

2 Concrete cross sections:
a normal concrete
b lightweight concrete
c glass foam concrete

INFRA-LIGHTWEIGHT CONCRETE

Infra- or ultra-lightweight concrete can be used for single-leaf wall construction. Its dry specific weight is <800 kg/m³. It can currently be produced as light as 350 kg/m³. These types of concrete not only have a low specific weight, but also low thermal conductivity. Their production involves various lightweight concrete aggregates (e.g. clay granulates).

GLASS FOAM CONCRETE

Glass foam concrete ⤳ 2c has very good thermal insulation properties (thermal conductivity of 0.38 to 0.12 W/mK). The additive used is glass foam. With a specific weight of 800 to 1600 kg/m³ the concrete achieves high compressive strength and is suitable for use in loadbearing structures.

SELF-COMPACTING CONCRETE

The special properties of this concrete in liquid form make it ideal for casting complex shapes. Self-compacting concrete will flow, release air bubbles and fully fill all spaces in the formwork simply as a result of gravity, without additional vibration. Its surface quality is good enough to be suitable for fairfaced applications. In addition, it is possible to save time and labour in the construction process. Its cured properties are not significantly different from those of normal concrete. In its composition, self-compacting concrete has a higher content of very fine grain, which results in extremely good flow characteristics. When casting this concrete into formwork, it is important to ensure that air can escape from the formwork in order to prevent the formation of cavities. In addition, the formwork is exposed to higher pressure which means that appropriate measures must be taken to strengthen it (e.g. greater frequency of formwork ties).

SPRAYED CONCRETE

Sprayed concrete is suitable for applications where it is difficult or impossible to build the necessary formwork, or where it is intended to make a structure loadbearing as quickly as possible. Typical applications are the temporary reinforcement of slopes or building pits, the lining of excavations such as tunnels, or the reinforcement of existing structures. Sprayed concrete (EN 14487) is conveyed directly to the point of application via hoses or pipes, and is applied by spraying; this automatically causes it to be compacted. Applications are possible in a dry or wet spray process.

FIBRE CONCRETE

In order to increase the strength of concrete (tensile strength, impact resistance, resistance to deformation), it is possible to add fibres consisting of steel, glass or plastic.

RAMMED CONCRETE

Rammed concrete is one of the oldest types of concrete. It is generally used without reinforcement and is compacted by ramming. Recent examples of this archaic construction method in use are the Bruder-Klaus Chapel (2007) by Peter Zumthor and the housing development in Samedan by Mierta and Lazzarini (2007). Rammed concrete consists of a dry (earth-moist) mixture of cement and pieces of natural stone. The material is placed in the formwork in layers, and it is important to observe the necessary drying times. Rammed concrete has a high density and is therefore very resistant to cracking and changes in shape. The appearance clearly reflects the layered installation.

WATERPROOF CONCRETE

By selecting a special concrete composition and limiting the width of cracks with the help of stronger reinforcement, it is possible to achieve a high density. The volume of capillary pores must be <20% of the overall volume. This can be achieved by adjusting the water/cement ratio (w/c 0.5). In order to achieve a vapour-proof structure for dry interiors it is necessary to use additional vapour barriers, e.g. an externally applied sealing membrane. Waterproof concrete is required for watertight concrete constructions. Where such structures are exposed to water pressure, it is common to use wall thicknesses of 30 cm and a 25 cm thick base slab.

RECYCLED CONCRETE

In recycled concrete the gravel aggregate is partly substituted with recycled construction material (crushed concrete, building rubble). This makes it possible to conserve gravel resources and save on disposal costs. Recycled concrete is less strong than normal concrete and is primarily used in road construction. By carefully sorting the concrete demolition material before re-use, it is possible to produce a concrete with improved properties. This material is still in the trial phase.

TRANSLUCENT CONCRETE

By inserting light-conducting fibres into concrete it is rendered translucent. Its appearance is determined by the way in which the fibres are arranged. The light-conducting property of the fibres makes it possible, irrespective of the wall thickness, to project colours and shadows through to the other side of the wall.

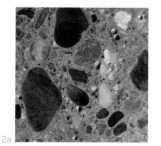
2a

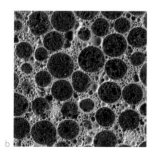
b

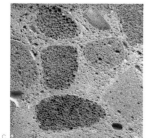
c

AGGREGATES

To a large extent, the size of stone grain and its grading curve determine the properties of the concrete. The size of grain, its strength and composition, the proportion of fines and resistance to frost together determine the application method, volume, surface texture, proportion of voids, specific weight and strength, proportion of paste and ultimately the field of application of the concrete. A more even distribution of the smaller and larger grain diameters in the aggregate results in a more highly interlinked and dense concrete structure, and hence a better quality concrete. In normal mixtures, the stone aggregate accounts for about 70% of the concrete volume. Lightweight concrete uses porous lightweight aggregate, such as pumice or expanded clay. Grain sizes of <0.125 mm are referred to as very fine grain. They aid the installation of fresh concrete and contribute to a dense structure of the concrete.

BINDING AGENT

The binding agent used in concrete production is cement, which is used in powder form. Through its reaction with water, it forms cement paste, which hardens to hydrated cement and binds the aggregate. Cement consists of finely ground limestone, clay, sand or iron ore. There are five main types of standard cement (DIN 1164-1), CEM I (Portland cement), CEM II (Portland composite cement comprising Portland cement and blast furnace slag), CEM III (blast furnace cement), CEM IV (Pozzolana cement) and CEM V (composite cement). There are also different strength classes.

White cement is a type of Portland cement with a low iron oxide content and is mainly used for light fairfaced concrete or white renders. It is therefore more expensive than ordinary types of cement.

WATER/CEMENT RATIO

The water/cement ratio (w/c ratio) refers to the proportion of water to cement in fresh concrete; it determines the quality of the concrete. Together, both these components form cement paste. The loadbearing capacity of concrete (tensile and compressive strength) increases with lower water/cement ratios. Cement can bind only a limited amount of water. A w/c ratio of approx. 0.40 is the optimum ratio for the hydration process (curing) of the concrete. This means that a water quantity of 40% in weight of the cement is chemically and physically bound. Fresh concrete with a higher w/c ratio will excrete the excess water (bleed); the cured concrete will then have numerous capillary pores and can therefore absorb more water. A higher proportion of cement leads to quicker shrinkage and drying out, resulting in cracks. This in turn increases the risk of corrosion. A light appearance of the concrete surface indicates a high w/c ratio, a dark appearance a low ratio.

ADDITIVES

Additives affect the workability of fresh concrete and the strength (compression, tension) and density of cured concrete, as well as its different chemical and physical properties. Additives must not interfere with the curing process and must not reduce the strength of the cured concrete. Possible additives are mineral-based (stonemeal, pigment, Pozzolana, limestone, trass, flue ash, silicate dust) or organic (synthetic resin dispersions) and fibrous materials (steel, glass or plastic fibres).

ADMIXTURES

Admixtures (liquid, powdered, granulated) can modify the properties of fresh or cured concrete through chemical or physical reactions. Compatibility with the concrete and reinforcement must be proven.

1   Different kinds of aggregate:
a   crushed stone
b   gravel
c   course sand

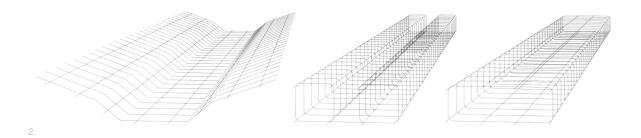

2

2 Bending reinforcement mesh to form cages

3 Spacers for formwork:
a for ties
b made of plastic
c made of fibre concrete

REINFORCEMENT AND CORROSION

Reinforced concrete components are reinforced with mesh, bars and stirrups so that they can absorb any tensile forces. There are different steel grades: basic, quality and special. Steel types commonly used for reinforcements are BSt 420 and BSt 500. The reinforcement of slabs usually consists of steel mesh. The reinforcement is capable of absorbing both tensile and compression stress; reinforced concrete can absorb about 3 to 5 times the force of 'plain' concrete, which has compressive strength only. In addition to steel bar, reinforcement may consist of steel fibres, textile fabric and, more recently, also glass-fibre reinforced plastic bar. Normally, reinforcement is inserted in its untensioned state and will not transmit any force until after the formwork has been removed and the concrete components are exposed to load and deform (deflection). An important factor affecting the bonding between steel and concrete is the profile or ribbing of the reinforcement steel (friction and shear bond). By prestressing the reinforcement it is possible to increase the loadbearing capacity of the concrete. The reinforcement is placed where the component is expected to be exposed to the heaviest load (deformation), such as at the periphery of a concrete floor. Some reinforcement is used not for structural reasons, but in order to stabilise the internal structure of the component and to avoid surface cracks (e.g. due to creep or shrinkage). Reinforcements are also available in prefabricated configurations such as cages, anchor plates, or fixing strips for a more economical construction.

3a   b   c

INSTALLATION METHODS

Concrete should be poured not in heaps, but in horizontal layers (approx. 50 cm each) with the concreting best carried out without interruption in order to ensure proper bonding between the layers. Concrete should not be dropped from a height of more than 2 m; it may be necessary to use a chute. In the case of fairfaced concrete, the height from which concrete is dropped should be reduced to 1 m.

Concrete remains workable only for a limited time. For this reason, it should be compacted as quickly as possible using suitable equipment. For in-situ concrete it is usual to use immersion vibrators ⬎ 1. External vibrators ⬎ 2 are used where confined space makes it impossible to use immersion vibrators, and also in precast concrete factories. The vibration process drives out any cavities and air inclusions through the mechanically generated vibrations in order to produce a dense internal structure with a low proportion of pores. When the process is applied correctly and with appropriate consistency, a thin layer of fine mortar will be created on the surface. The vibrator should not come into contact with the reinforcements since this would interrupt the bonding process between the reinforcements and the concrete.

Depending on requirements, fresh concrete is produced in different consistencies. These range from F1 (stiff, rammed concrete), F2 (plastic, components with few reinforcements), F3 (soft, most common consistency), F4 (very soft, for highly reinforced components), F5 (fluid, requiring minimal compaction) and F6 (very fluid). The temperature of the concrete should be between 5° and 30 °C when poured. Ideal temperatures are between +18° and +25 °C. When the air temperature is between +5° and –3 °C, the temperature of the fresh concrete must be at least +5 °C. No concreting should be carried out at temperatures below –3 °C; alternatively, a winter construction site has to be set up. At temperatures above 30 °C the fresh concrete must be prevented from heating up or setting too soon. The pouring and compaction of the concrete must be carried out in such a way that no gravel pockets ⬎ 3 are created and the concrete cannot separate.

The solidification and hardening process is the result of a chemical reaction between the cement and the water. The drying process involves a reduction in volume of the fresh concrete. This is called shrinkage. The strength of concrete is the result of the crystallisation process of its clinker components. This takes several months, which means that the concrete will not attain its final strength until long after it has been poured. Under normal temper-

ature and humidity conditions, the specified standard strength is achieved after 28 days. In order to produce a dense and durable concrete surface, it is necessary to protect the fresh surface against too rapid drying out, i.e. the areas near the surface must have sufficient water for the hydration process. For this reason it is important to ensure that water does not evaporate too quickly as a result of solar radiation, frost or wind. Suitable preventive measures include: placing a water-retaining foil or thermal insulation layer (e.g. vapour barrier membrane or thermal insulation); spraying the fresh concrete with water; leaving it in the formwork, and covering fresh work with a heated construction tent. In the case of fairfaced concrete, these preventive measures may continue for between 5 and 10 days. Furthermore, fresh concrete must be protected against mechanical impact such as from rain or vibration. Concrete surfaces that dry out unevenly may develop cracks or a patchy appearance.

1 Vibrations generated by immersion vibrators compact fresh concrete.

2 External vibrators are attached to the formwork wall and are used in confined spaces as well as in the prefabricated component industry.

3 Gravel pocket

4   Joint design options:
a   dummy joint as design element, no structural effect
b   open joint (for back-ventilated facade elements)
c   joint sealer (joint sealing compound and foam strip)
d   joint with plastic plug profile

5   Crackling;
the permissible width of cracks is specified in DIN 1045-1; a crack ruler can be used to measure these widths.

6   Formation of cracks in concrete:
a   separation cracks
b   bending cracks
c   shear cracks
d   longitudinal and fissure cracks
e   compound cracks

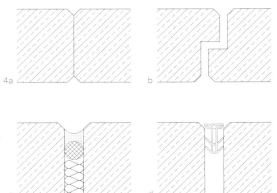

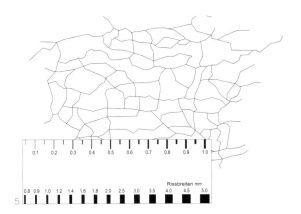

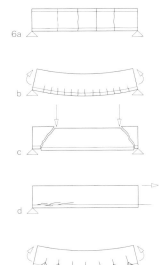

DEFORMATION

Building components are subject to deformation during their service life. Causes include expansion due to changes in temperature, shrinkage and creep, foundation settlement, the concrete's own weight, imposed loads, earth pressure, wind, snow and earthquake forces. The type and degree of deformation depends on the composition of the concrete and the strength of the reinforcement, as well as the size of the components. Permanent exposure to load can eventually cause concrete to undergo plastic deformation, which however will reverse when the load is removed. Deformation of concrete as a result of constant tension is referred to as creep. This is the result of exposure to compression, which causes a change in the internal structure and a reduction in the volume, due to changes in the cement gel. Creep deformation will reduce as the concrete increases in age and will finally stop after several years. Creep needs to be taken into account particularly when calculating the loadbearing capacity of slender columns or the deformation of floors.

JOINTS

If the deformation of concrete is restricted by parts of the construction, tensions and cracks result. For this reason it is important to provide adequate movement joints in the design. Joints are a complex design issue, and where visible should be integrated into the aesthetic concept. ⌐ 4 Continuous building components, which are favourable from the point of view of transferring horizontal loads, are interrupted by intersecting joints. In this case it is necessary to provide calculation evidence for the bracing of both parts of the building. Joints represent a not insignificant cost factor and should be restricted to what is necessary in terms of number and dimension. A distinction is made between expansion joints (every 10 to 60 m, depending on requirements), settlement joints (continue down to the foundations; used to separate different development phases or building sections of different heights), slip joints (bearing at the top level to allow differential movement of the structure above) and construction joints (between separate concreting sections, may be sealed with waterstop profiles).

CRACKS

In general, it is not possible to avoid cracks in concrete. They are, however, not detrimental unless they impair the component's loadbearing capacity, durability, or suitability for purpose. In the case of external walls, it is important to distinguish whether cracks are on the surface only or penetrate the component. Typical crack patterns ⌐ 5, 6 are crackling, crazing, shrinkage, bending, tension, shear, hair or fissure cracks, or cracks along the reinforcements. These cracks are caused by shrinkage, or during the settling process of the fresh concrete and the dispersion of hydration heat, through temperature differentials between the core and the surface of the fresh concrete, external temperature effects (frost, heat), exposure to loads, differential restraining conditions, or corrosion. DIN 1045 specifies limits for the width of cracks, which range between 0.1 and 0.4 mm, depending on the application. Whether such cracks have to be repaired depends on aesthetic criteria and structural requirements.

TIMBER CONSTRUCTION

1

1 Sunken House, London, 2007, David Adjaye:
The architect chose a solid timber construction, which provided freedom in terms of spans, beams and posts. Openings can be placed where they are wanted for a certain view or cardinal direction. The large-format window openings form flush edges with the cedar-wood facade, and thus underscore the homogeneity of the building.

In recent decades, the construction of timber buildings has moved away from the long members of traditional frame and skeleton construction towards elements that function like stiff plates or walls. One of the reasons for this change is the development of modern, engineered-wood materials. The objective is the optimum utilisation of this raw material, as well as an extension of its applications. This has led to products and formats which do not occur in nature in that form. Homogeneous, monolithic structures in solid construction can be produced using nail-laminated or glued laminated timber elements, cross-laminated timber box or other box elements made of plain softwood. Oriented strand boards (OSB), glued laminated (glulam), laminated veneer or parallel strand timber has significantly better technical properties than natural board timber, and their structural properties are easier to calculate. Another aspect is that the external appearance of modern timber buildings has its own pattern language, which is not reminiscent of historic building styles. Compared to steel, concrete and brick, the production of timber components uses less fossil fuel. As a renewable raw material, timber has the potential to make a sustainable contribution to climate protection.

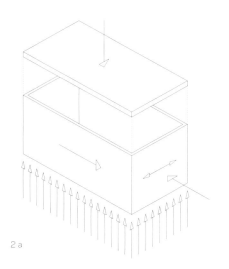

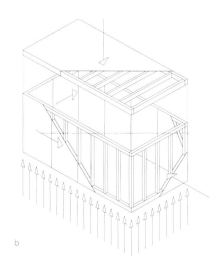

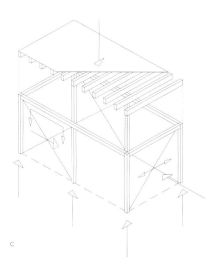

2 a   b   c

2a Solid panel construction
Solid timber: the reinforced concrete slab transfers the loads to
the walls, which in turn transfer
the loads into the ground v a strip
foundations.
Timber frame construction: the
walls form a rigid joint with the reinforced concrete slab and are thereby able to withstand the horizontal
forces acting on them from all
sides.

b Frame construction
(balloon frame und platform frame)
Solid timber: the loads are transferred from the timber deck via
the head plates to the timber
frame. The closely spaced studs
of the timber frame walls transfer
the loads via a footplate to the
strip or pad foundations.
Timber frame construction: the
floor acts as a rigid plate in conjunction with the walls with their
rigid planking, forming a rigid
structure.

c Post-and-beam construction
Solid timber: the timber deck transfers the loads to the secondary
beams spanning between the main
beams. The main beams span from
post to post, transferring the loads
to these posts. From these posts,
point loads are transferred into the
ground.
Timber frame construction: the
timber deck, together with the
secondary beams, forms a rigid
horizontal plate. At least three of
the structurally supporting fields
must be sufficiently braced so
as to form a rigid structure with
the timber deck.

LOADBEARING CAPACITY

In its loadbearing behaviour, natural wood is directional.
It has its highest strength in the direction of the fibres
(along the fibre) and can absorb both tensile and compressive forces. Across the fibre, its loadbearing capacity is reduced. For the purpose of building construction,
this means that timber should be installed so as to bear
the main loads in the direction of its longitudinal axis.
DIN 4074 specifies different strength grades of timber:
grade I (construction timber with exceptionally good loadbearing capacity), grade II (construction timber with
ordinary loadbearing capacity) and grade III (construction timber with low loadbearing capacity). For designing and dimensioning, it is usual to work with grade II
construction timber. Cellulose makes up 40% to 50%
of its volume and is primarily responsible for its tensile
strength. Hemicellulose (which is a fill material) accounts
for 20% to 30% and lignin makes up another 20% to
30%. Together, these compounds determine the material's compressive strength. Additional components may
include resins, waxes, fats, tanning and colouring compounds, carbohydrates, proteins and minerals which together determine the smell, colour, strength and durability of timbers. A timber element that has the same
loadbearing capacity as a steel element will have a larger
cross section, but will weigh significantly less. It is capable of absorbing compressive and tensile forces and
therefore has one of the best loadbearing capacities of
the thermally insulating materials.
Each of the different timber construction methods has
its own principles. The main and secondary beams, the
load transfer principle and bracing method vary depending on the system. They are distinguished by the position, connection and jointing of their individual parts and
elements. DIN 1052 includes rules for the structural stability and hence the sizing of the respective elements.
In Germany, Austria and Switzerland, the construction
height for timber buildings is limited to 5 to 6 storeys, depending on the respective building regulations, whereas
in Great Britain, 9 full storeys are permissible.
The basic element in modern timber construction is the
sheet. The manufacture of a typical sheet would include
a minimum of three layers of crosswise glued timber
veneers. The layers consist of sawn timber, slats or battens for which it is not necessary to use high-quality timber. Placing these layers crosswise results in sheets that
have great rigidity and strength, and which structurally
function as plates. The loadbearing capacity of sheet
products is directionally neutral and not tied to the direction of growth, as with solid timber. The properties of
the elements can be influenced to a large extent by the
quality of the individual components.

1a   b   c   d   e

BRACING

As a general principle, bracing follows the same rules as in masonry and concrete construction. In skeleton and frame construction, solid timber profiles are used to form frames and sub-divisions. The loadbearing timber profiles are arranged in a certain grid. The plate effect is achieved through triangular bracing using either thin bracing profiles or steel cables. These can only absorb tensile forces however, which is why it is always necessary to provide two diagonals. Alternatively this function can be fulfilled by cladding, in the form of sheet material or diagonal clapboard. Parallel boarding does not fulfil a bracing function. Wall connections and openings must be integrated in the bracing system.

In timber construction with logs, nail-laminated or plywood elements, the wall structure consists of solid timber. The crosswise arrangement of the laminated board layers creates stable and rigid wall plates which can absorb higher horizontal loads and, at the same time, be used for bracing purposes. In addition, these elements are suitable for larger spans. An advantage is that openings and wall connections can be placed relatively freely. This results in cost-effective systems that make efficient use of the material and that are well suited for use in multi-storey construction. In order to transfer horizontal and vertical loads in this construction method, floors or roofs made with beams must also be constructed so as to function as plates.

OPENINGS IN WALLS

With sheet-type elements it is possible to 'punch out' openings in the walls. In frame construction, openings are specially built by inserting trimmers and other frame members in the stud wall. In sheets or plates manufactured in layered construction, openings can be placed more freely owing to the homogeneous nature of the material.

SERVICES INSTALLATIONS

Pipes and wires within external walls must be arranged on the room side of the vapour barrier in order to ensure adequate air and wind integrity of the wall structure. A good solution is to install them within an additional, inner skin. → 2

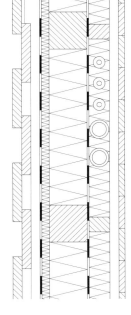

1 Timber construction methods with different forms of bracing:
a timber frame construction
b large span frames
c large span frames
d timber stud construction
e log construction

2 Horizontal section through stud wall, 1:10:
vertical weatherboarding 48 mm,
support battens 24 mm,
sheathing paper,
insulation board 20 mm,
timber studs interspaced with insulation 100 mm,
vapour check,
services installation cavity with insulation and battens 55 mm,
support battens 24 mm,
internal wall finish 16 mm

2

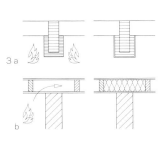

3 a

3 Risk scenarios and fire safety
measures:

a Bearings
As a measure to prevent fire from
destroying bearings and thus
destabilising the structure, it is
possible to fit fire-protection
cladding to bearing elements.

b Hollow spaces
By placing insulation material such
as mineral wool (melting point
1000 °C) into hollow spaces it is
possible to counteract the risk
of fire spreading through voids to
the next fire compartment.

4 Fire protection of internal walls:

a F30 – studwork with a single
layer of fire-resistant plasterboard
on both sides, including internal
mineral fibre insulation
(d = 40 mm / > 40 kg/m³),
melting point > 1000 °C.

b F60 – studwork (studs 60/60
or 80/60) with a double layer
of fire-protection plasterboard
(2 × 12.5 mm), mineral fibre
insulation (d = 40 m / > 40 kg/m³),
melting point > 1000 °C

c F90 – studwork (studs 60/60
or 80/60) with a double layer
of fire-protection plasterboard
(2 × 12.5 mm), mineral fibre
insulation (d = 80 mm / > 100 kg/m³),
melting point > 1000 °C

FIRE PROTECTION

Wood is classified as a combustible material (class B of DIN 4102). The defining parameter is its load-bearing behaviour when exposed to fire. Timber burns slowly and in a predictable way as it contains 15 % moisture, which first needs to evaporate before the solid matter can burn. Solid timber elements can therefore resist fire for a very long time. The top layer of the timber chars during burning and then acts as a protective coat for the underlying layers so that the remaining cross section will continue to retain its strength, even at high temperatures (up to 1000 °C). The burning speed of softwood is approx. 0.7 mm and that of hardwood, approx. 0.5 to 0.6 mm per minute. By comparison, steel loses its loadbearing capacity at 450 to 500 °C and concrete loses one third of its compressive strength at about 650 °C.

In Germany, regulations now permit multi-storey buildings in timber construction up to 5 storeys high (building class 4) and in exceptional cases, up to 6 storeys high. Their loadbearing and bracing building components have to comply with the 'highly fire-resistant' fire classification. If timber is only used for the facade material, approval can even be obtained for up to 8 storeys. Fire protection should be included in the design considerations as early as possible. When timber components are encased, it is important to clarify whether the fire-resistance requirements must be complied with by the entire structure or only by the casing, as this affects the structural sizing of the timber sections, their specific weight and the detailing of the connections. It is possible to construct fire walls by selecting appropriate layers and materials in the necessary sizes. If a building's use, design/construction, or dimensions require a degree of fire protection that cannot be provided by its built components, additional technical measures have to be provided, for example sprinkler systems.

Fire protection as part of the building construction has to be documented as part of the structural calculations; in more complex cases it may be necessary for a specialist engineer to produce a fire protection concept. For cost reasons (construction, maintenance and servicing costs), it is desirable to restrict fire protection to construction measures by complying with the relevant standards. This can be achieved by increasing the cross section of the respective building component or by cladding loadbearing timber elements (without cavities) with non-combustible materials such as insulation material, plaster, plasterboard, or gypsum fibre board (DIN 4102-4).

THERMAL INSULATION

Owing to its fine-pored internal structure, timber has good thermal insulation properties. The thermal conductivity of softwood is 0.13 W/mK and that of hardwood (oak) is 0.23 W/mK. In timber construction, thermal insulation layers can be placed between the timber studs nearest the outside or the inside, either continuously or in a combination of two arrangements. In external walls, the insulation and structural planes often coincide. This has advantages compared to other constructions, since the wall thicknesses can be kept smaller with the same insulating effect. Timber sections interrupting the thermal insulation cause thermal bridging, which must be taken into account in calculations. Common construction details include several layers, with the outer skin consisting of a continuous insulation layer (such as thermally insulating sandwich systems or back-ventilated designs). For this purpose, mineral insulation materials are particularly suitable (felts, quilts, boards). By contrast, foam materials in the shape of boards can be problematic and should only be specified in particular installation situations. Where these materials are subject to shrinkage or deformation under load, they may no longer fully

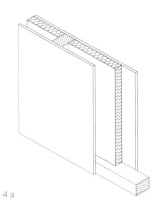

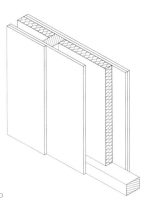

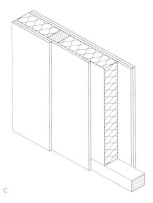

4 a   b   c

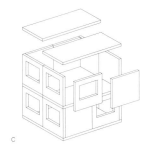

1a

b

c

1 Construction systems:
a log construction
b timber frame construction
c panel construction

2 Wall construction details:
a timber frame construction
b solid timber construction

3 Wall systems (from top to bottom):
Nail-laminated wall
Cross-laminated timber wall
Board system wall
Stud wall
Single-sided stud wall

fill the space between timber profiles, which leads to thermal bridging within the wall cross section (risk of convection). Well insulated timber constructions can achieve a U-value of 0.3 W/m²K with as little as 20 cm wall thickness. A timber frame wall with a thickness of approx. 30 cm can achieve 0.15 to 0.2 W/m²K, which meets the standard of a low-energy house.

CONSTRUCTION SYSTEMS

In modern timber construction, factory prefabrication is gaining ground because the production of standardised construction systems can take place regardless of weather conditions.

Owing to good processing quality and CNC-controlled production, products comply with exacting size tolerances. Products available include semi-finished components (compound elements with timber frame and planking material, on one or both sides) through to complete elements (with windows, doors, linings and facades). These products can be used as part of a cost-efficient construction method, involving short installation times and no waiting periods due to drying-out processes. For the design, this means that all details have to be completely established and defined at the beginning of the construction stage. For this reason many system providers include certain preliminary design services, such as standard construction details and typical structural calculations.

WALL SYSTEMS

The detailing of wall constructions varies with the different systems. Today, it is quite common to combine different systems rather than using one system for both walls and floors. Typical timber wall constructions include block and solid wood construction, stud and frame construction. These wall constructions may consist of stud-type elements which are combined with the help of the cladding to form a loadbearing element, or they may involve solid timber constructions (e.g. nail-laminated or cross-laminated timber). There are also some systems which – similar to the block formats in masonry construction – consist of similarly sized elements that are easy to handle. Depending on the size and installation of the elements, the grid and module dimensions of the industrially produced serial products (building sheets, timber lengths etc.) are relevant.

In order to comply with the different requirements in terms of structure and building physics, external walls built with a standardised system today usually consist of several layers. Here, the insulation is applied in two layers: one in the fields between the loadbearing profiles and one fixed on the outside (e.g. wood-fibre insulation board without slat substrate) in order to create a continuous insulation plane. The vapour barrier is always fitted on the warm side of the insulation and must not be pierced or interrupted.

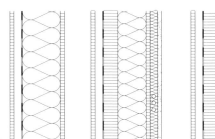
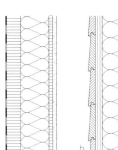
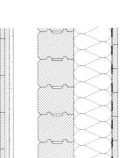
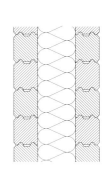

2a

b

3

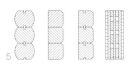

4 Construction of a log house

5 Solid timber wall constructions
(from left to right):
round logs with fillet joints,
square-sided logs,
square-sided logs with fillet joints,
solid timber glulam wall

6 Section through log
construction, 1:20
a Wall construction:
loadbearing log wall 120 mm,
insulation and battens 120 mm,
vapour check, insulation and
services cavity 40 mm,
double layer plasterboard 25 mm

b Floor construction, upper floor:
solid timber parquet 28 mm,
impact sound insulation 60 mm,
planed floorboards 28 mm,
floor joists 160 mm with
insulation in void 80 mm,
battens 30 mm,
double layer plasterboard 25 mm

c Floor construction, ground floor:
solid timber parquet 28 mm,
floating screed 60 mm,
vapour barrier,
insulation 200 mm,
damp-proof membrane,
reinforced concrete slab 200 mm,
blinding layer

d Roof construction:
roof tiles, counter battens,
battens, fibre board 30 mm,
rafters with interspaced insulation
180 mm, vapour check,
battens with interspaced insulation/
services cavity 40 mm,
double layer plasterboard 25 mm

LOG CONSTRUCTION

Log construction, which in Alpine regions is also known as 'strickbau', is rightly referred to as a solid construction (solid timber component > 50 %) in its original sense. It is traditionally popular in wooded regions. It requires good craftsmanship and the careful selection of timber. It has a typical appearance, as the timber logs remain visible. Owing to current thermal insulation regulations, classic single-skin log construction is no longer viable today. The increased requirements can be met by log buildings using cavity construction, in which insulation is inserted either on the inside or within the cavity.

The loadbearing structure, the insulation, and the external and internal finishing are all provided by the stacked round logs or planks, which are structurally linked with the help of corner joints (cogged or dovetailed). This type of construction does not rely on technical fasteners. The bracing is achieved via the friction resistance in the bearing joints. Spans depend on the available length of the solid timber, usually up to 4 or 5 m. Settlement can be up to 25 mm per storey and must be accommodated in the design of connections, such as those with walls or chimneys. It must also be taken into account for the design of services installations. The headers of door and window openings have a tongue-and-groove joint along the top surface, which allows enough play to prevent settlement from buckling the frames. The layout design of these buildings is limited in its possibilities; a rectangular arrangement of walls makes economic sense. Multi-storey buildings are not favoured, on grounds of both construction and cost.

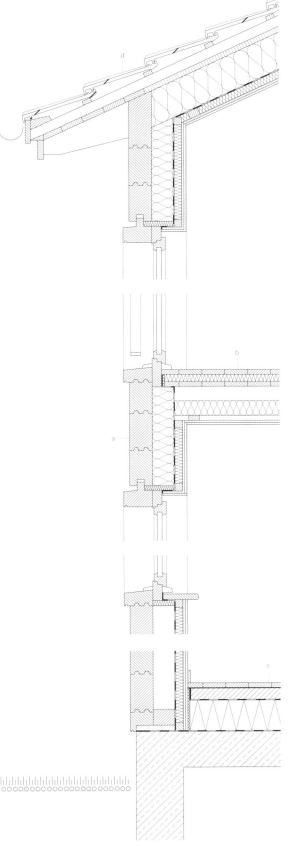

6

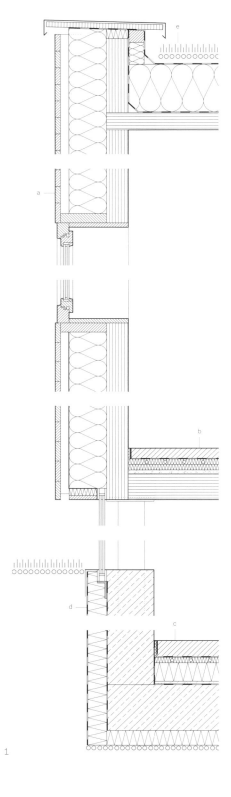

SOLID TIMBER CONSTRUCTION

Walls, floors and ceilings have both space-forming and structural functions and consist of plate-like elements made of firmly connected boards, planks or sheets (wood-based materials). They may be bonded by gluing, nailing or dowelling and be put together simply, crosswise or diagonally. In cross section they may be combined as a solid or a hollow box section, overall forming a plate-type structure. The advantage of the latter option is the reduced material cross section and the lower weight. The elements are very dimensionally stable, owing to the layered construction with well dried-out timber. Usually there is no gradual shrinkage and cracking. The advantage of the large quantity of timber (e.g. a good room climate) can thus be used to the full. Crosswise glued systems feature very little shrinkage and swelling; with single-layer, nail-laminated timbers it may be necessary to provide shrinkage and expansion joints.

Owing to the high strength of the elements, it is also possible to insert openings afterwards. Bracing is achieved through the plate-type structure. Depending on the load and buckling length, plate thicknesses between 60 and 120 mm are common. Any point loads may have to be transferred via additional posts. The elements are manufactured at the factory, including openings (windows, doors). Services can be fitted in cut recesses or behind an additional cladding layer. The structure of the external wall with its solid elements is often enough to provide an adequate seal. In view of the fact that the loadbearing elements usually do not provide the thermal insulation required today, an additional thermal insulation plane is needed. ➘ 1

1 Section, solid timber construction 1:20

a Wall construction:
Douglas fir cladding painted 24 mm,
battens/ventilation gap 50 mm,
thermal insulation 200 mm,
cross-laminated spruce 115 mm,
white acrylic paint coat

b Floor construction, upper floor:
cement-based screed sealed/black 60 mm,
impact sound insulation with heating tubes 30 mm,
insulation board 30 mm,
loose perlite 16 mm,
cross-laminated spruce 146 mm

c Floor construction, ground floor:
cement-based screed sealed/black 90 mm,
impact sound insulation with heating tubes 30 mm,
insulation board 98 mm,
loose perlite 16 mm,
vapour check,
reinforced concrete 250 mm,
insulation 80 mm,
gravel 100 mm

d Plinth sealing finish:
external perimeter insulation 100 mm,
reinforced concrete ledge 250 mm

e Roof structure:
extensive greening 80 mm,
two-layer waterproof membrane 5 mm,
sloping insulation 200 to 300 mm,
vapour barrier,
cross-laminated spruce 95 mm,
white acrylic paint

2 Construction of a house using solid timber elements, Hamburg, 2007, Kraus Schönberg Architects

3

3 Construction of a building in
timber panel construction

4 Different jointing methods for
the vertical joints of wall elements.
It is important here that the joints
between the elements are structurally effective (plate effect) and
that the substrate for fixing internal
and external cladding is flush and
smooth.

PANEL CONSTRUCTION

In panel construction, timber elements are manufactured ready for installation as walls or floors/ceilings. The load-bearing structure, thermal insulation, cavities for services, and concealed linings are combined in one component. The prefabrication may even include items such as windows, doors and tiles on the walls. Entire wall construction systems are combined with panels or plates to form a structural unit. It is important that the loadbearing structure of the plates is non-directional. The very strong and rigid solid plates can be joined together rather like a model to create rooms.

Openings can be cut almost anywhere and do not require a change in construction, provided there is still enough material remaining above the opening. In this way panel construction is clearly different from classical skeleton-type timber construction. The objective is to achieve a low-priced and quick construction method, which is suitable particularly for temporary buildings. Wall, floor and roof plates are constructed as a composite system. From a structural point of view, frame and panel construction are nearly identical, the essential difference being that the cladding on at least one side has not only a bracing, but also a loadbearing function. The two layers together (studs and cladding on both sides) provide the full load-bearing capacity of the element. For this reason, the cladding material must be very strong and rigid (e.g. cross-wise glued blockboard). The plates are non-directional as a structural system. The grid spacing of the studs or ribs can vary from case to case (depending on the structure and openings) and thus allows greater design freedom.

The bracing of the building is achieved through the combined rigidity of floor, wall and roof plates. Fasteners can be nails, screws, bolts, brackets and glue. Care must be exercised in the detailing of the individual element joints.

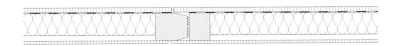

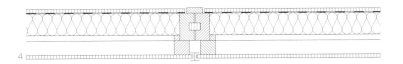

4

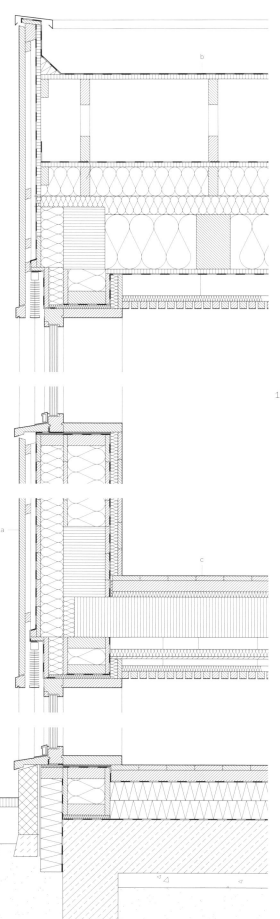

1 Community centre in timber frame construction, St. Gerold, 2009, Cukrowicz Nachbaur Architects

2 Section, timber frame construction 1:20

a Wall construction:
silver fir face battens 30 mm,
base battens 30 mm,
counter battens 30 mm,
breather paper,
diagonal boarding
(spruce/fir) 25 mm,
timber battens 125 mm
with cellulose insulation in between,
diagonal boarding
(spruce/fir) 25 mm,
timber battens 200 mm
with cellulose insulation in between,
diagonal boarding
(spruce/fir) 25 mm,
vapour check,
timber battens,
installation cavity,
silver fir board

b Roof structure:
bitumen roofing membrane,
mineral chippings,
spruce/fir close-boarding,
back ventilation 500 mm,
spruce/fir close-boarding,
timber battens 180 to 300 mm
with cellulose insulation in between,
loadbearing timber joists 300 mm
with cellulose insulation in between,
spruce/fir close-boarding,
vapour check,
installation cavity,
sheep's wool acoustic insulation 30 mm,
dust membrane,
timber battens 40 mm

c Floor construction:
floorboards 27 mm,
packing timbers
with insulating felt,
vapour barrier,
packing timbers
with wood-fibre insulation
100 mm in between,
moisture barrier membrane,
priming coat,
reinforced concrete slab 300 mm,
blinding layer 80 mm

TIMBER FRAME CONSTRUCTION

Timber frame construction has the advantages of being quick and easy to put up and of allowing considerable design freedom. For this reason it is the most commonly practised timber construction method today. The facade cladding can be chosen to suit the project. Interior finishes on the walls may consist of wood-based board material, gypsum-fibre board or plasterboard.

In frame construction, similar to post-and-beam construction, the loadbearing elements are composed of slender profile sections. The individual timber frame elements, which are formed from vertical studs and horizontal frames, are usually prefabricated at the factory and fitted storey by storey. The timber members required for the frame elements consist of rectangular solid sections with slender profiles, preferably standardised, (e.g. 60/120 mm), usually of whitewood or redwood. The grid spacing is normally between 50 and 70 cm; common dimensions are 62.5 and 65 cm. The spans are usually approx. 4.50 m to a maximum of 7 m. Wall connections and window or door openings can be arranged relatively freely; studs crossing the planned opening can be interrupted and bridged with trimmers. Where structurally required, the adjacent studs have to be reinforced. The individual wall plates are joined with butt joints. The elements are usually installed storey by storey with the floors inserted in between. Since any settlement is determined by the horizontal timbers, it is particularly important that these consist of dry wood. The panels are filled with thermal insulation as required; today it is common practice to install a second insulation layer that is independent of the loadbearing plane. In this way it is possible to significantly reduce thermal bridging.

1

2

3 Basic timber frame element
a head plate
b base plate
c stud
d planking / siding

4 Load transfer in timber frame
construction:

a Siding prevents studs from
breaking
b Studs prevent siding from
breaking
c Studs carry vertical loads
d Siding absorbs wind load
through bending
e Head plate transfers horizontal
load to rigid deck
f Studs prevent buckling of
planking/siding
g Head plate transfers horizontal
load into bracing wall
h Siding creates rigid wall
construction and transfers
horizontal loads
i Vertical load is transferred to
deck and floor

5 Nail connection detail

6 Timber frame construction

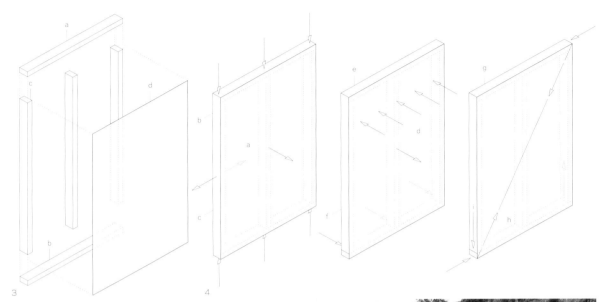

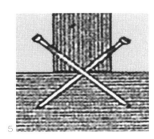

The frame elements are lined on one or two sides with sheet material (OSB, chipboard, plasterboard or gypsum-fibre board) in one or several layers (if necessary, fitted diagonally). The cladding should span at least two frame fields. The material can be selected to suit the conceptual, construction, building physics, and service installation requirements. It is important that the plates are connected with the ribs on their four peripheral edges and therefore that joints between plates are not made in the=middle of a panel. The interior may be lined with chipboard, OSB or multi-layer wood-based material; the exterior may be clad with soft wood-fibre board or diffusive MDF board.

The plates are needed for the transfer or horizontal loads from walls and floors. Depending on requirements, an air or vapour barrier has to be integrated. Vertical ribs transfer the vertical loads; due in contrast to skeleton construction, their slenderness necessitates bracing of the individual ribs with cladding on at least one side. This also transfers the horizontal loads resulting from wind and other horizontal forces and derives its rigidity in turn from the ribs. This construction method is also referred to as a composite system. The timber components are butt jointed and connected with nails or screws. The bracing of the entire building is achieved through the combined rigidity of the floor, wall and roof plates.

SOUND INSULATION

Timber construction relies primarily on lightweight materials with a relatively low mass per unit area. On the other hand, the walls are in the main constructed of several layers which, together with the creation of flexible skins (mass-spring principle), gives them sound reduction properties similar to heavy walls in solid construction. Important parameters are the material of the skins, the grid and stud properties, the dimension of the spacing between skins, the fixing of the skins and the attenuation in the cavities within the construction. The best values are achieved with flexible facing skins and with constructions in which the different skins of the wall are separated. The vertical sound insulation between storeys can be improved by installing floating screeds or additional suspended ceilings, or by adding weight to the loadbearing structure.

AIR-TIGHTNESS

An air-tight building envelope reduces heat loss. To a large extent, the sense of comfort depends on air flows (draught) perceived by the user. In timber construction there are many joints and there is also the fact that timber moves over time. Whereas tongue-and-groove connections are not considered air-tight, board materials (wood-based boards, plasterboard, building paper) with sealed joints (using filler or adhesive tape) and vapour-check membranes (e.g. polyethylene foils) usually provide the required air-tightness. A wind barrier is required on the outside in order to prevent the external air from flowing through the thermal insulation. Suitable materials are bitumen felt on timber cladding, softwood-fibre board, roofing underlay, or insulation board with a high flow resistance.

DIFFUSION

If diffusion causes condensation within the wall, the result can be a reduction in the insulation value and, in the long term, damage to the loadbearing structure (mould or fungus attack). Where walls consist of several layers, the sequence of layers is important. The denser layers on the warm side (inside) should limit or prevent the penetration of water vapour. Towards the cold side (outside) the materials should be increasingly more open to diffusion. A vapour barrier on the inside of the wall will normally prevent any diffusion through the wall. It is imperative to protect this layer against mechanical damage, for example resulting from the installation of wiring or pipes. In view of the fact that this can be difficult, and also taking into account the long-term risk that users may damage this layer with screws or nails, a wall construction that allows diffusion may be preferred. In that case the layers are arranged such that any moisture entering the wall can be fully discharged again to the outside. An example of this arrangement is a construction with OSB board on the inside acting as a vapour check, and MDF board on the outside, which allows any trapped moisture to diffuse to the outside.

ROOM CLIMATE

Today, timber construction systems are commonly open to diffusion. Owing to the hygroscopic property of timber it will absorb any excessive moisture in the air and thereby balance the relative humidity, which helps to create a comfortable interior climate. A design with good thermal insulation ensures that the temperature on the inside of external walls is comfortable. There is also the fact that timber itself has good insulation properties and – at its surface – adjusts easily to the ambient temperature. That means that the surface does not attract condensation. Users perceive wood as comfortable because it feels warm (no loss of body heat through radiation to building components with cold surfaces).

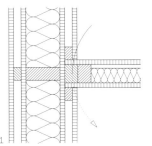

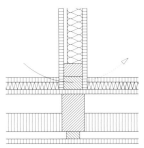

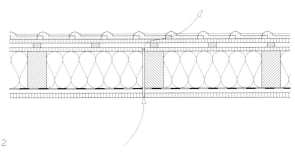

1 Detailing to protect timber

2 Mechanisms of water vapour transport through building components:
substantially more water vapour is carried by convection airflow through joints than is carried by diffusion

3 Use classes in buildings as per DIN 68800-3 or as per EN 335-1:

Use Class 01
Wood-based product under cover and fully protected from the weather –not exposed to wetting

Use Class 02
Wood-based product under cover and fully protected from the weather – but where high environmental humidity can lead to occasional but not persistent wetting

Use Class 03
Component is exposed to the weather but not in contact with the ground – subject to frequent wetting

Use Class 04
Component is in constant contact with fresh water and/or the ground – constant wetting

Use Class 05
Component is permanently in contact with salt water – constant wetting

4 Timber protection methods: Important factors are the depth of penetration and the even distribution of the timber treatment agent. Simple processes involve brush coating, spraying, dipping, hot and cold immersion. Other common methods are pressure impregnation or vacuum impregnation. Not all types of treatment are suitable for all types of timber.

5 Solid planks of pressure impregnated timber

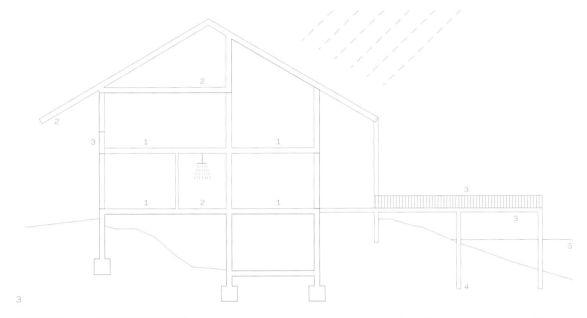

3

4

5

PROTECTION AGAINST DAMPNESS
When timber is exposed to moisture (>25%) for long periods it will rot and lose its structure and strength. It is however possible to remove and replace any damaged parts and still achieve a close fit. Adequate passive protection can be provided by overhanging roofs, slanting surfaces, or cover materials (for which wear is accepted). Special protection is required for the end-grain, i.e. where the timber has been cut perpendicular to the direction of the fibre. These cuts leave the capillary pores open, allowing moisture to penetrate deep into the wood.

TIMBER PROTECTION
There are many timber houses that are four hundred years old or more. Most of the wood pests that may be present in green timber are killed off as timber is processed and dried out. Likewise, the timber's tendency to swell and shrink reduces over time. For this reason, attacks are only likely to occur – apart from mould and fungus – from wood-boring insects (primarily furniture beetle and house longhorn beetle) although these attacks only occur at low temperatures and require a minimum moisture content in the timber of >10%. When the moisture content rises to >20% it is also possible for fungus and mould to develop. However, in walls without thermal bridges and with good insulation these conditions are rare. It is therefore very important to protect timber from permanent exposure to water. If timber does get wet, it should be possible for it to dry out as quickly as possible. External building components that are regularly exposed to moisture should be made of timber species that are resistant to the effects of the weather. Preventive measures during the construction (DIN 68800-2) protect the timber through appropriate detailing, taking building physics into account. Measures include appropriate transport and storage, as well as carrying out the construction so as to avoid the formation of condensate, protect the fabric from moisture from the outside (e.g. driving rain), allow the timber to dry out and prevent pests from entering. The selection of the timber can also be a protective measure; a durable timber species may not require chemical timber treatment. Generally speaking, heartwood is more resistant than sapwood. Particularly durable European timber species are e.g. robinia, oak, larch and Douglas fir. With correct detailing, chemical timber treatment is not absolutely necessary, but it can extend the service life compared to untreated timber. Where timber is heavily exposed or has to remain dimensionally true, it may be opportune to apply a preventive timber treatment.

DIN 68800-3 contains a listing of different hazard classes (GK0 to GK4) for loadbearing components and the respective requirements for chemical timber treatment or, alternatively, the choice of a suitable timber species which does not require chemical treatment. The finishing and appearance of the completed surfaces should be taken into account when choosing a timber treatment system. On interior surfaces it is usually possible to omit extensive application of chemicals. In the case of an existing attack of either mould or insects, chemical treatment offers one avenue of dealing with the problem.

WOOD AND WOOD-BASED MATERIALS

Natural wood is an inhomogeneous construction material. The heartwood (nearest the core) has different characteristics compared to the sapwood (outer layers). The strength depends on the width of the annual growth rings (speed of growth) and the number of branches. Hard timber comes from slow-growing trees and soft timber from fast-growing trees. As a natural material, timber always moves. By absorbing or giving off moisture from or into the air, it expands or contracts. Its specific weight is responsible for the physical characteristics and varies according to the species. It is also affected by the moisture content of the timber, which is why this must be included in a specification. The most common wood for the construction of timber buildings is softwood from domestic coniferous species. For external applications it is prudent to use more durable timbers such as larch, oak, or Douglas fir. The term 'solid wood' refers to wood that is cut from a log. The term 'wood-based material' refers to material that is manufactured using layers of strips, chips or fibres in different thicknesses. A wide range of wood-based materials and composite building components is available, such as nail-laminated timber boards, pressed woodchip profiles, board construction elements and composite deck materials, which provide new design and construction options essential for modern timber buildings. Owing to completely new production methods, timber is nowadays available in many different forms, as solid boards, battens, or sheet material. Whereas in traditional timber construction the sizes of components were determined by the size of the trees, today the sizes are determined by the restrictions imposed by the available transport and installation options.

MOISTURE CONTENT OF TIMBER

The moisture content of timber is affected by its hygroscopic properties and the prevailing relative humidity. When it absorbs moisture, timber will swell and when it releases moisture it will shrink. The difference in volume resulting from this movement is called the shrinkage coefficient. DIN 1052 contains a definition of use classes 1 to 3, depending on the climate conditions, the ambient air (temperature, humidity) and the moisture content of the timber. Green timber has an inherent moisture content of about 60 %. The fibre saturation point is between 25 % and 35 %. Below this value, timber starts to shrink and the direction of shrinkage depends on the direction of the annual growth rings. In order to prevent defects and damage in timber constructions, the timber is dried before it is used (air-dried, kiln-dried). One advantage of construction with timber is that no water is used and therefore no time is lost waiting for components to dry out. Wood-based materials are grouped into material classes according to their resistance to moisture. In Germany, V20 is the designation for timber not suitable for exposure to moisture and V100 is suitable for short-term exposure to moisture.

QUALITY AND MARKING

Construction materials are subjected to quality checks in order to ensure that they are mechanically and physically fit for purpose and that they neither present a health hazard nor are harmful to the environment. Of special relevance for materials from renewable sources are the RAL quality seal, the Ü-mark and the CE-mark.

FORMATS OF WOOD-BASED PANEL PRODUCTS

Common sheet material sizes are based on a 62.5 cm grid. Typical wood-based material sheet sizes therefore range from 1.25 m to 5.0 m. It is obviously advantageous, at the design stage, to select a construction grid that minimises cutting waste.

SAWN TIMBER

Most construction timber is softwood from coniferous species (fir, pine, spruce, larch); the most common hardwoods are oak and beech. Timber grades are classified as solid timber, solid timber with dovetail connection, and structural solid timber. In accordance with DIN 68252, sawn timber is produced from naturally grown logs by cutting parallel to the axis of the log. Various names are used to describe different sizes, e.g. batten, board, plank and scantling. These timber sections have a residual moisture content of 20 %. Owing to their durability and weather resistance, larch and Douglas fir sections are often used as thresholds in timber houses.

STRUCTURAL SOLID TIMBER

The term 'solid timber' is defined in DIN 1052. The term refers to technically dried (residual moisture content approx. 15 %) dimensionally stable solid timber from coniferous species that has been sorted and sawn to exclude the pith of the log. Owing to its dimensional stability, the development of shakes and cracks is minimised. It usually has a planed surface and is therefore suitable for constructions where the material is exposed to view. The minimum dimensions are 60/120 mm, the maximum dimensions 120/240 mm.

1 Wood and wood-based products:
a solid construction timber
b DUO beam
c three-layered timber beam
d four-section glued timber beam
e glulam timber

2 Quality seals
(from top to bottom):
CE mark
RAL quality mark
PEFC logo

1a

b

c

d

e

0672 - CPD - | 14.21.33
EN 14080 Brettschichtholz der Festigkeitsklasse
GL 24h GL 28h Fichte (Picea abies), Lärche (Larix)
Klebstoff Typ I nach EN 301

2

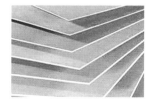

3

3 Wood and wood-based products
(from top to bottom):
Tree trunks
Battens
Planks
Tongue-and-groove boards
Plywood
Cross-laminated timber

TWO AND THREE-LAYERED TIMBER BEAM (LAMINATED TIMBER)

These beams are manufactured by gluing together two or three equal planks or scantlings with the flat sides facing each other in the direction of the fibre. As the glued joints' thickness is minimal, the solid timber character is retained. Laminated timber is grouped into use classes 1 and 2 and should not be exposed to fluctuating climate conditions.

FOUR-SECTION GLUED TIMBER BEAM

As the name implies, four square or similar softwood timber sections are glued together in parallel with the direction of the fibre. Four quarter sections are joined together with the outside facing inwards. This configuration creates a continuous cavity in the centre of the rectangular cross section. Four-section glued timber beams are suitable for loadbearing and bracing building components; they have good dimensional stability and a low moisture content.

GLUED LAMINATED TIMBER (GLULAM)

A cross section consists of a minimum of three horizontally glued solid timber planks (dovetail joint, usually fir) and is particularly suitable for heavy-duty structures with large spans. Depending on the timber used, the dried and planed planks are 3 to 4 cm thick and 20 cm wide. The maximum height and length of these beams is determined by the available production technology. Lengths of 30 to 35 m and heights of 2.20 m are possible. The geometry of the cross section and the shape of the beam (straight or curved) are variable. For the selection of the gluing process it is necessary to take the exposure conditions of the beam into account.

PLYWOOD AND BLOCKBOARD

In these sheet materials the layers are glued at right angles to each other; plywood is manufactured in a range of different thicknesses, numbers of layers and timber species, including softwood and hardwood outer layers; blockboard has a thicker inner layer of battens faced with a thin outer layer on either side. These manufactured board materials have good resilience. Board thicknesses from 8 to 30 mm are suitable for use as bracing material for timber constructions and loadbearing walls.

PARTICLE BOARDS

The base material of particle boards (chipboard, parallel strand lumber, OSB, flat-pressed particle board) consists of timber strands, wood peelings, wood sawings or similar. By applying pressure and heat these materials – together with binding agents (cement, mineral or synthetic resin) – are formed into medium-strength board material in different thicknesses and finishes. Many are suitable as a bracing material in timber structures. Depending on the size of the chips or strands the resulting board will be directional or – in the case of small chips – non-directional. OSB board is significantly stronger in the direction parallel to the strands than across. In contrast to the – non-directional – chipboard, it can be used where directional strength is required, e.g. for roof sheathing. In wood-based board material bonded with inorganic or mineral binding agent (gypsum or cement) the wood fibres function as reinforcement. Various types are available and can be used in situations requiring thermal and sound insulation, as well as fire and moisture resistance. Chipboard has many uses in construction, refurbishment, fitting out and furniture making. It can be used for lining walls or ceilings and also as carrier for veneers and laminates.

SOFTBOARD AND FIBRE BOARD

In fibre board the timber structure is no longer recognisable. It consists of a mixture of processed wood fibres and filler materials which is pressed together with or without adhesive (binder), sometimes with water. Board materials of different strengths are produced, depending on the degree of compaction. A wide range of board material is produced for various applications and different requirements, including softwood-fibre insulation board, porous fibre board, medium hard fibre board, hardboard and bituminous fibre board. Soft fibreboard or softboard is used as thermal and sound insulation material or to improve fire safety. By adding bitumen emulsions it is possible to create water-repellent board for external applications or for use as impact sound insulation material. This material allows diffusion and contributes to controlled and balanced moisture levels.

The fibres used in MDF board have been dried, sprayed with glue and processed in presses to form board material. This produces a wood-based material with equal strength in the longitudinal and transverse directions. MDF and HDF are mostly used for furniture-making and for fitting out interiors. It is also good as a carrier material for veneer or laminates, or for paint finishing. MDF board is not suitable for external application as its resistance to moisture is very limited. HDF and hardboard can be used in facade cladding.

FLOOR CONSTRUCTION

Floors have a double function, as they form both the lower and the upper horizontal enclosure of a room. On the ground floor they form the barrier between the lowest storey and the ground. In buildings with flat roofs, the uppermost deck forms the ceiling as well as the roof. In combination with floor finishes and suspended ceilings, floor decks fulfil both loadbearing and bracing functions; they also have to meet acoustic and – sometimes – thermal insulation requirements, and have to be fire and moisture-resistant. The loadbearing deck can be constructed in a number of ways, depending on the building task, the conceptual design approach, structural factors such as span and structural system, and other factors such as type of use, material, costs, construction time and the locality. In addition to the structural function, decks are also used for other functions, making them a rather complex building component, which may also be used for the installation of items such as ventilation ducts or services pipes, or as a cooling ceiling, whereby the mass of the structure is used to absorb excessive heat. The most common deck constructions today are flat slabs, consisting of reinforced in-situ concrete, or prefabricated or partially prefabricated components. The installation of prefabricated floor components requires very careful design and planning, and heavy lifting gear; in addition, the delivery period needs to be taken into account. Constructions with partially prefabricated components involve semi-finished reinforced girders or slabs (e.g. filigree precast floor slabs) which are finished off with in-situ concrete. The installation of fully prefabricated elements, such as reinforced element floor decks (e.g. hollow concrete planks) or floor decks with steel girders, is more expensive. An advantage is that prefabricated components are fully ready for service immediately after installation. Generally speaking, flat slab decks are more economical than ribbed decks or constructions with beams, because the cost of the formwork for the latter is considerable. As fire regulations evolve and there is increasing interest in renewable building materials and the careful use of resources, prefabricated timber floors are becoming more popular, particularly in housing developments. Advantages are the relatively low weight, easy processing and the fact that the material is dry.

1

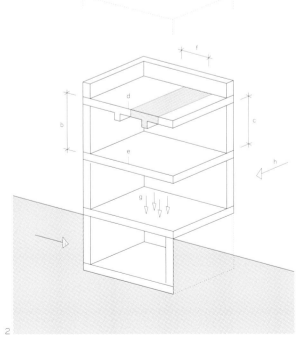

2

1 Roof construction of company canteen, Ditzingen, 2008, Barkow Leibinger Architects. The loadbearing structure is modelled on elements from nature and, with its leaf-like structure, creates an impressive ceiling. The primary steel structure is filled with honeycomb-like timber cells of different heights, some of which penetrate the roof as rooflights.

2 Legend:
a footprint area
b storey height
c clear storey height
d ribbed slab floor
e flat slab
f loaded area
g loads
h wind load
i earth pressure

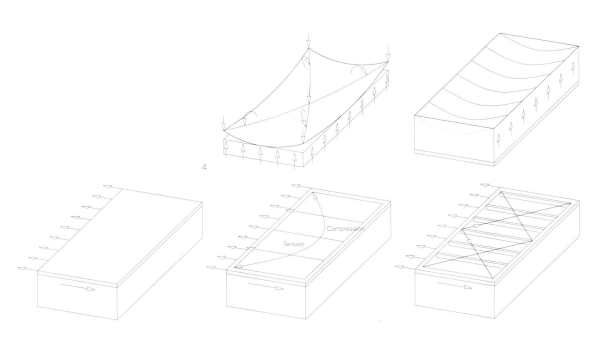

CONSTRUCTION SYSTEMS

Floors and ceilings should only have very limited deflection and should therefore consist of rigid horizontal structural members. All vertical forces, such as that from the weight of the structure and the imposed loads (DIN 1055-3), are transferred into horizontal beams or girders and vertical loadbearing walls or uprights. In order to prevent excessive deflection, floor decks have to have adequate rigidity. With appropriate detailing as bracing slabs with shear strength, floor decks can transfer horizontal forces (e.g. from wind or earth pressure) to the bracing walls. In the case of floors constructed of individual elements (e.g. timber beams), this can be achieved by inserting cladding or cross members. Floor decks can be constructed using reinforced concrete, timber, masonry or steel, or a combination of these materials. From the cost efficiency point of view, the construction should have the least possible weight and construction height, in order to make the best possible use of the available space in a building. Different load transfer principles apply, depending on the design of the floor deck. The two main systems are: solid slab floor decks; floors resting on beams. The type of construction depends primarily on the overall structural system and the resulting bearing situation; the dimension of the cross section depends on the length and direction of the span, and the loads to be supported. The choice of floor construction also needs to take into account whether the floor has to support non-loadbearing partition walls. With some types of floor, such walls can be placed anywhere; with others they may only run parallel or crossways to the direction in which the floor structure spans. It may be necessary to provide additional means of support in the form of reinforcements, trimmers, strips with greater loadbearing capacity, or beams.

LOAD TRANSFER

In the case of beamed floors or ribbed floors, the beams (ribs) are the structurally relevant elements which support the secondary loadbearing elements, such as timber boarding (on joists) or fill elements. A plate effect cannot be achieved unless additional measures are provided. Homogeneous floor slabs normally have the effect of plates. They are mainly exposed to bending stress and have substantial loadbearing reserves. In the case of a beam-and-slab floor, the beams and slab both contribute to the transfer of loads. They act as a plate without requiring additional measures. Vaulted ceilings are primarily subjected to compression. Single-axis floors transfer loads in the direction of the span. Where additional transverse forces have to be transferred for structural reasons, additional support has to be provided. Uni-directional reinforced concrete floors will include transverse reinforcements, which ensure that forces are evenly distributed. Bi-directional floors transfer loads in both directions. In that case the ratio of the span in the two directions is important (favourable <1:2).

3 Directions of span and orientation of layout:
a, b one-directional span, support at two ends
c two-directional span, supported on three sides
d cross span, supported on four sides
e point bearing

4 Vertical load transfer via bending moment:
the vertical loads from the floor slab are transferred vertically to the bearing points.

5 Bracing of buildings
The effect of floor slabs/decks: floor slabs or decks stabilise a building by absorbing and transferring horizontal forces into bracing walls, frames or similar.

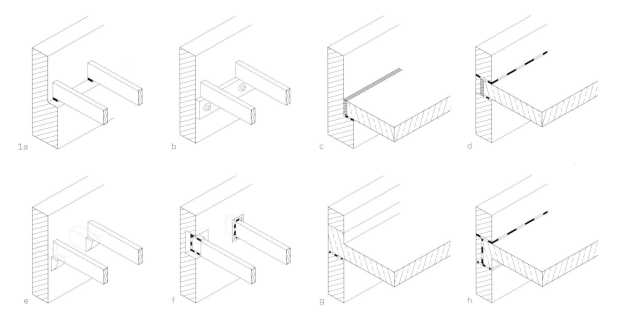

Left-hand page

1   Floor bearings:
a   with ledge
b   with border joist
c   with ledge and edge insulation strip to buffer thrust movement from the floor
d   with soldier course and thermal insulation, floor and upper part of the wall bearing on bituminous sheeting strip, edge strip with centring strip inside
e   individual solid bearing pads
f   joist heads bearing in the wall, moisture protection with diffusive building paper
g   flat roof upstand, bearing with sliding joint
h   tie beam with sliding joint beneath

DEFLECTION AND DEFORMATION

Floors in the interior of buildings are not likely to be subject to thermal deformation. More important is elastic deformation resulting from loads, and different kinds of material deformation at the bearings. When exposed to evenly distributed loads, floors with support on all sides will bend in the form of a paraboloid. The permitted deflection of floors is limited. If the deflection is excessive, it is possible that non-loadbearing partition walls will be exposed to too much stress and will crack.

FLOOR BEARINGS/SLIDING BEARINGS

In small-scale buildings, floors usually rest on the walls in a linear formation. Where larger spans are required, intermediate beams have to be introduced. It is also possible to provide direct support in the form of uprights. In that case it may be necessary to reinforce the floor at the point of support (risk of punching shear). In order to ensure an adequate load tranfer, the bearing points in a floor have to be thick enough or adequately reinforced to be able to absorb the loads. The maximum permissible compression must not be exceeded in the bearing area. If the floor is not thick enough at the point of bearing, the deflection of the floor may cause increased edge pressure at the bearing and hence spalling. In order to avoid this and centralise the forces to be transferred into the wall, it may be appropriate (with larger spans) to insert a felt strip at the edge of the bearing. Sliding bearings avoid restraints and the formation of cracks. At the point of bearing, the force vector within the floor changes: the compression and tension zones are inverted. In reinforced concrete floors, the reinforcement is therefore bent so that it occupies the upper part of the floor cross section; alternatively a reinforcement mesh can be placed (mesh reinforcement). Reinforced concrete floors are subject to deformation due to creep and shrinkage. Reinforced concrete roof slabs can be subject to significant deformation when exposed to larger temperature fluctuations.

SERVICES INSTALLATIONS

Horizontal services installations (electric cables, heating and water pipes, ventilation ducts) can be conveniently placed in the void of raised floors or suspended ceilings. It is also possible to install such services in solid reinforced concrete floor decks, but their position has to be designed in detail and the structural calculation adjusted accordingly. In buildings requiring many services, a better solution may be to designate a special zone for their installation. At the Salk Institute by Loius Kahn, this zone takes the form of a separate walk-in room. Recesses and apertures for vertical services installations in concrete floors are often prepared by inserting polystyrene spacer blocks into the formwork. Smaller holes can also be made subsequently using the core drilling process. However, holes should be placed such that they do not cut through major reinforcement bars.

Right-hand page

2   Thermal protection:
a   thermal insulation masonry at floor level with soldier course and additional insulation strip
b   thermal insulation sandwich system
c   cavity wall construction with thermal insulation in the cavity
d   internal insulation with horizontal edge insulation above and below floor
e   internal insulation with thermal break cage connector

3   Heat flow from floor to outside wall with external insulation

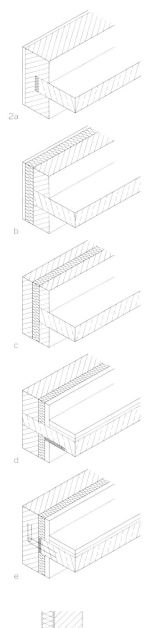

2a

b

c

d

e

3

FLOOR DECK DESIGN

Different requirements apply to purely internal floors (between storeys or between a top floor and attic) and external decks (e.g. flat roofs or floors over open passageways). The cross section of a floor is primarily designed to carry the relevant load. Additional layers may be required where a floor has to perform additional functions, such as fire protection and sound or thermal insulation. In general it is desirable however to fulfil as many of the required purposes as possible with the main, loadbearing part of the floor.

THERMAL INSULATION

Normally, no thermal insulation measures are required for purely internal floor decks. But this is not so with floors over unheated passages or cellars, loggia floors or flat roofs. In these cases additional internal or external insulation is required, sometimes both. In addition to providing thermal insulation, it is also important to avoid the formation of condensate. Components without insulation can attract condensate on the inside owing to their low temperature. For thermal protection during the hot season it is primarily the storage capacity of concrete floors that can be utilised. The perimeter face of floors can represent a significant point of thermal bridging – which should be counteracted by placing appropriate thermal insulation on the outside. Cantilevered floor areas should be thermally separated from internal floor areas. Special reinforcement cages have been developed for this purpose in which only the reinforcement steel bridges the gap, thus minimising the cold bridge effect.

FIRE PROTECTION

Floors form the horizontal fire compartments. No special fire protection requirements exist for the floors in buildings of up to two storeys; in buildings of three to five storeys all floors must be at least fire-resistant, and in buildings of more than five full storeys, all floors must be fireproof. The fire resistance of floors should be such that, in the event of a fire, they are sufficiently loadbearing for the duration of the rescue work (approx. 90 minutes). Where a floor does not have this required fire resistance, additional measures must be undertaken. Solid (mineral-based) floors offer the best fire protection. Steel will fail at temperatures of 450–650 °C. For this reason, load-bearing steel components are usually lined or coated. In the case of timber, the burning speed plays an important role. In fact, the entire detailing must be taken into consideration. Timber floors can be made adequately fire-resistant through appropriate detailing or by making the cross sections larger than required for the structural duty.

AIRBORNE AND IMPACT SOUND INSULATION

Sound insulation in floors is required in order to stop noise from travelling vertically between rooms above each other. A distinction is made between airborne and impact sound.

For protection against airborne sound it is primarily the mass of a building component that is relevant. A high weight per unit area, such as that of solid floors, results in a good sound reduction index (Rw). In the case of timber floors, airborne sound insulation is usually achieved when there is sufficient impact sound insulation. In most cases this requires a multi-layer construction in which at least two layers are separated by an insulating element (e.g. floating screed). Acoustic bridges contribute significantly to a loss of insulation.

Good sound insulation can be provided by heavy floor toppings (screed or mineral fill), elastic or impact-sound insulating intermediate layers, mineral wool inserts in cavities, or by a suspended ceiling on resilient bearings. In the case of a solid timber floor, the underside of which is not to be clad, it is possible to achieve the necessary sound insulation with an additional, heavy layer on top (mineral fill, additional boarding). However, these layers also add to the weight of the floor and may in turn lead to larger timber sections.

UTILISING COMPONENTS FOR COOLING

Current developments in cooling ceilings involve the installation of capillary tube meshes in the reinforced concrete of the floor (utilising the concrete's large storage capacity). This makes it possible to reduce the room temperature in summer with a relatively small energy input as the water in the capillary tubes indirectly absorbs heat from the room air.

DESIGNS

Just as the layout design affects the vertical loadbearing system of walls and uprights, this in turn determines the structural system of the floors. The material of floors can be chosen independently of the construction and requirements for walls. In a construction with masonry walls, the traditional method of constructing a floor is with timber joists or beams. However, owing to the risk of fire, insect attack, rot, and the often only moderate sound insulation, solid reinforced concrete floors have become more popular. Today, flat floor slabs are the most common form of floor construction. These floors do not have any downstanding beams and thus offer a flat and unobstructed ceiling, which also helps with the installation of services. There are no restrictions on the layout design, and subsequent changes in layout are easy to accommodate. On the downside there is the fact that concrete floors are relatively heavy. If the weight becomes an issue, for example because of larger spans, beam-and-slab floors may be a viable alternative. Generally speaking there are now numerous floor construction systems on the market. Important factors for selecting a particular construction are the combination of spans, fire safety and sound insulation, construction height and room height, the installation situation, costs and time needed for construction.

SLAB FLOORS

Nowadays, solid floor slabs are mostly cast in reinforced concrete. These floors allow a flexible layout design, but require expensive formwork. This needs to be supported for the curing period of the concrete, during which time the support structure is a potential obstacle for the construction process. Slab floors can be prefabricated or constructed in situ on the building site. Floor construction on site requires the erection of formwork, the placing of reinforcements in accordance with the structural specification and finally the casting of the concrete. The formwork can be removed at the end of the curing period; it is then that the concrete reaches its loadbearing capacity and until then the temporary support structure needs to remain in place. The reinforcement is designed and placed to suit the spanning direction of the floor. ➘ 1 The objective is to distribute the loads as evenly as possible to the bearing points or lines. Depending on the geometry of the layout, floors can be supported on one, two, three or four sides. One-directional floors with a width-to-length ratio of > 1:2, as well as floors supported by beams and beamed floors, represent the basic principle of a beam supported by a post, wall or cross-beam on either side. Slab-type floors with a distributed load are normally supported on four walls and are reinforced in two directions. Using uni-directional, untensioned reinforcement and floor thicknesses of between 18 and 30 cm it is pos-

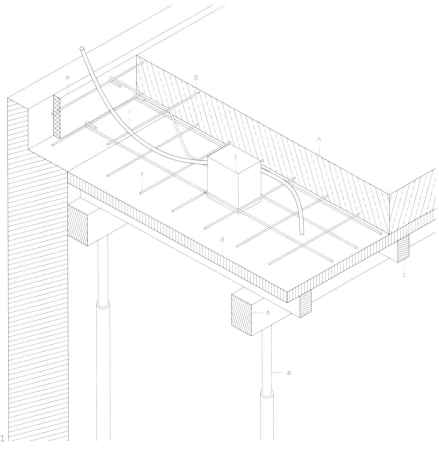

sible to produce floor spans of up to 6.5 m length. When bi-directional reinforcement is used, spans of 8 m length are commercially viable. Slabs that continue over several bearings ➘ 2 are called continuous slabs. According to DIN 1045 the minimum thickness of slabs is generally 7 cm, of slabs with transverse reinforcement 16 cm, and of slabs with transverse reinforcement and punchthrough reinforcement 20 cm. Flat floor slabs with thicknesses of > 25 cm are usually not commercially viable.

PRESTRESSED CONCRETE FLOORS

Where larger spans are needed (> 9 m) prestressed concrete is used rather than reinforced concrete. It is produced by combining concrete with high-tensile steel (braided wire), which is pretensioned in the building component and causes the component to be prestressed. The braided wires are mechanically tensioned in the concrete and create pressure at those points where the future tensile stress is expected. In this construction method it is possible to keep the cross section of concrete members small, even when used over large spans.

1 Conventional reinforced concrete floor construction:
a prop
b spreader beam
c beam
d formwork panel
e edge formwork
f lower reinforcement
g upper reinforcement
h in-situ concrete
i services conduit
j foam block for aperture

2 Reinforced concrete slab, floor bearing in wall

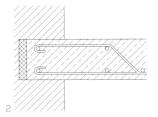

3 Hollow core floor with semi
prefabricated components,
Cobiax balls (void formers) and
reinforcement prior to casting
in-situ concrete.

4 Hollow-core floor elements

5 Filigree floor:
a large area slab (prefabricated)
b in-situ concrete
c lattice girder
d longitudinal reinforcement
e transverse reinforcement
f butt joint

HOLLOW CORE FLOORS

As a structural system, this consists of a flat floor with a thickness of 31.5 to 36 cm and a potential span of up to 12 m in one direction. The thickness of the floor is required in order to achieve the necessary rigidity and to avoid the formation of cracks. In the production process, hollow plastic balls are placed in the central 'layer' of the slab before concreting. This helps to reduce the weight of the planks by up to 30% compared to a solid slab and makes it possible to achieve longer spans. Owing to the sometimes complex positioning of the reinforcements, the manufacturing process is relatively costly. In order to prevent the plastic balls and the reinforcement from drifting upwards, concreting is carried out in two stages. There is also a semi-finished prefabricated option in which the reinforcement and the balls are already pre-installed on a thin concrete slab (similar to filigree floors). ⌁ 3

HOLLOW CORE SLABS OR PLANKS

These are prefabricated and pretensioned floor slabs or planks made of prestressed concrete with tubular voids

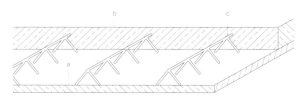

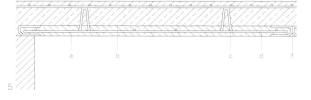

in the central zone of the cross section, where compressive and tensile stresses are lowest. ⌁ 4 These tubular voids are formed using cardboard tubes or foam balls. In this way the weight of the element can be reduced by 20% to 40%. Depending on the thickness of the slab (15 to 40 cm) it is possible to achieve spans of 7 to 16 m length. The planks come in widths of 120 or 240 cm. The tubular voids can be used for the installation of services. As they are fully prefabricated, these elements require only short installation times.

FILIGREE FLOORS

The system of filigree reinforced concrete floors was developed as a method for the industrial prefabrication of floor elements. In this system, large prefabricated, semi-finished, reinforced concrete slabs (width approx. 2.5 to 3 m, length approx. 12 m) are installed in the building before additional concrete is cast to make up the full thickness. ⌁ 5 During the concreting process the prefabricated floor element serves as shuttering to support the fresh concrete. The concrete part of the prefabricated element is 4 to 6 cm thick and is reinforced in both longitudinal and transverse direction so that it is sufficiently rigid for transport and for installation on site. The elements remain supported until the in-situ concrete has cured. The lattice girders in the completed floor provide the bond between the prefabricated part and the in-situ concrete as well as the necessary shear reinforcement. An additional joint reinforcement is provided at the joints between the slabs. All necessary penetrations, recesses and apertures etc. are prepared at the factory. The lower surfaces of the elements are smooth from the formwork, with bevelled edges, and the upper surfaces are rough so as to provide a good key for the in-situ concrete. When completed, the prefabricated part and the in-situ layer together form a composite element that is structurally effective over its whole cross section.

BEAM FLOORS

Beamed floors consist of wholly or partially prefabricated loadbearing beams spanning the longer distance, with the space between beams (the field) filled with transverse-spanning units. ⤳ 1 The beams may be of reinforced concrete or steel profiles. Each carries the load of one field and is dimensioned accordingly. The distance between beams is determined by the spans of the material used to fill the gap, which is selected and sized to suit the required loadbearing function. Production is similar to that of prefabricated or semi-prefabricated elements, allowing a range of different construction methods. Alternatively it is also possible for beams to be placed close together so that they form a loadbearing bond and cover a complete part of the space to form part of the floor.

HOLLOW TILE FLOORS

These types of floor represent another form of partially prefabricated floor construction. In this case, tiles approx. 25 cm wide or hollow concrete blocks are inserted between the beam elements and contribute to the loadbearing function. ⤳ 2 They are designed to be able to absorb compressive forces in the upper part, sometimes also throughout the entire height. As they contain many cavities, these elements keep the weight of the floor low. The bearing points and butt joints are filled with concrete on site. Alternatively, it is also possible to prefabricate these floor elements. Hollow tile floors can also be prefabricated in factories and are usually 16.5 to 24 cm thick (minimum thickness 9 cm). Elements are usually manufactured in widths of 2.50 m, and lengths of up to 7.3 m are possible. When dealing with larger loads or longer spans, it is possible to add transverse reinforcement to strengthen the butt joint. The tile elements have to absorb compressive and shear forces and sustain stress only in one direction. Ideally the imposed loads should be evenly distributed. Special structural measures are required for larger imposed loads and where recesses or apertures are needed; floors of this type may also perform a bracing function, but then special structural calculations are required. During construction it may be necessary to provide temporary support.

The underside of the floor can be designed to be completely level, with beams and elements finishing flush. When completed, the ceiling may be finished with plaster or left unfinished. Alternatively it is possible to mount timber battens on the underside of the beams, which can be used as fixing points for a suspended ceiling. Owing to the voids in the floor, the fire resistance is not as good as that of solid floors, so proof of compliance with the regulations is required.

Owing to the low weight of the elements making up these floors, they are suitable for manual installation and are

therefore often chosen in situations where it is not possible to use a crane or large formwork elements.

POT-AND-BEAM FLOORS

Prefabricated concrete beams in the shape of an inverted T-section are placed on loadbearing walls or girders. ⤳ 3 Depending on the 'pots' used, the distance between beams is between 50 and 75 cm. Beams consisting of steel profiles are rarely used today because of the lack of fire resistance. The space between the beams is filled with hollow elements (made of concrete, lightweight concrete or fired clay). Depending on the respective structural requirements, reinforcement bars or mesh can be installed on site. The installation is completed by casting in-situ concrete into the gaps between the elements at least or, in the case of more exacting requirements (structural, sound insulation), over the entire surface (layer thickness > 3 cm). In this way a flat composite slab is formed.

PLANKS

In contrast to hollow core slabs, planks have a solid concrete cross section. In order to keep their weight down, they are manufactured in lightweight concrete and, in Germany, require building control approval. The reinforcement is subject to special regulations. Planks come in thicknesses of 15, 20, 24 or 30 cm and are 62.5 cm wide; the maximum span is 6 m. The imposed load is limited to 3.5 kN/m².

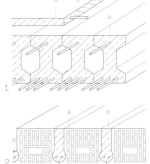

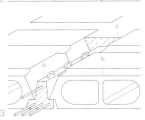

1 Beamed floor:
a prefabricated reinforced concrete components closely spaced
b in-situ concrete
c transverse reinforcement

2 Hollow block floor:
a in-situ concrete
b floor block
c reinforcement:

3, 4 Pot-and-beam floor:
a prefabricated concrete beam
b hollow block
c in-situ concrete

5   Ribbed slab floor:
a   rib
b   compression slab
c   transverse reinforcement
d   stirrup
e   stirrup hook
f   reinforcement bar

6   Composite trapezoidal sheet
metal floor:
a   in-situ concrete
b   anchor
c   trapezoidal steel sheet

7   Mushroom floors:
In order to avoid the risk of the
upright piercing the floor slab in the
bearing area, the reinforcement is
strengthened around the top of the
upright. The name of this floor is
derived from the strengthened area
around the head of the upright,
which creates a mushroom-shaped
transition between the upright and
the floor.

a   classic shape
b   technical shape
c   flat mushroom

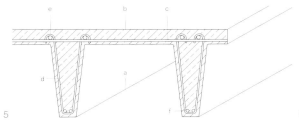

5

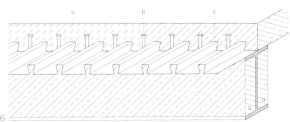

6

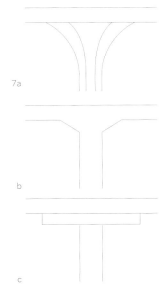

7a

b

c

BEAM-AND-SLAB FLOORS AND RIBBED SLAB FLOORS

These floors consist of an upper continuous reinforced concrete slab with several parallel concrete beams underneath. These can be rectangular or trapezoidal in cross section. ⌐5 The layer of concrete placed on top of the floor (compression plate) spans at a right angle to the ribs and its thickness is at least 7 cm or 10% of the clear distance between the ribs. The clear distance between the ribs is usually between 65 and 75 cm, and the minimum width of the underside of the rib is 5 cm. The slab thickness of beam-and-slab floors is between 10 and 16 cm. Beams or ribs are also reinforced for shear so that they can transfer transverse forces. This reinforcement is connected with the compression plate and ensures a reliable transfer of forces. Such floors can be constructed to have a bracing (plate) effect. Beams have a minimum width of approx. 15 cm. The prefabricated elements are approx. 2.50 m wide. With ribbed floors it is possible to achieve spans of 6 to 20 m length. Common construction heights measure between 30 and 85 cm. Services can be installed between the ribs or beams. Alternatively there are flooring systems with loadbearing and non-loadbearing fill elements, which result in level upper and lower surfaces.

COMPOSITE TRAPEZOIDAL SHEET METAL FLOORS

The underside of these flat floors consists of steel profile sheets that also function as lost formwork. The surfaces of the profiles are factory-protected against corrosion (galvanised, plastic-coated). A structurally effective connection can be achieved through the profiling of the metal sheeting. There are trapezoidal steel sheet floors with and without a bonding connection. Downturn beams are usually steel beams or girders that are connected to the deck via structurally effective dowels or anchors. The steel beams are made fireproof by encasing them in concrete. Where a structurally effective connection exists between the metal sheeting and the slab the sheeting acts as the lower layer of reinforcement steel. The loadbearing characteristics of these floors are similar to those of solid slab floors. The profile sheeting can be used to install services and light fittings etc. or to attach suspended ceilings.

In floors without a structurally effective connection between the metal sheeting and the slab, the sheeting is used as lost formwork only and does not have any structural function. Owing to their profiled cross section, composite trapezoidal steel sheet floors have larger surfaces than flat floors and are therefore particularly suitable for activating the thermal mass as part of a cooling concept. ⌐6

Another floor construction is that of composite steel beam floors. They have similar loadbearing characteristics to beam-and-slab floors. The steel beams are the longitudinal loadbearing members. They are structurally connected with the floor slab using fasteners such as headed shear studs. The tensile forces are absorbed by the steel beam, acting as the lower chord, and the compressive forces by the reinforced concrete slab.

WAFFLE FLOORS

These floors have been developed on the basis of ribbed floors, resulting in a bi-directional floor slab. Spans of up to 12 m are possible with floor thicknesses of between 30 and 45 cm. As the installation of formwork on site is costly, prefabrication may be a preferable alternative. The size of the waffle squares varies between 50 × 50 cm and 150 × 150 cm.

MUSHROOM SLABS

Where a flat slab floor is supported by a column, the transition between the floor and the column can be strengthened in the form of a mushroom, in order to prevent the small bearing surface of the column punching through the slab. ⌐7 The cost of the formwork and reinforcements is relatively high. For this reason – and in order to achieve greater freedom in the layout design (also of grid systems) – a construction method has been developed which provides the reinforcement within the thickness of the slab (internal column-head reinforcement). This may require a significantly thicker floor slab. It is obviously advantageous to keep the thickness of the floor slab to the minimum structurally required dimension (15 to 30 cm). Spans of between 4 and 8 m are possible. An advantage is that no downstand beams are required, which might be desirable from the conceptual design point of view. Mushroom floor decks are a method of creating

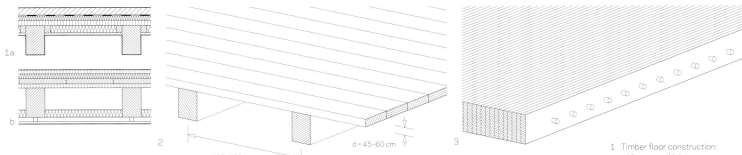

1a

b

2

a = 120–180 cm

d = 45–60 cm

3

large open spaces while keeping the construction height of the deck to a minimum.

HOURDIS FLOORS
These thin-walled hollow clay blocks are between 4 and 10 cm thick and measure 50 to 100 cm in length and can be placed as horizontal members on beams of steel or timber. Such a floor may be finished off with a 3 to 5 cm thick in-situ concrete layer. Nowadays, this type of construction is not often used in new buildings.

TIMBER BEAM (JOIST) FLOORS
Unlike solid floors, timber floors ⌐ 1, 2 do not have a compression slab that can distribute loads. Therefore point loads can only be distributed over several beam or joist fields to a limited extent. A classic timber floor is normally one-directional in its span. It is however also possible to span timber floors in two directions (e.g. coffered). In buildings with walls in masonry construction, traditional spacing distances between beams are 70 to 120 cm. In modern timber constructions, spacings tend to be between 40 and 80 cm. This means that the floor joists can be slimmer, it is easier to achieve a low moisture content and is therefore possible to reduce the tendency of the floor to shrink. For construction heights of between 17 and 30 cm, the spans are between 3 and 5 m. Where ducts, pipes or staircases interfere with one or several joists, a trimmer needs to be inserted to form the required opening. Depending on the type of floor construction, the underside can either be left exposed or has to be lined. Although this choice has a strong visual impact, fire safety and sound insulation also need to be considered. In order to complete the floor, its joists need to be covered with boarding. Where these boards are joined, the joint must be over a joist or beam. In order to achieve thermal and sound insulation in traditional construction, the spaces between joists were filled with slag or clay, while nowadays mineral wool insulation is more common. The top of the floor can be finished off with floorboards. However, today it is more common to use chipboard placed on felt strips for acoustic decoupling. In order to improve sound insulation it is possible to increase the weight of the floor and lay out prefabricated concrete slabs. This can then be followed up with a 'floating' (acoustically decoupled) screed and a floor finish.

FLOORS IN PANEL CONSTRUCTION
As with panel construction in walls, this type of floor structure is a composite construction. The ribs and panelling together form the loadbearing component, with the panel either carrying part of the load or just performing a bracing function. The construction grid plays an important role in the design. The height of the beams is the same throughout the floor area. Beams or joists should be spanning across the shorter distance.

CROSS-LAMINATED TIMBER FLOORS
In these floors, several layers of timber are glued crossways under pressure to make floor panels with thicknesses of between 12.5 and 17 cm. Panel formats can be up to 4.50 wide and 16 m long. Special lengths of up to 30 m can also be manufactured. Panels can be manufactured for mono-directional and bi-directional applications. Services can be installed in ducts, which must be planned at the design stage; openings for wiring or pipes can simply be drilled. The joints between elements can be either in the form of a stepped rebate, or as tongue and groove for a structurally effective connection.

NAIL AND SPIKE-LAMINATED TIMBER FLOORS
In order to build a solid timber floor, boards, planks, or scantlings are placed upright next to each other and connected with a structurally effective method. ⌐ 3-5 Heights can vary between 6 and 24 cm and elements can be 60 to 125 cm wide. These floors are very strong, have good loadbearing properties for point loads and only have minimal deflection. Single spans of up to 6 m are feasible, and when spanning several fields it is possible to achieve approx. 7.5 m. Fire safety and sound insulation can only be achieved by applying additional layers, such as floating screeds or suspended ceilings. The large mass of wood has a positive effect on the room climate.

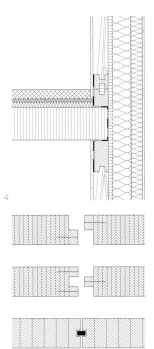

4

5

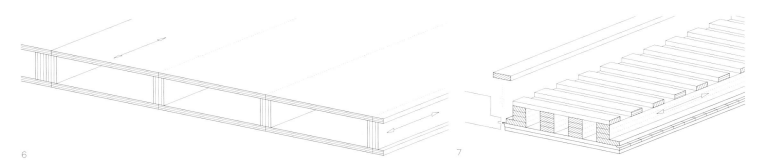

6

7

6 Hollow box floor

7 Timber brick panel floor

8 Vault constructions
(from top to bottom):
cross vault
cloister vault
pendentive dome
barrel vault

9 Prussian vault:
a tapered brick
b concrete
c bearing timber 70/100 mm
d floorboards 30 mm
e sand

8

HOLLOW BOX FLOORS

In this construction the flooring elements consist of hollow boxes glued together from wooden slats. ↘ **6** The box elements are available individually for placing by hand, or in the form of large-format floor elements which have to be placed by crane. They are suitable for monoaxial loadbearing floor or roof constructions and are characterised by their rigid and slab-like loadbearing behaviour. A plate-like bracing effect can be achieved by adding bracing struts or OSB sheets, or by fitting shear connectors. The construction height is similar to that of a concrete floor (12 to 32 cm), and the floors provide good sound insulation and fire protection. They also perform a thermal storage function. To enhance the storage capacity, the cavities can be filled with a range of different fill materials. The elements can be used in timber construction as well as in masonry construction buildings. The floor elements are placed on a bearing consisting of a ring beam or of steel angles.

TIMBER BRICK PANELS

The floor elements consist of glued board layers with or without cavities. Where there are cavities, the fibres of the layers of the solid parts run in the same direction and the floor elements span in one direction. Depending on the type of construction, the upper side can be open or closed and the surface of the closed underside can be smooth or profiled. ↘ **7** The thickness of the floor depends on the structural and building physics requirements. The cavities can be used for the installation of services or can be filled with heavy aggregate in order to improve sound insulation.

COMPOSITE TIMBER AND CONCRETE FLOORS

In multi-storey timber construction there are strict requirements relating to structure, sound insulation and fire protection. These are well met by composite timber and concrete floors. As a result of structurally effective bonding between the monolithic reinforced concrete floor (compression zone) and the timber beam or nail-laminated floor (tension zone), the floors are very rigid in terms of vibration. The concrete slab has a thickness of between 6 and 14 cm, depending on requirements. The connection between the concrete and timber is created using bonding screws, shear connectors, bonding anchors or nail plates.

VAULTED FLOORS

Vaulted constructions ↘ **8** are the original method of building floors with solid materials. Imposed loads are transferred to the bearings in the form of compressive forces. In vaulted brick constructions either the bricks or the joints are wedge-shaped. In order to prevent loss of compression stress through settlement or as a result of the vault thrust over the long term, tensile anchors or imposed loads can be used as a means of stabilisation. In traditional multi-storey structures it is still common to find 'Prussian vault' ceilings/floors. ↘ **9** These are segments of rather shallow brick arches which bear on steel I-beams. The connecting piece between the bricks and the steel beam has to have a special shape and is either made of a purpose-designed brick or concrete. In order to improve fire resistance, it is common to encase the metal parts. The rise of the arc is normally 10% to 15% of the length of span between two steel beams. Standard spans are about 2 m. Barrel vaults are significantly more rounded. They are semi-circular in cross section and rest on parallel bearings. Two barrel vaults intersecting each other at right angles form a cross vault.

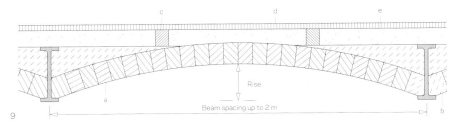

c   d   e

Rise

a   b

Beam spacing up to 2 m

9

SUPPORT | MATERIALISE
EXAMPLES

ASSEMBLY AND ADMINISTRATION CENTRE IN SENDEN, GERMANY, 2007
GERKEN ARCHITECTS, ULM

The assembly centre's foundations are those of an existing basement structure. In view of the fact that the imposed load was to be kept as low as possible, steel was the obvious construction material. Another requirement was that the ground floor had to be free of columns for the assembly process. This means that the entire building is supported on a kind of 'table' consisting of four main columns for transferring the load and, bearing on these, storey-high lattice girders, with spans of 18 m. A peripheral reinforced concrete gallery was used to perform the bracing function.

The four upper storeys are built as composite constructions using Vierendeel girders and fairfaced concrete walls, which are braced with the help of additional ties. Each level contains six loadbearing structures in the form of tables which, together with the corner columns and the peripheral ring beam, are supported on the storeys below. In spite of the strong bending forces, it was possible to keep the steel nodes small.

The central 16 m high atrium above the assembly storey has been designed as the company's informal meeting area. The design and administration offices have been arranged on both sides of the atrium and the second floor is used for the assembly of small equipment. The facade is glazed on all sides, allowing visitors and employees to view the production process.

The facade gives the building a certain elegance; during the daytime it produces primarily a mirror effect, while at night the building appears transparent. The insulating glass used in the facade is a new development and achieves a g-value of only 36% with seventy percent light transmission; about 40% of the facade has been rendered opaque with the application of silkscreen printing. This has been designed in the form of a net filter which is denser at the building corners and disappears almost completely towards the centre. Ventilation flaps in the facades ensure rapid smoke dispersal from the atrium in the event of a fire and the entire building is protected with a sprinkler system. For heating and cooling the building, water is pumped from the ground through the fairfaced concrete ceilings; the electric energy required for operating the heat pumps comes from a photovoltaic installation and modular CHP unit running on rapeseed oil.

View from the peripheral reinforced concrete gallery – which gives the building rigidity – over the large machine assembly hall.

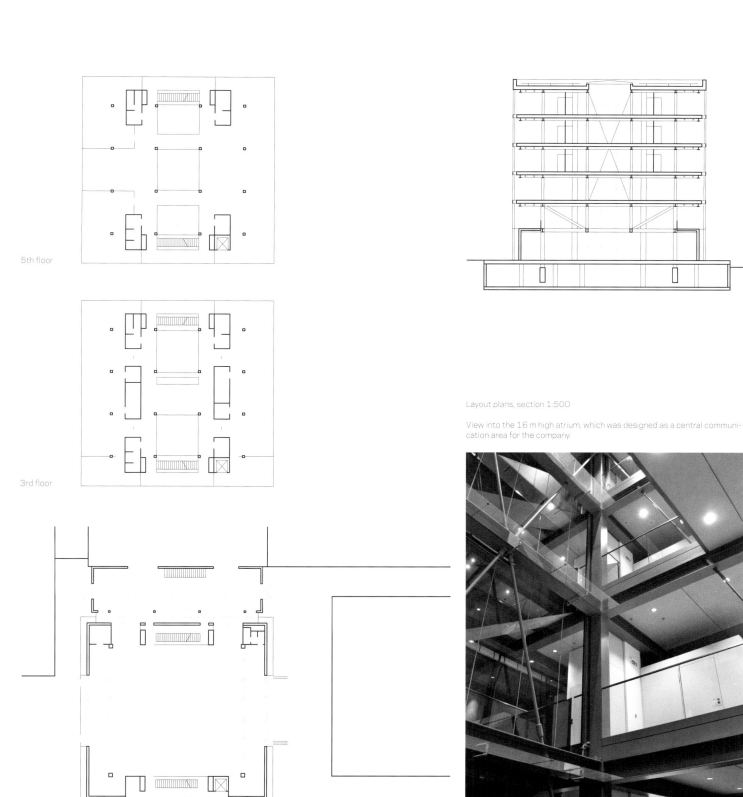

5th floor

3rd floor

Ground floor

Layout plans, section 1:500

View into the 16 m high atrium, which was designed as a central communication area for the company.

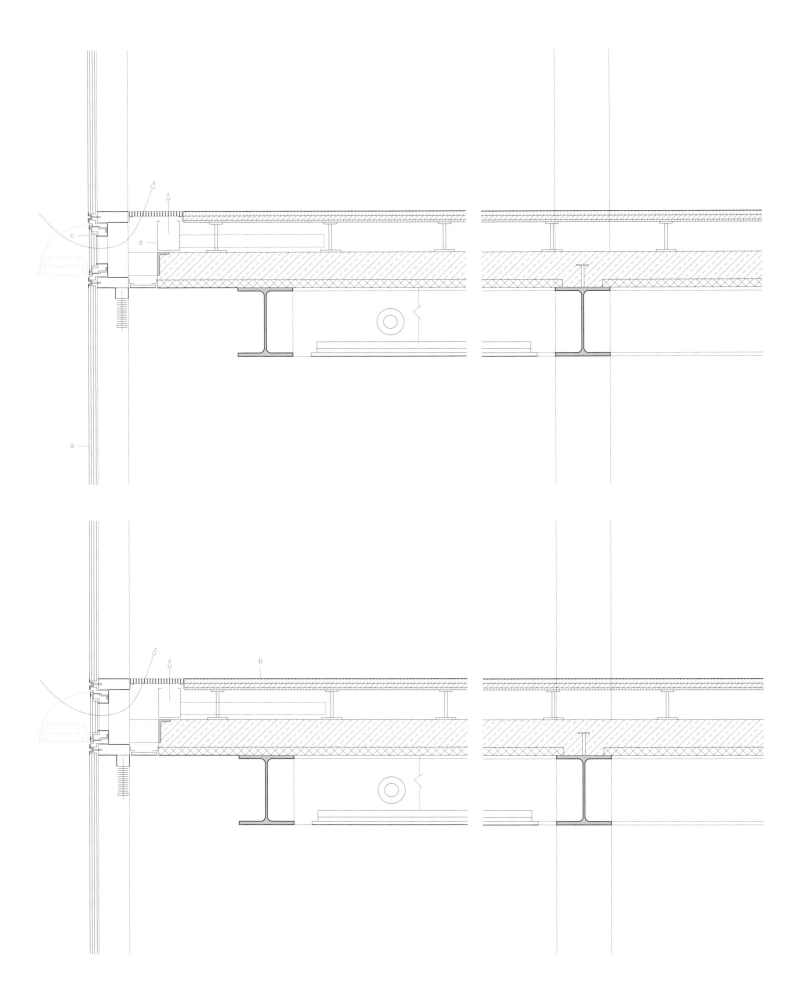

The building at night; isometric of structural system, 1:100
The entire building is supported on a kind of 'table' consisting of four main
loadbearing columns and storey-high lattice girders bearing on these.

Section 1:20

a   Wall construction:
double insulation glazing with selective solar screening
coating and silkscreen printing (g = 0.35),
steel girder 160 mm

b   Floor construction, upper floors:
Kugelgarn fleece carpet 25 mm,
mineral insulation board 23 mm,
services cavity 175 mm,
semi-prefabricated deck with in-situ concrete as
compound steel construction with headed shear studs
and concrete core activation 190 mm,
steel girder 380 mm with F30 coating,
cooling ceiling with acoustic insulation effect

c   Ventilation flaps for natural air intake

d   Fresh-air intake duct

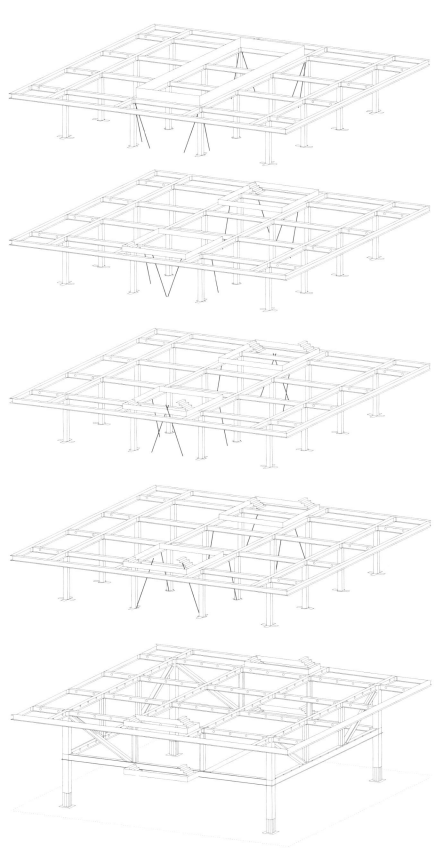

VOCATIONAL TRAINING CENTRE
IN BADEN, SWITZERLAND, 2006
BURKARD MEYER ARCHITECTS, BADEN

The new vocational training college in Baden provides state-of-the-art training facilities for over 2000 students in a wide range of vocational subjects. Different parts of the college complex have been inserted as components into the built fabric of an existing industrial area. The starting point for the design was the conversion of the former welfare premises of BBC (Brown, Boveri & Cie.) into a new college, administration and infrastructure facility. This building, which was designed by the architect Armin Meili in 1954, was retained, as it represents a notable example of Baden's industrial culture. In front of it is a large sports complex, which has been dug into the sloping terrain. Placed on a new three-storey car park, the sports facility opposite the industrial quar-

ters rises to a height of twenty metres. The floor structure of the sports halls conveys the image of an artificial landscape, reflecting the power of the impressive filigree main facade of the old welfare building. While diffused daylight fills the halls during the day, artificial lighting illuminates the artificial landscape during the hours of darkness.

The loadbearing structure of this building consists of fairfaced concrete columns in the form of a skeleton construction, which is surrounded by a glass-and-bronze facade. The skeleton construction remains visible through the layering of columns and facades and contributes to the almost ephemeral appearance of the building. The simple loadbearing principle of the structure and its floors and columns shines through. Modern forms of teaching have been accommodated together with the requirements for fire safety, sound insulation and energy efficiency, while an adequate architectural expression has evolved from the regular pattern of the structural members and related components.

At night, the aesthetic principle of stacked structural layers is particularly apparent.

The structure projects graphic
patterns of light and shadow that
enliven the long facades
Layout plans 1:1000

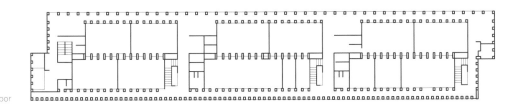

3rd floor

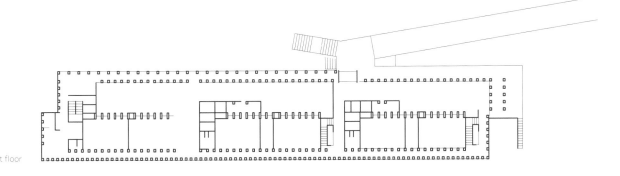

1st floor

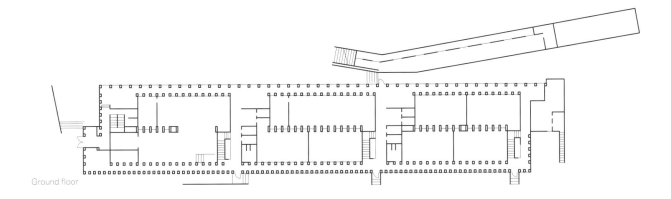

Ground floor

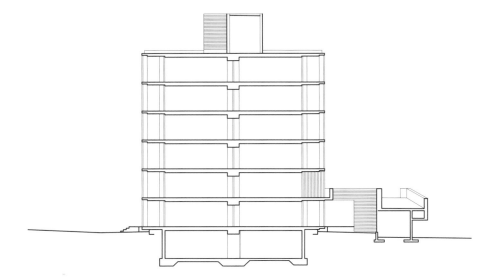

Sections 1:200, 1:20

a Wall construction
Outer row of columns:
bronze façade metal profiles, triple glazing units,
thermal insulation, prefabricated concrete column
with 460 × 330 mm reinforcement insert.
Inner row of columns:
prefabricated concrete element columns with
560 × 330 mm reinforcement insert – some with
ventilation slots, glazing with integrated slatted blind,
room doors coated with synthetic resin,
natural fibre BSB.

b Floor construction:
5 mm granolithic concrete, 30 mm xylolite flooring,
260 mm compound in-situ concrete floor,
100 mm concrete element
coloured white with white cement,
underside trapeze-shaped,
with 35 mm white acoustic foam insert

c Concrete element, prefabricated and coloured white
with white cement

d Sprinkler pipeline combined with light fittings

e Electric duct for floor boxes

Classrooms and common rooms alternate.

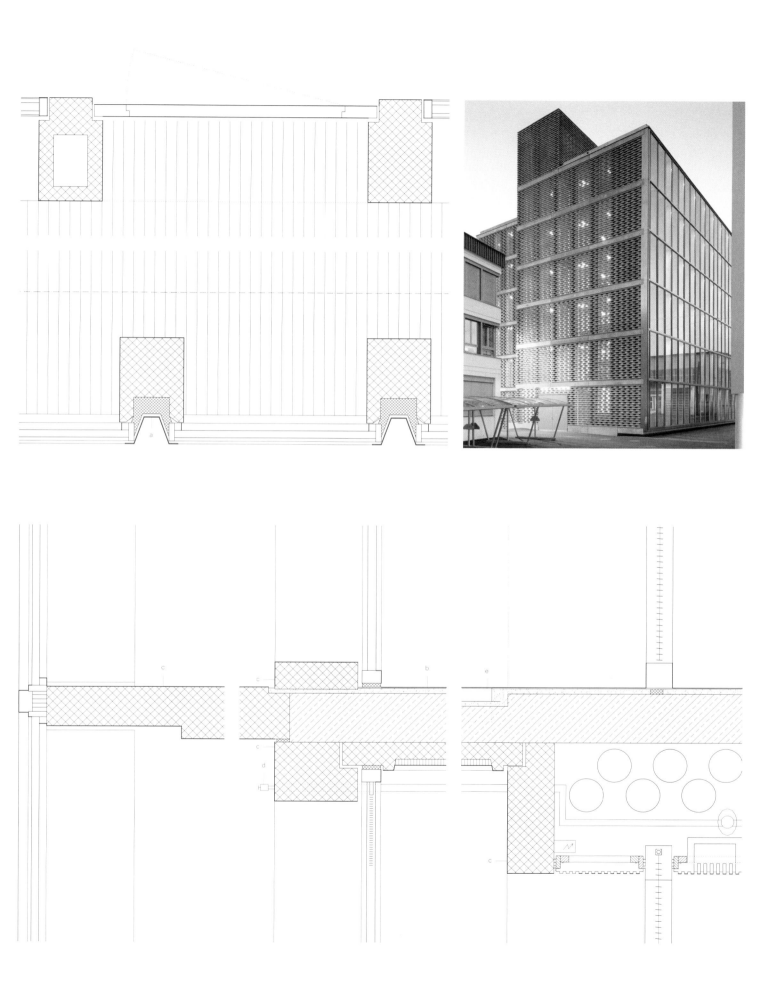

MÜLIMATT SPORTS TRAINING CENTRE
IN BRUGG-WINDISCH, SWITZERLAND, 2006
STUDIO VACCHINI, LOCARNO

The sports training centre comprises two triple gymnasia in a compact volume measuring 80 m in length and 55 m in width. A characteristic feature of the building is its fairfaced-concrete folded-shell structure. Built using prestressed components, it consists of 27 monolithically joined frame units with a constant cross-sectional height of 2.59 m and a uniform span of 52.60 m. In addition to the triple gymnasia, the central section accommodates grandstands, gymnastics rooms, changing rooms, teaching rooms and work areas. Large external facilities with parking spaces were not required because of the nearby field and track stadium with a cycle race track and sufficient car parking spaces.

The sports training centre clearly demonstrates what can be achieved with prefabrication. A total of 135 prestressed concrete elements were prefabricated, with the uprights weighing 35 tonnes each, and the roof segments 50 tonnes each. Each frame unit comprises five segments, and the roof area alone is made up of a total of 81 elements. Rainwater is conducted along the valleys of the folded shell structure and then down the uprights to land drains along the sides of the building.

The design of the facade resulted from the loadbearing requirements and the need to admit as much daylight as possible to the interior. The gymnasia were not only to be generous in size, but also bright and, with the large glazed elements, open to the landscape. In order to control glare and excessive solar radiation, some of the elements are fitted with solar control glass. The glass facade is located within the folded shell structure, connecting with the reveals of the prefabricated concrete frame uprights, and the gymnasium ceiling is attached to the underside of the horizontal members of the folded structure.

The pattern of the prefabricated frame elements is expressed in the facade to a uniquely striking effect.

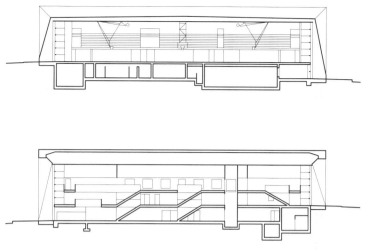

Floor plan,
sections 1:750

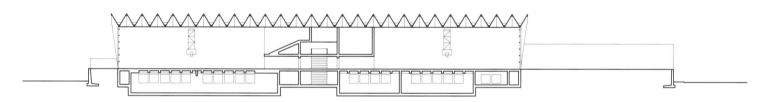

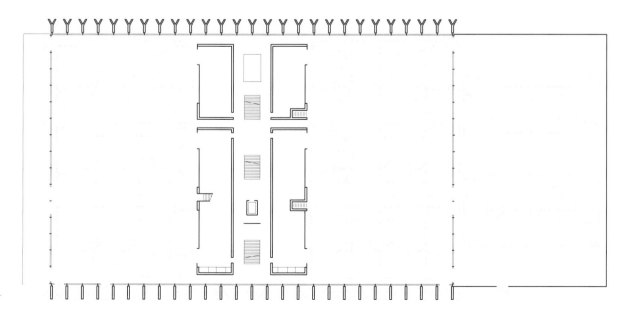

Ground floor

Sections 1:50

a   Upright member of prefabricated concrete frame:
self-compacting concrete, pre-tensioned 160 to 380 mm

b   Plastic coating seal 2 mm,
pre-cast concrete component, self-compacting concrete,
pre-tensioned 160 to 380 mm

c   Steel connection lug, apertures closed with concrete

d   Stainless steel tracks inserted in concrete, 18 mm OSB board,
timber sections 180/80 mm, mineral fibre thermal insulation 180 mm,
OSB board 22 mm, vapour barrier, cement-bonded wood-wool acoustic
ceiling panel 50 mm

e   Mullion / transom facade:
profiled steel tube 70/70/4 mm,
insulation glazing: toughened glass 6 mm + gap 14mm +
float glass 6 mm + laminated safety glass 12 mm

f   Floor construction:
EPDM/PUR layer 5 to 8 mm, reinforced cement screed 95 mm,
PE membrane 0.2 mm, impact sound insulation 40 mm,
PE membrane 0.2 mm

Isometric of the structure (project phase)

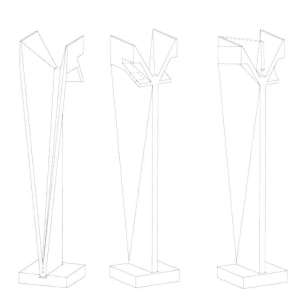

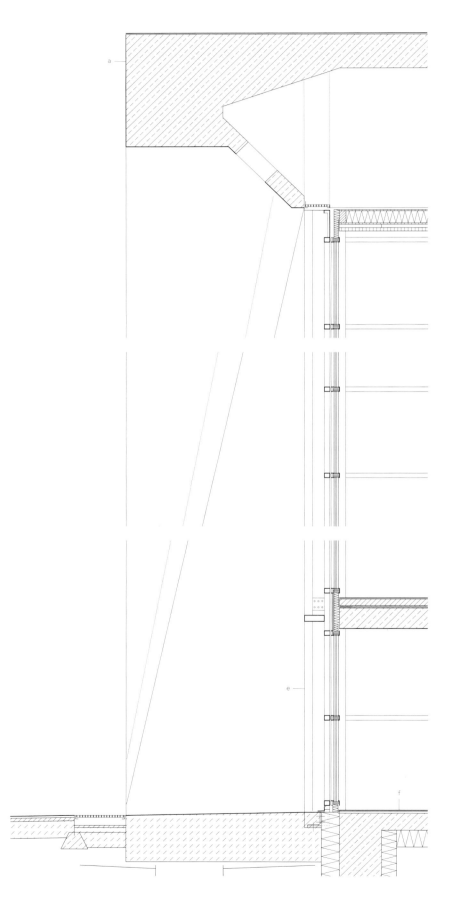

Section through roof structure
1:50

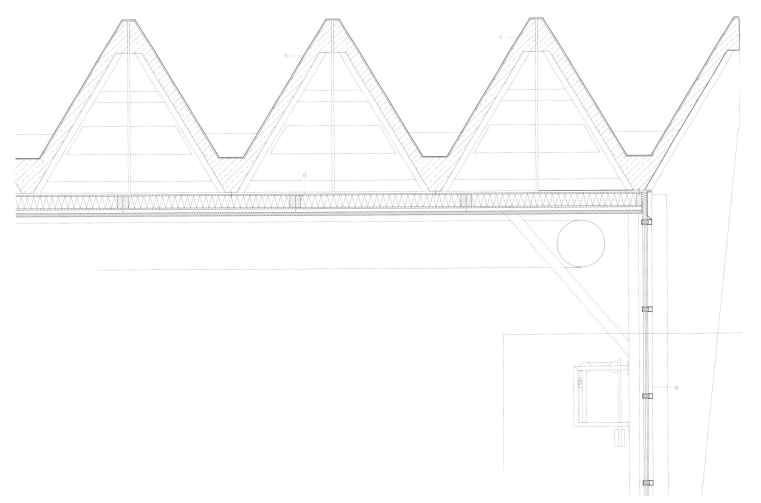

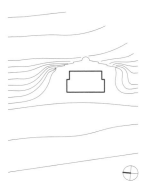

HOUSE IN HÜTTINGEN, GERMANY, 2006
NIKOLAUS BIENEFELD, SWISTTAL-ODENDORF

The hunting lodge-cum-holiday home in the Eifel mountains measures just 62 m² and has been built mostly of brick. A solid structural wall built of vertically perforated brick with a good insulation performance is lined on the outside by a skin of facing brick in traditional German format (24 cm × 11.5 cm × 6.3 cm) which – with the extra-wide horizontal joints – lends the building an archaic appearance.

The interplay between delicacy and monumentality, which is evoked through the arrangement and rhythm of the deeply inset window reveals and the scale-distorting proportions of the facades, continues in the interior: from the two-storey hall – which has a sacral feel about it – a narrow library staircase leads up to a gallery, which provides access to the rooms on the first floor via equally narrow door openings. The clear height of the rooms on the ground floor is just 2,1 m.

Every detail of this unusual building reveals the architect's deep understanding of brick as a building material. From the floor via the window sills and lintels through to the joint between wall and roof, an ancient tradition of building is evoked which is largely absent in modern-day construction.

Site plan 1:1000 (see top of page)
view of house on the mountain slope

Ground floor   Upper floor

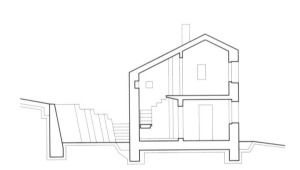

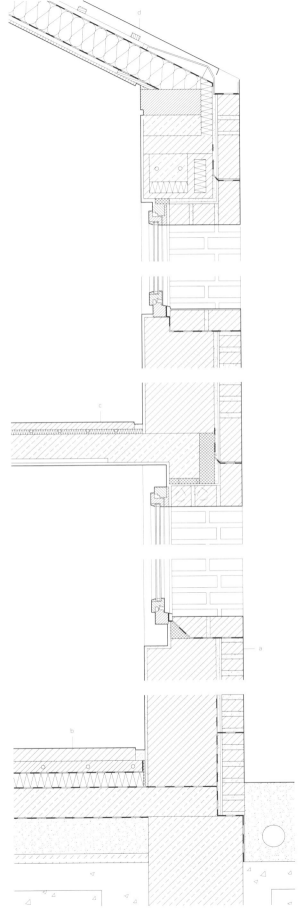

West and north elevations, layout plans 1:500
Section 1:200

Section 1:20

a Wall construction:
face brick 115 mm, cavity 10 mm, render coat 20 mm,
highly insulating vertically perforated blocks 365 mm, internal plaster 15 mm

b Floor construction in living area:
flooring brick 71 mm, screed with underfloor heating 65 mm, thermal insulation 80 mm,
levelling screed 30 mm, bitumen topping, floor slab 160 mm waterproof concrete,
gravel 200 mm, lean-mix concrete 50 mm

c Floor construction, bathroom:
screed with underfloor heating 40 mm, bitumen paper,
thermal insulation 25 mm with thermal conduction profiles as underfloor heating system,
reinforced concrete slab 160 mm

d Roof construction:
roof tiles, battens, counter-battens, under-slating,
rafters 120/160 mm, thermal insulation 160 mm, vapour barrier,
counter-battens 24/48 mm, three-layer blockboard 16 mm

HOUSE IN MÜNSTER, GERMANY, 2007
HEHNPOHL ARCHITECTURE, MÜNSTER

This family home for artists with two children is located in an established residential area to the south of the city of Münster, the Geistviertel, which features a haphazard development of individual homes. The simple cuboid is a reference to the shape of bricks from which the facades of the neighbouring houses have been built. From this basic shape, apertures and recesses have been cut by a process of subtraction, which further emphasises its cubic nature – from the recessed entrance area via the stairwell with a large rooflight through to the roof terrace. The angular new house picks up on numerous design features of the neighbouring homes and translates them into a modern pattern language: the planter in the lounge, the roof terrace, the full-height balcony doors and the terrace with its outside staircase.

The layout of the house follows a strict pattern: all secondary and services rooms face north and the living and sleeping quarters face the south, opening on to the garden and a nature conservation area. This explains the contrast between the block-like, closed street elevation and the much looser, transparent garden side of the building. So as to increase the sense of enclosure, the brick skin has been extended as perforated filter brickwork in front of the windows, which generates attractive light moods on the inside. The outer brick skin consists of hard-fired facing bricks, the irregularities of which create a contrast (especially in sunlight) to the formal severity of the house. The loadbearing part of the walls has been built with calcium silicate blocks and the floors consist of reinforced concrete.

Inside the house, all walls and ceilings have been finished with a coarse lime cement plaster, which has been painted with white mineral paint. This is contrasted by a matt black basalt lava floor and the warm hues of oiled, solid oak floorboards, which have been laid on cross bearers.

The shape of the bricks is repeated in the basic shape of the house, the squareness of which is further accentuated by the stark shape of the openings.

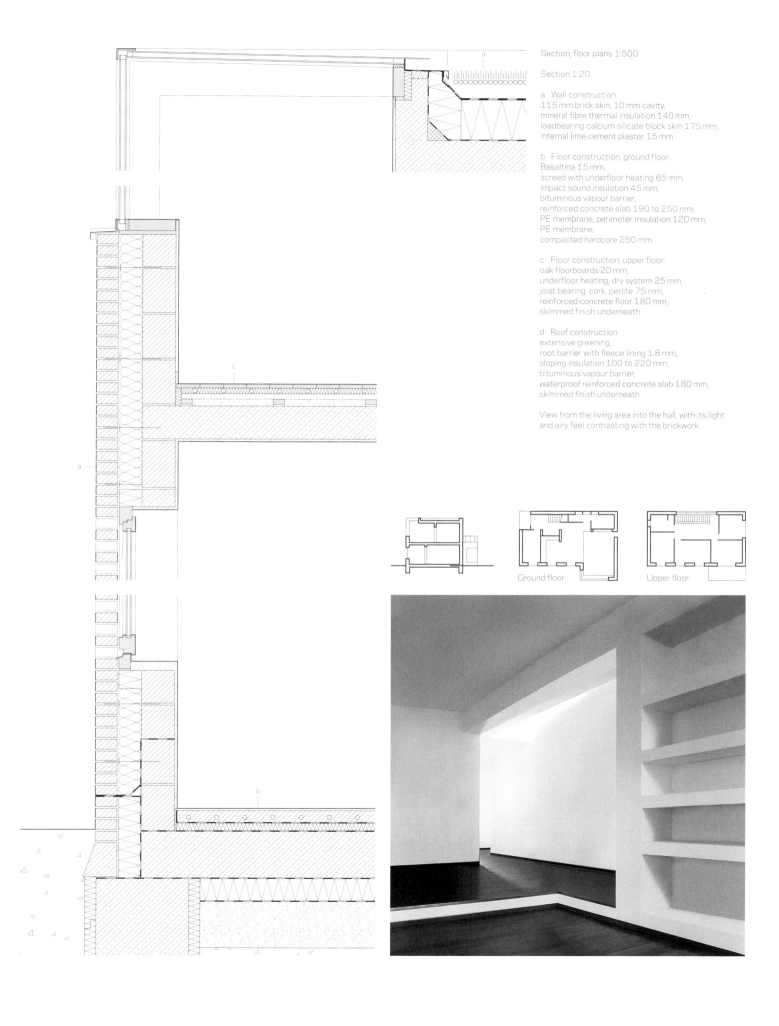

Section, floor plans 1:500

Section 1:20

a   Wall construction:
115 mm brick skin, 10 mm cavity,
mineral fibre thermal insulation 140 mm,
loadbearing calcium silicate block skin 175 mm,
internal lime cement plaster 15 mm

b   Floor construction, ground floor:
Basaltina 15 mm,
screed with underfloor heating 65 mm,
impact sound insulation 45 mm,
bituminous vapour barrier,
reinforced concrete slab 190 to 250 mm,
PE membrane, perimeter insulation 120 mm,
PE membrane,
compacted hardcore 250 mm

c   Floor construction, upper floor:
oak floorboards 20 mm,
underfloor heating, dry system 25 mm,
joist bearing, cork, perlite 75 mm,
reinforced concrete floor 180 mm,
skimmed finish underneath

d   Roof construction:
extensive greening,
root barrier with fleece lining 1.8 mm,
sloping insulation 100 to 220 mm,
bituminous vapour barrier,
waterproof reinforced concrete slab 180 mm,
skimmed finish underneath

View from the living area into the hall, with its light
and airy feel contrasting with the brickwork.

Ground floor

Upper floor

OFFICE AND TRAINING BUILDING
IN RIED, AUSTRIA, 2008
FINK THURNHER ARCHITECTS, BREGENZ

———————

The two-storey office and training building has been designed as a succinct and simple building volume and forms its own ensemble with existing buildings on the Ried Trade Exhibition ground. The different kinds of room are grouped around the two central atria. The facade, which is clad with vertical louvres all round, acts as a filter to the adjoining exhibition site and also as structural solar screening for the offices. The timber construction of the office and training building consists of untreated spruce. Solid timber floors inside permit large clear spans and a flexible layout design. The facade ribs are fitted with openable and fixed glazing elements, as well as high-performance insulating panels. Spruce is used for the walls, floors, ceilings, windows, doors and furniture.

The only insulation material used is sheep's wool. The building does not have a basement and is built on both a slab foundation and strip foundations. The ground floor ceiling is a solid timber deck consisting of nail-laminated elements with a maximum span of approx. 7 to 8 m; the roof has been constructed in the form of a timber beam deck. The external walls comprise glulam posts at 60 cm spacing. The non-loadbearing timber louvres are externally fixed and give the facade its distinct appearance. On the inside, timber-clad steel stanchions support the beams, which are flush with the ceiling. Around the stairwell, sanitary rooms and lift, cross-laminated timber elements are used as loadbearing and bracing walls.

The fire safety requirements are met thanks to a special fire protection concept, developed in cooperation with the IBS (Institute for research into fire protection and safety) in Linz. Heat is generated by a woodchip boiler plant, which also heats the neighbouring buildings. The general areas and the hall are heated with underfloor heating, and the offices via the ventilation system.

The spruce boards of the facade have been fitted as closed siding or vertical louvres, depending on the needs of the spaces behind.

View of the atrium
Site plan 1:2000,
Layout plans 1:500

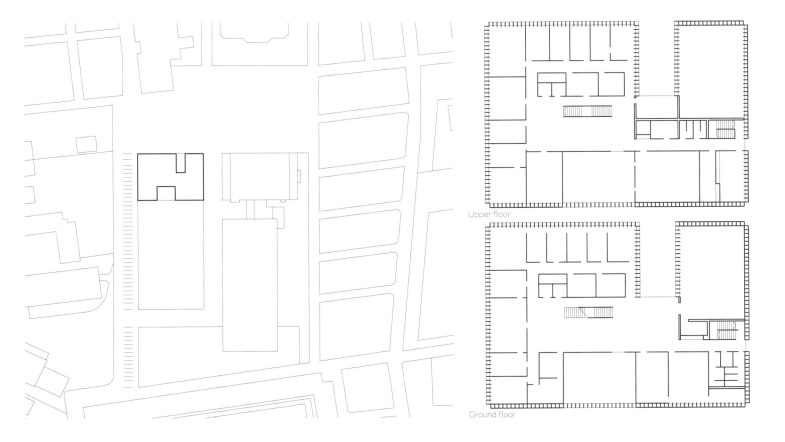

Upper floor

Ground floor

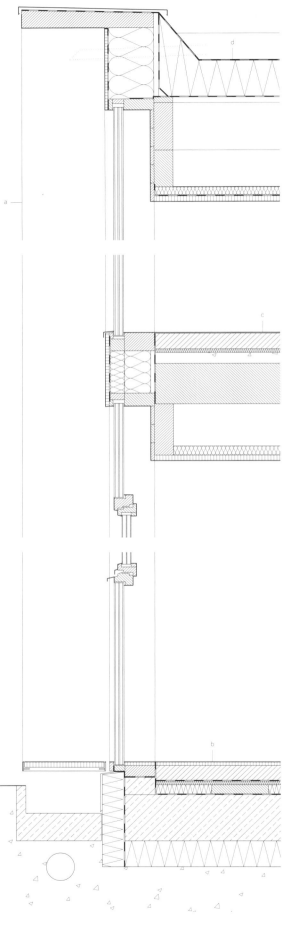

Cross section and part of layout plan 1:20

a   Wall construction, mullion/transom facade:
timber louvres 440/70 mm,
non-structural and replaceable,
laminated veneer timber 120/27 mm,
aluminium glazing bracket,
triple-glazing,
steel stanchions 120/80 mm with F30 coating,
bonded timber cladding

b   Floor construction, ground floor:
xylolite flooring 20 mm,
screed 80 mm in parts with underfloor heating,
vapour barrier,
impact sound insulation 25 mm,
impact sound insulation 50 mm with electrical installation duct,
bituminous sealing layer,
waterproof reinforced concrete slab 250 mm,
insulation, hardcore

c   Floor construction, upper floor:
mineral coating 5 mm,
base screed 85 mm,
impact sound insulation 20 mm,
mineral chippings with electrical installations 60 mm,
solid timber floor 280 mm,
ventilation void 180 mm,
sheep's wool 50 mm,
suspended ceiling 30 mm with open joints

d   Roof construction:
bituminous sealing layer with fitted gutter,
mineral chippings on top layer,
sloping insulation 200 to 350 mm,
bituminous vapour barrier with aluminium lining,
timber decking 30 mm,
ceiling joists 260 mm,
services void 200 mm,
sheep's wool 50 mm,
black acoustic fleece,
suspended ceiling 30 mm with open joints

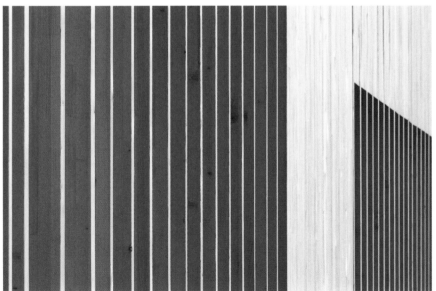

The non-loadbearing solar
screening louvres reveal the inner
structure and give the building
its striking appearance.

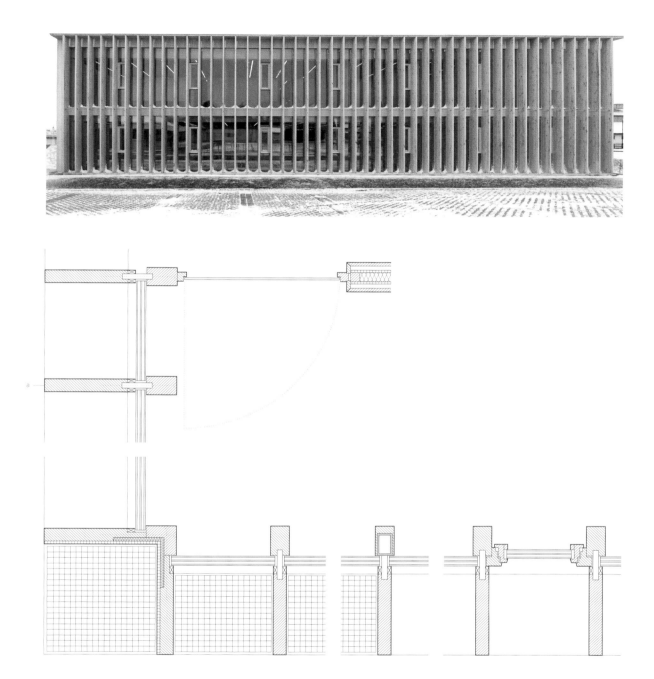

SUMMER HOUSE IN OBERBERGEN, AUSTRIA, 2011
JUDITH BENZER, VIENNA

———————

The shape and size of the summer house in southern Burgenland is based on the 'Kellerstőckl', a vinicultural building typical of the area, used for the storage of wine and occasional accommodation. It is planned to accommodate a wine cellar with production area. The simple shape is reminiscent of the existing buildings in the region. The cellar contains the rooms for wine storage and production and the rooms above ground provide living accommodation. Building up from the reinforced concrete basement,

the ground and first floors of the building are built in timber: a stud construction braced with timber panels. The cross-laminated timber elements are in fairfaced quality and, in addition to their structural function, are used as design elements in the interior. The construction principle of the walls is emphasised by the horizontal larchwood boarding used for cladding the building envelope on the outside. In this project, timber is used for the structure, the design and the envelope all in one. The material is used extensively and contrasts with the fairfaced concrete and steel elements. The materials have been deliberately left untreated and without cladding; in combination, they create a homogenous spatial effect. In view of the fact that the house is not inhabited during the winter months, the building can be completely closed with folding shutters.

The archetypal shape of the house is highlighted by its stark outlines.

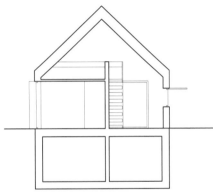

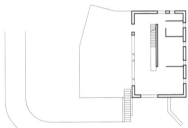

Ground floor

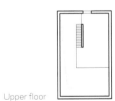

Upper floor

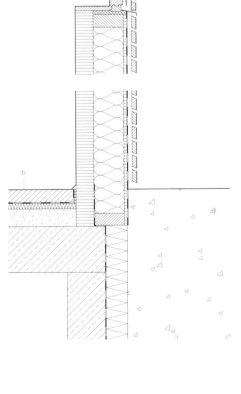

Floor plans, west and south elevations (from top to bottom)
1:500

Section 1:200

Section 1:20

a Wall construction:
open bevel siding, larch wood,
black-painted fixing battens 26/70 mm,
sheathing paper, fibreboard 16 mm,
timber studs 80/160 mm filled with mineral wool 160 mm,
cross-laminated timber 95 mm

b Floor construction, ground floor:
cement screed with ground top layer 70 mm,
PE membrane, impact sound insulation board 30 mm,
reinforced concrete slab 250 mm

c Roof construction:
open bevel siding, larch wood,
aluminium girt system 20/50/2 mm,
roofing membrane,
aluminium girt system 70/50/2 mm,
tongue-and-groove boarding 27 mm,
counter-battens 60/80 mm, under-slating,
tongue-and-groove boarding 20 mm,
rafters 80/120 mm,
with mineral wool 120 mm fitted between,
cross-laminated timber 140 mm

FIRE SAFETY
TABLES AND INFORMATION

Fire resistance class	Fire resistance duration in minutes
F30	≥30
F60	≥60
F60	≥90
F90	≥120
F120	≥180
F180	≥180

1

Construction material class	Building control terminology
A	
A1	non-combustible materials
A2	
B	combustible materials
B1	hardly flammable materials
B2	normally flammable materials
B3	highly flammable materials

2

1 Fire resistance classes in accordance with DIN 4102

2 Construction material classes in accordance with DIN 4102

3 Definition of fire resistance classes in accordance with DIN 4102

4 European classification of building components – designations in accordance with DIN EN 13501

Fire resistance class	Construction material class to DIN 4102 Part 1 of the materials used in the tested building components for:		Code	Building control terminology
	Important components	Other components		
F30	B	B	F30-B	fire resistant (fr)
	A	B	F30-B	fire resistant (fr) and essential components consisting of non-combustible material
	A	A	F30-A	fire resistant (fr) and of non-combustible material
F60	B	B	F60-B	-
F90	B	B	F90-B	-
	A	B	F90-AB	fireproof (fp)
	A	A	F90-A	fireproof (fp) and of non-combustible material

3

Code	Criterion	Range of application
R (Résistance)	Loadbearing capacity	
E (Étanchéité)	Space enclosure	
I (Isolation)	Thermal insulation (exposed to fire)	For the description of fire resistance
W (Radiation)	Limitation of passage of radiation	
M (Mechanical)	Mechanical impact on walls (impact load)	
S (Smoke)	Limitation of smoke permeability	Smoke protection doors (as additional requirement, also for fire doors), ventilation systems incl. flaps
C (Closing)	Self-closing characteristic incl. permanent function	Smoke protection doors, fire doors incl. door sets for conveyor systems
P	Maintaining energy supply and/or signal transmission	Electric cable installations generally

4

MASONRY
TABLES AND INFORMATION

5 Application of masonry mortar in accordance with DIN 1053-1

6 Types of block
* Masonry blocks and bricks are considerably at variance in the UK. The abbreviations do not apply.

Range of application	Standard mortar			Lightweight mortar	Thin-bed mortar
	MG I	MG II/IIa	MG III/IIIa		
Vaulting	not permissible[2]	permissible	permissible	not permissible	permissible
Basement masonry	not permissible[2]	permissible	permissible	permissible	permissible
>2 full storeys	not permissible[2]	permissible	permissible	permissible	permissible
Wall thickness < 24 cm[1]	not permissible[2]	permissible	permissible	permissible	permissible
Non-loadbearing outer leaf of external double-leaf walls					
– external leaf	not permissible[2]	permissible	not permissible[3]	not permissible	permissible
– rendered external leaf	not permissible[2]	permissible	not permissible[3]	permissible	permissible
Face brickwork, outside with flush pointing	not permissible[2]	permissible	permissible	not permissible	permissible
Weather conditions (precipitation, low temperatures)	not permissible[2]	permissible	permissible	permissible	permissible
Masonry blocks with vertical dimensional deviation > 1 mm	permissible	permissible	permissible	permissible	not permissible
Masonry to performance test DIN 1053-2[4]	not permissible[2]	permissible	permissible	permissible	permissible

5

1   In double-leaf walls with or without continuous air cavity, the thickness is deemed to be that of the inner leaf.
2   Application is permitted for the repair of natural stone masonry with MG I.
3   Except subsequent pointing and for masonry sections with structural reinforcement.
4   Hitherto not introduced under building regulations.

Type of block	Abbreviation*	Specific weight classes available (kg/dm³)	Compressive strength classes available (N/mm²)
Calcium silicate block:			
solid block (standard large size)	KS, KS (P)	1.6-2.2	4-60
perforated and hollow-core block (standard large size)	KS L, KS L (P)	0.6-1.6	4-60
tongue and groove system	KS R, KS R (P) KS L-R, KS L-R (P)	0.6-1.6	4-60
facebrick	KS Vm, KS VmL	1.0-2.2	12-60
brick slips	KSVb, KSVb L	1.0-2.2	20-60
Aerated concrete block (aircrete):			
coursing bricks, standard large blocks	PB, PP	0.35-0.5	2
		0.5-0.8	4
		0.65-0.8	6
		0.8-1.0	8
panel, standard large panel	Ppl, PPpl	0.35-1.0	–
Lightweight concrete block:			
hollow core slab	Hbl	0.5-1.4	2-8
solid block/brick, solid block with slots	V, Vbl, Vbl S	0.5-2.0	2-8
solid block with slots with special thermal insulation properties	Vbl S-W	0.5-0.8	2-12
Concrete blocks:			
hollow core block	Hbn	0.9-2.0	2-12
solid block	Vbn, Vn	1.4-2.4	4-28
facing block	Vm, Vmb	1.6-2.4	6-48
Granulated slag blocks:			
solid granulated slag block	HSV	1.6-2.0	12-28
perforated granulated slag block	HSL	1.2-1.6	6-12
hollow core granulated slag block	HHbl	1.0-1.6	6-12

6

CONCRETE, REINFORCED CONCRETE TABLES AND INFORMATION

Concrete strength class	Nominal strength ß wN [N/mm²] (minimum value for compressive strength ßw28 of each cube)	Serial strength ßwN [N/mm²] (minimum value for average compressive strength ßw28 of each cube series)	Manufactured to	Application
B5	5	8	Recipe or design mix see DIN 1045 Sec. 6.5.5	only for un-reinforced concrete
B10	10	15		
B15	15	20		
B25	25	30		
B35	35	40	Performance test, see DIN 1045 Sec. 6.5.5	for un-reinforced and reinforced concrete
B45	45	50		
B55	55	60		

1

Compressive strength class	f ck,cyl[1] [N/mm²]	f ck, cube[2] [N/mm²]	Type of concrete
C8/10	08	10	
C12/15	12	15	
C16/20	16	20	
C20/25	20	25	Standard concrete
C25/30	25	30	
C30/37	30	37	
C35/45	35	45	
C40/50	40	50	
C45/55	45	55	
C50/60	50	60	
C55/67	55	67	
C60/75	60	75	High-strength concrete
C70/85	70	85	
C80/95	80	95	
C90/105	90	105	
C100/115	100	115	

2

Compressive strength class	f ck,cyl[1] [N/mm²]	f ck, cube[2] [N/mm²]	Type of concrete
C8/9	08	09	
C12/13	12	13	
C16/18	16	18	
C20/22	20	22	Lightweight concrete
C25/28	25	28	
C30/33	30	33	
C35/38	35	38	
C40/44	40	44	
C45/50	45	50	
C50/55	50	55	
C55/60	55	60	
C60/66	60	66	High-strength concrete
C70/77[3]	70	77	
C80/88[3]	80	88	

3

1   f ck, cyl = characteristic strength of cylinders, 150 mm diameter, 300 mm length, age 28 days
2   f ck, cube = characteristic strength of cubes, 150 mm edge length, age 28 days
3   National Technical Approval or approval required on a case-by-case basis

Exposure class[1]	Bar diameter[2] 2 ds (mm)	Minimum dimensions cmin (mm)	Nominal dimensions cnom (mm)
XC1	up to 10	10	20
	12, 14	15	25
	16, 20	20	30
	25	25	35
	28	30	40
XC2, XC3	up to 20	20	35
	25	25	40
	28	30	45
XC4	up to 25	25	40
	28	30	45
XD1, XD2, XD3[3]	up to 28	40	55
XS1, XS2, XS3	up to 28	40	55

4

1   Should several exposure classes apply to a building component, the exposure class with the highest requirement must be selected for design purposes
2   In the case of bar bundles, the comparative diameter dSV is relevant for design purposes
3   In the case of XD3, special corrosion protection measures may be required for the reinforcement

1 Strength classes of concrete

2 Compressive strength classes of standard concrete

3 Compressive strength classes of lightweight concrete

4 Concrete cover on reinforcement for reinforced concrete depending on exposure class, in accordance with DIN 1045-1

5 Exposure classes in accordance with DIN 1992 (2011-01) – Eurocode 2

Exposure class	Environmental conditions	Example for assignment in accordance with national appendix, DIN EN 1992-1-1/NA (2011-01)
No risk of corrosion or attack		
X0	No risk of corrosion or attack	Unreinforced foundations without frost, unreinforced internal components
Reinforcement corrosion, triggered by carbonation		
XC1	Dry or constantly wet	Components indoors with common relative humidity (kitchen, bathroom in residential buildings or sim.)
XC2	Wet, rarely dry	Parts of water containers, foundations
XC3	Moderate humidity	Components with frequent or constant contact with external air (open buildings), interiors with high r.h. (commercial kitchens, bathrooms), wet rooms (indoor swimming pools)
XC4	Alternating wet and dry	External components with direct exposure to rain, components in areas with changing water levels
Reinforcement corrosion, triggered by chloride, except seawater		
XD1	Moderate humidity	Components exposed to spray mist near transport routes
XD2	Wet, rarely dry	Pool basins, components exposed to industrial effluent containing chloride
XD3	Alternating wet and dry	Parts of bridges, road surfaces, car park surfaces
Reinforcement corrosion, by chloride from seawater		
XS1	Salt-laden air, no direct contact with seawater	External components near the coast
XS2	Underwater	Components in port structures, constantly underwater
XS3	Tide areas, spray and spray mist areas	Quay walls in port structures
Concrete attacked by frost, with and without de-icing agent		
XF1	Moderate water saturation without de-icing agent	External components
XF2	Moderate water saturation with de-icing agent or seawater	Concrete components near the spray mist area of transport surfaces treated with de-icing agent. Concrete components near seawater spray mist
XF3	High water saturation without de-icing agent	Open water containers, components exposed to changing fresh water levels
XF4	High water saturation with de-icing agent or seawater	Road surfaces treated with de-icing agent, components near spraywater from road surfaces treated with de-icing agent. Components in sewage treatment plants, components exposed to changing seawater levels
Concrete attacked by chemicals in the environment		
XA1	Weak chemically aggressive environment	Containers in sewage treatment plants, sewage containers
XA2	Medium chemically aggressive environment and sea structures	Concrete components exposed to seawater, components in soils that are very aggressive to concrete
XA3	Strong chemically aggressive environment	Industrial effluent structures with strongly aggressive effluent
Additional exposure classes in accordance with National Appendix, DIN EN 1992-1-1/NA (2011-01) Concrete corrosion owing to alkaline/silicic acid reaction		
W0	Concrete that stays largely dry after curing (dry)	Internal component in a high-rise building, components exposed to external air but no precipitation, surface water or ground dampness and/or not constantly exposed to a relative humidity of >80%
WF	Concrete that is damp frequently or for prolonged periods after curing (damp)	Unprotected external component exposed to precipitation, surface water and ground dampness, internal components in high-rise buildings used for wet rooms with relative humidity predominantly higher than 80%, components frequently exposed to temperatures below dew point e.g. chimneys, bulky components in acc. with the DAfStb guideline with minimum dimensions >0.80 m (irrespective of exposure to moisture)
WA	Highly aggressive chemical environment	Components exposed to seawater, components exposed to de-icing salt without additional high dynamic loading (e.g. surfaces on roads and multi-storey car parks), components in industrial and agricultural structures (e.g. sewage containers) exposed to alkaline salt
WS	Class WA concrete with additional high dynamic loading (damp + alkaline exposure from outside + high dynamic loading)	Components exposed to de-icing salt with additional high dynamic loading
Additional exposure classes in accordance with DIN 1045-2 (2008-08) Concrete exposed to the effects of wear		
XM1	Moderate wear	Road surfaces in residential areas
XM2	Heavy wear	Road surfaces on main roads, transport surfaces with heavy forklift traffic
XM3	Extreme wear	Surfaces frequently exposed to track vehicles (barrack yards), Hydraulic structures exposed to geological movement (upper course of rivers, stilling basins)

STEEL
TABLES AND INFORMATION

Corrosion category	Loss of thickness* in 1st year [µm] Binding agent base		Examples of typical environments		Target thickness of coating [µm]	Binding agent base suitable coating
	C-steel	Zinc	External	Internal		
C1 insignificant	≤1.3	≤0.1	-	insulated building ≤60% relative humidity		
C2 small	>1.3-25	>0.1-0.7	slightly polluted atmosphere, dry climate, e.g. rural areas	buildings without insulation and intermittent heating with intermittent formation of condensate, e.g. warehouses, sports halls	K: 80 M: 120 L: 160	AY, CR PUR, AK-PUR, AK
C3 moderate	>25-50	>0.7-2.1	urban and industrial atmosphere with moderate SO_2 pollution or moderate coastal climate	rooms with high relative humidity and small amounts of pollution, e.g. breweries, laundries, dairies	K: 120 M: 160 L: 200	AK (160 µm); AY (200 µm) PVC PUR, AK-PUR, EP, CR
C4 high	>50-80	>2.1-4.2	industrial and coastal atmosphere with moderate exposure to salt	swimming pools, chemical plants, boat houses above seawater	K: 120 M: 160 L: 200	PVC, PUR, EP, CR (200 µm)
C5 very high I	>80-200	>4.2-8.4	industrial environment with high relative humidity and aggressive atmosphere	buildings or areas with almost constant condensation and high levels of pollution	M: 280-500 L: 500	PUR, CR, PVC, EP, SI with sacrificially protecting Zn primers
C6 very high M	>80-200	>4.2-8.4	coastal and offshore areas with high exposure to salt	buildings or areas with almost constant condensation and high levels of pollution	K: 120 M: 160 L: 200	CR, PVC, EP, PUR EP, PUR

* also stated as loss of mass [g/m²] 100 µ corresponds to 0.1 mm
Protection period to DIN EN ISO 12944-1:
K   short 2-5 years
M   medium 5-15 years
L   long, over 15 years

Type	Material designation			Tensile strength[1] [N/mm²]	Min. yield point[3] [N/mm²]	Min. breaking elongation[5] $L_o = 5\,d_o$ [%]
	to EN 10027-1 and CR 10260	to EN 10027-2 and CR 10260	previous national			
General construction steel to DIN EN 10025	S185[2]	1.0035	St 33	290-510	185	18
	S235JR	1.0037	St 37-2	340-470	235	26
	S235JRG1	1.0036	USt 37-2			
	S235JRG2	1.0038	RSt 37-2			
	S235J0	1.0114	St 37-3U		235[4]	
	S235J2G3	1.0116	St 37-3N			
	S235J2G4	1.0117	-			
	S275JR	1.0044	St 44-2	410-560	275	22
	S275J0	1.0143	St 44-3U			
	S275J2G3	1.0144	St 44-3N			
	S275J2G4	1.0145	-			
	S355JR	1.0045	-	490-630	355	22
	S355J0	1.0553	St 52-3U			
	S355J2G3	1.0570	St 52-3N			
	S355J2G4	1.0577	-			
	S355K2G3	1.0595	-			
	S355K2G4	1.0596	-			
	E295	1.0050	St 50-2	470-610	295	20
	E335	1.0060	St 60-2	570-710	335	16
	E360	1.0070	St 70-2	690-830	360	11

Type	Material designation			Tensile strength[1] [N/mm²]	Min. yield point[3] [N/mm²]	Min. breaking elongation[5] $L_o = 5\,d_o$ [%]
	to EN 10027-1 and CR 10260	to EN 10027-2 and CR 10260	previous national			
High-strength fine-grained structural steel suitable for welding to DIN EN 10113 Part 2[6]	S275N	1.0490	StE 285	370-510[7]	275[8]	24
	S275NL	1.0491	TStE 285			
	S355N	1.0545	StE 355	470-630[7]	355[8]	22
	S355NL	1.0546	TStE 355			
	S420N	1.8902	StE 420	520-680[7]	420[8]	19
	S420NL	1.8912	TStE 420			
	S460N	1.8901	StE 460	550-720[7]	460[8]	17
	S460NL	1.8903	TStE 460			
Hollow profiles for steel construction[9]	S235JRH	1.0039	RSt 37-2	340-470[11]	235	26
	S275J0H	1.0149	St 44-	410-560[11]	275	22
	S275J2H	1.0138	St 44-3			
	S355J0H	1.0547	St 52-3U	490-630[11]	355	21
	S355J2H	1.0576	St 52-3N			
	S275NH	1.0493	StE 285	370-510[11]	275[12]	24
	S275NLH	1.0497	TStE 285			
	S355NH	1.0539	StE 355	470-630[11]	355[12]	22
	S355NLH	1.0549	TStE 355			
	(S420)[10]		(StE 420)	(500-660)	(420)	(19)
	S460NH	1.8953	StE 460	550-720[11]	460[12]	17
	S460NLH	1.8956	TStE 460			

[1]   For product thicknesses of 3 mm up to and including 10 mm; higher values for smaller thicknesses; for thicknesses over 100-250 mm, values reduced by up to 10-50 N/mm²
[2]   Only available in nominal thicknesses ≤25 mm.
[3]   For thicknesses up to 16 mm. For >16 to ≤40 mm value reduced by 10 N/mm², for >40 up to ≤63 mm value reduced by 20 N/mm².
[4]   For thicknesses >63 to ≤80 mm, >80 to ≤100 mm, >100 to ≤150 mm, >150 to ≤200 mm, >200 to ≤250 mm value reduced by additional 10 N/mm² for each increment. Exception: see footnote[5]
[5]   The values apply to longitudinal samples of product thicknesses of ≥30 to ≤40 mm. Lower values apply to cross samples and smaller and larger thicknesses.
[6]   Thermo-mechanically rolled steels are governed by DIN EN 10113 Part 3. These types are identified by the letter M (instead of N).
[7]   Applies to thicknesses up to 100 mm.
[8]   Applies to thicknesses up to 16 mm. Above that thickness, values reduced by 10 to 60 N/mm²
[9]   The data apply to hot-rolled hollow profiles to DIN EN 10210-1 (Issue 09.94) and cold-produced welded hollow profiles to DIN EN 10219-1 (Issue 1997). DIN EN 10219-1 also contains definitions for profiles with the MH and MHL designations (thermo-mechanical treatment of input products).
[10]   Only in DIN EN 12019 when supplied as MH and MHL.
[11]   For thicknesses ≥3 to ≤65 mm or max. 40 mm for cold-produced hollow profiles.
[12]   For thicknesses up to 16 mm; for >16 to ≤40 mm values reduced by 10 N/mm², for >40 to ≤65 mm by 20 N/mm².

1   Corrosion exposure – classification of environmental conditions in accordance with DIN EN ISO 12944-2

2   Designation and key data of construction steels

TIMBER
TABLES AND INFORMATION

3 Hazard classes and application areas in accordance with DIN 68800-3

4 Planed timber classification in accordance with DIN 4074-1:08

5 Construction softwood in accordance with DIN 4070-1:58

Hazard class	Hazard from				Application area	Exposure	Measures
	Insects	Mould	Elutriation	Fungal decay			
Timber parts not exposed to precipitation, spray water or similar							
0	no	no	no	no	internal components in heated and unheated rooms with effective ventilation and circulation in the construction (average relative humidity up to 70%) or similarly exposed components a) inaccessible to insects due to all-round cover or b) controllable, since open to the room	constantly dry, long-term moisture content not more than 20% (measured locally)	none
1	yes	no	no	no	as hazard class 0, but not covered on all sides and therefore accessible to insects and not controllable	as hazard class 0	use of coloured heartwood with a sapwood content < 10% or chemical timber treatment of test class Iv[1]
2	yes	yes	no	no	internal components in rooms with restricted ventilation and circulation in the construction (average relative humidity over 70%) and similarly exposed components internal components in wet areas with water-repellent cover external components without direct exposure to the weather	timber not exposed to the weather or ground, however temporary wetting possible	use of sapwood-free coloured heartwood of resistance classes 1, 2 or 3 to DIN 68364 e.g. afzelia, azobe, Douglas fir, oak, greenheart, larch, keruing, mahogany, makore, meranti, red cedar, robinia, teak or chemical timber treatment to test class Iv, P 2
Timber components exposed to precipitation, spray water or similar							
3	yes	yes	yes	no	external components exposed to the weather but not in constant contact with the ground and/or water, internal components in wet rooms	timber exposed to the weather or condensation	use of sapwood-free coloured heartwood of resistance class 1 or 2 to DIN 68364 e.g. afzelia, azobe, oak, greenheart, keruing, makore, meranti, red cedar, teak, or chemical timber treatment to test classes Iv, P, W[1]
4	yes	yes	yes	yes	timber components constantly exposed to the ground and/or fresh water e.g. in hydraulic engineering or owing to dirt deposits in cracks	timber constantly exposed to heavy wetting	use of sapwood-free coloured heartwood of resistance class 1 to DIN 68364 e.g. afzelia, azobe, greenheart, keruing, makore, robinia and teak or chemical timber treatment to test classes Iv, P, W, E[1]

3

1   Test classes as defined by the Institute for Building Technology, Berlin: Iv = insect preventive, P = mould resistant, W = weather resistant, E = decay resistant

Designation	Thickness (d) or height (h)	Width (w)
Batten	d ≤ 40 mm	w ≤ 40 mm
Board (thickness ≥ 6 mm)	d ≤ 40 mm	w ≥ 80 mm
Plank	d > 40 mm	w > 3 d
Timber section, quarter timber, beam	d ≤ h ≤ 3 w	w > 40 mm

4

Roof battens:	A ≤ 32 cm², w:h max 1:2
Construction planks:	w:h = 1:3 and greater
Timber section:	w and h ≥ 6 cm; w:h less than 1:3
Beam:	largest side of section ≥ 20 cm
Boards, un-planed (to DIN 4071):	d = 16–38 mm
Planks, un-planed (to DIN 4071):	d = 44–75 mm

5

STANDARDS AND GUIDELINES (SELECTION)

DIMENSIONS
- DIN 1055   Basis of structural design
- DIN 4172   Modular co-ordination in building construction
- DIN 18 000   Modular co-ordination of building components
- DIN 18 202   Tolerances in building construction

FIRE SAFETY
- DIN 4102   Fire behaviour of building materials and components
- DIN 18234   Fire safety of large roofs of buildings
- DIN 18320   Fire safety in industrial buildings

SOUND INSULATION
- DIN 4109   Sound insulation in buildings
- DIN 18 005   Noise abatement in town planning

THERMAL INSULATION
- DIN 4108   Thermal insulation in building construction
- WschVO   Thermal Insulation Ordinance
- EnEV   Energy Conservation Directive

CONCRETE CONSTRUCTION
- DIN 1045   Structures made of concrete, reinforced concrete and pre-stressed concrete
- DIN 1164   Special cement
- DIN 4235   Compacting of concrete by vibration
- DIN 18 203-1   Tolerances for building; precast ordinary, reinforced and pre-stressed concrete components
- DIN 18 215   Timber form boards for concrete and reinforced concrete structures
- DIN 18 216   Formwork ties; requirements, testing, use
- DIN 18 217   Concrete surfaces and formwork surface
- DIN 18 331   German construction contract procedures (VOB) Part C; General technical specifications in construction contracts – concrete and reinforced concrete
- DIN 18 333   German construction contract procedures (VOB) Part C; General technical specifications in construction contracts – cast stone work
- DIN EN 197   Cement
- DIN EN 206-1   Concrete; specification, performance, production and conformity
- DIN EN 1992-1   Design of reinforced and pre-stressed concrete structures; Part 1 General rules
- DIN EN 1992-1   Part 2 Requirements for fire resistance
- DIN EN 10 080   Steel for the reinforcement of concrete – weldable reinforcement steel
- DIN EN 12 350   Testing fresh concrete
- DIN EN 12 390   Testing hardened concrete
- DIN EN 12 620   Aggregates for concrete
- DIN EN 13 055-1 Lightweight aggregates – Part 1: Lightweight aggregates for concrete, mortar and grout
- DIN EN 13 139   Aggregates for mortar
- DIN EN 13 369   Common rules for precast concrete products
- DIN EN 13 747   Part 1 Floor plates for floor systems; common requirements
- DIN EN 14 216   Cement – composition, specifications and conformity criteria for special very low heat cement
- DiN V 18 197   Sealing of joints in concrete with water stops
- DIN V ENV 1992 Design of reinforced and pre-stressed concrete structures

MASONRY CONSTRUCTION
- DIN 105   Clay masonry units
- DIN 106   Calcium silicate bricks
- DIN 398   Granulated slag aggregate concrete blocks; solid, perforated, hollow blocks
- DIN 1053   Masonry
- DIN 1164-1   Special cement
- DIN 4103   Non-loadbearing internal partition walls
- DIN 4165   Autoclaved aerated concrete blocks and flat elements

- DIN 4166   Autoclaved aerated concrete slabs and panels
- DIN 4211   Plaster and masonry binder - requirements, control
- DIN 18 153   Concrete masonry units (normal weight concrete)
- DIN 18 162   Solid lightweight concrete blocks for walls; without reinforcement
- DIN 18 195   Sealing of buildings
- DIN 18 330   Masonry work
- DIN 18 554-1   Testing of masonry; determination of compressive strength and of elastic modulus
- DIN 18 555-8   Testing of mortars with mineral binding agents; fresh mortar
- DIN 18 557   Factory mortar; production, control and delivery
- DIN EN 197-1   Cement; composition, specifications and conformity criteria; Part 1 Common cement
- DIN EN 413   Plaster and masonry binder
- DIN EN 771   Specification for masonry units
- DIN EN 1996   Design of masonry structures; Part 1-1: General rules for reinforced and unreinforced masonry structures
- DIN EN 1996-1   Part 2 Requirements for fire resistance
- DIN EN 1996-2   Design considerations, selection of materials and execution of masonry
- DIN EN 1996-3   Simplified calculation methods
- DIN V 106   Calcium silicate units with specific properties
- DIN V 18 164   Rigid cellular plastics insulating building materials
- DIN V 18 165   Fibre insulating building materials

TIMBER CONSTRUCTION
- DIN 1052   Design of timber structures
- DIN 4070   Coniferous timber
- DIN 4074   Grading of timber by strength
- DIN 4103   Non-loadbearing internal partition walls
- DIN 18 334   German construction contract procedures (VOB) Part C; General technical specifications in construction contracts; carpentry and timber construction works
- DIN 68 364   Properties of wood types – bulk density, modulus of elasticity and strength
- DIN 68 365   Structural timber for carpentry; quality grading
- DIN 68 800   Wood preservation
- DIN EN 335   Durability of wood and wood-based products
- DIN EN 338   Structural timber; strength classes
- DIN EN 350   Durability of wood and wood-based products
- DIN EN 635-1   Classification of plywood by surface appearance; general
- DIN EN 622-1   Wood-based panels, performance specifications
- DIN EN 1912   Structural timber; strength classes; assignment of visual grades and species
- DIN EN 1995   Design of timber structures; Part 1-1: Design and calculation principles
- DIN EN 1995-1   Part 2 Requirements for fire resistance
- DIN EN 13 171/A1 Thermal insulation products for buildings; factory-made wood fibre (WF) products
- DIN EN 13 353   Solid wood panels (SWP); requirements
- DIN EN 13 501   Fire classification of construction products and building elements
- DIN EN 13 986   Wood-based panels for use in construction

STEEL CONSTRUCTION
- DIN 18335   Structural steelwork
- DIN 18360   Structural metalwork
- DIN 18800   Steel structures; design and construction
- DIN 18807   Design of trapezoidal sheeting in building construction
- DIN 55928-8   Protection of steel structures from corrosion by organic and metallic coatings
- DIN ENV 1993   Design of steel structures
- DIN V ENV 1994 Design of composite steel and concrete structures (Eurocode 4)
- DIN EN ISO 12944 Corrosion protection of steel structures by protective paint systems·

BIBLIOGRAPHY

Ackermann, Kurt: Grundlagen für das Entwerfen und Konstruieren, Stuttgart 1983

Ackermann, Kurt: Tragwerke in der konstruktiven Architektur, Munich 1988

Belz, Walter: Zusammenhänge – Bemerkungen zur Baukonstruktion und dergleichen, Cologne 1999

Bergmeister, Konrad (ed.); Fingerloos, Frank; Wörner, Johann-Dietrich: Beton Kalender 2009

Bundesverband Kalksandsteinindustrie: Kalksandstein, Planung - Konstruktion - Ausführung, Hanover 2009

Cheret, Peter: Baukonstruktion – Handbuch und Planungshilfe, Berlin 2010

Deplazes, Andrea (ed.): Constructing Architecture, Basel 2013

Dierks, Klaus; Schneider, Klaus-Jürgen; Wormuth, Rüdiger: Baukonstruktion, Cologne 2006

Döring, Wolfgang: Arbeitsblätter zur Baukonstruktion, Aachen 1998

Dworschak, Gunda; Wenke, Alfred: Der neue Systembau, Holz/Beton/Stahl – Skelett-, Tafel-, Zellenbauweisen, Cologne 1999

Eggen, Arne; Sandaker, Bjørn Normann: Steel, Structure, and Architecture, New York 1995

Engel, Heino: Tragsysteme/Structure Systems, Stuttgart 2006

Fachvereinigung Deutscher Betonfertigteile e.V.: Betonfertigteile im Geschoss- u. Hallenbau, Bonn 2009

Friedrich-Schoenberger, Mechthild; Heider, Katharina; Widmann, Sampo: Holzarchitektur im Detail, Munich 2003

Hauschild, Moritz: Konstruieren im Raum/Spacial Construction, Munich 2003

Hegger, Manfred; Fuchs, Matthias; Rosenkranz, Thorsten; Griese, Marion: Construction Materials Manual, Basel 2006

Hegger, Manfred; Drexler, Hans; Zeumer, Martin: Basics Materials, Basel 2006

Hegger, Manfred; Fuchs, Matthias; Stark, Thomas; Zeumer, Martin: Energy Manual, Basel 2008

Henninger, Dirk; Stehr, Holger: Baukonstruktion im Planungsprozess, Wiesbaden 2002

Herzog, Thomas; Natterer, Julius; Volz, Michael; Schweitzer, Roland; Winter, Wolfgang: Timber Construction Manual, Basel 2004

Homann, Martin: Porenbeton Handbuch, Planen und Bauen mit System, Berlin 2008

Hugues, Theodor; Steiger, Ludwig; Weber, Johann: Timber Construction, Details, Products, Case Studies, Munich 2004

Hugues, Theodor; Greilich, Klaus; Peter, Christine: Building with Large Clay Blocks, Details, Products, Examples, Munich 2004

Jäger, Wolfram: Mauerwerk-Kalender, Berlin 2009

Kind-Barkauskas, Friedbert; Kauhsen, Bruno; Polonyi, Stefan; Brandt, Jörg: Concrete Construction Manual, Basel 2002

Kindmann, Rolf: Stahlbau Kompakt, Düsseldorf, 2008

Knaack, Ulrich; Klein, Tillmann; Bilow, Marcel; Auer, Thomas: Façades, Principles of Construction, Basel 2007

Knaack, Ulrich; Meijs, Maarten: Components and Connections, Principles of Construction, Basel 2009

Knaack, Ulrich; Chung-Klatte, Sharon; Hasselbach: Prefabricated Systems, Principles of Construction, Basel 2012

Kolb, Josef: Systembau mit Holz, Bern 1998

Kolb, Josef: Systems in Timber Engineering, Loadbearing Structures and Component Layers, Basel 2008

Kummer, Nils: Basics Masonry Construction, Basel 2006

LeCuyer, Annette: Steel and Beyond: New Strategies for Metals in Architecture, Basel 2003

Lindner, Gerhard; Schmitz-Riol, Erik: Systembauweise im Wohnungsbau, Düsseldorf 2001

Meier, Ulrich: Moderne Holzhäuser – Systeme, Konstruktionen, Beispiele, Cologne 2004

Meistermann, Alfred: Basics Loadbearing Systems, Basel 2007

Müller, Harald; Nolting, Ulrich; Haist, Michael: Sichtbeton – Planen, Herstellen, Beurteilen, Karlsruhe 2005

Neumann, Dietrich; Weinbrenner, Ulrich; Hestermann, Ulf; Rongen, Ludwig: Frick/Knöll: Baukonstruktionslehre, Wiesbaden 2006

Pech, Anton; Kolbitsch, Andreas; Zach, Franz: Decken, Vienna 2005

Pech, Anton; Kolbitsch, Andreas: Wände, Vienna 2006

Pech, Anton; Kolbitsch, Andreas; Zach, Franz: Tragwerke, Vienna 2008

Peck, Martin: Concrete – Design, Construction, Examples, Munich 2006

Pfeifer, Günter; Liebers, Antje; Reiners, Holger: Der neue Holzbau, Munich 1998

Pfeifer, Günter; Ramcke, Rolf; Achtziger, Joachim: Masonry Construction Manual, Basel 2001

Pottgiesser, Uta: Prinzipien der Baukonstruktion, Stuttgart 2008

Reichel, Alexander; Ackermann, Peter; Hentschel, Alexander; Hochberg, Anette: Building with Steel - Details, Principles, Examples, Munich 2006

Röhling, Stefan; Eifert, Helmut; Kaden, Reinhard: Betonbau, Berlin 2000

Ronner, Heinz; Rysler, Emil; Kölliker, Fredi: Baustruktur – Baukonstruktion im Kontext des architektonischen Entwerfens, Basel 2000

Rüegg, Arthur; Gadola, Reto; Spillmann, Daniel: Die Unschuld des Betons, Zurich 2004

Ruske, Wolfgang: Timber Construction for Trade, Industry, Administration, Basel 2004

Sandaker, Bjørn Normann; Eggen, Arne: The Structural Basis of Architecture, New York 1992

Schmitt, Heinrich; Heene, Andreas: Hochbaukonstruktion. Die Bauteile und das Baugefüge. Grundlagen des heutigen Bauens, Wiesbaden 2001

Schulitz, Helmut C.; Sobek, Werner; Habermann, Karl J.: Steel Construction Manual, Basel 2000

Schulz, Joachim: Sichtbeton Atlas - Planung, Ausführung, Wiesbaden 2009

Steiger, Ludwig: Basics Timber Construction, Basel 2007

Von Seidlein, Peter C.; Schulz, Christina: Skelettbau. Konzepte für eine strukturelle Architektur, Projekte 1981-1996, Munich 2001

INDEX

INDEX / IMAGE CREDITS

Architekturbüro Bienefeld: p. 154; p. 155
ArcelorMittal: p. 60 2
Architekturfotografie Gempeler: p. 108 2
Attali, Erieta: p. 140; p. 146; p. 147
Baselgia, Guido: p. 74 1
Bauer, Simon: p. 159; p. 160
Bestpix.ch: p. 77 3
BMW Group Archiv: p. 51 2b
Bühler, Beat: p. 45 5, 6
Casals, Luis: p. 48
Creative Commons 3.0: p. 11 3; p. 68 1; p. 108 1; p. 109 3; p. 110 1; p. 114 1, 2
Dilling, Jan: p. 104 1, 2; p. 127 4
Duckek, Martin: p. 60 1; p. 142
Fink Thurnher Architekten: p. 158; p. 161
Franck, David: p. 130 1
Frei, Roger: p. 148; p. 149
Gebauer, Henry: p. 80 1
Geco SA: p. 112 1a, b
Gerken Architekten: p. 143; p. 145
Graupner, Klaus: p. 13 3, 4

Havlova, Ester: p. 54 2
Hehnpohl Architektur: p. 156; p. 157
HeidelbergCement AG/ Steffen Fuchs: p. 101 4
Helfenstein, Heinrich: p. 106 1
Herschel, Andreas: p. 10 2
HHF Architekten: p. 100 1
Hochberg, Anette: p. 164
Holka Genossenschaft, 2013: p. 121 4
Holzherr, F.: p. 88 1
Holz Ruser: p. 129 3 (1, 3, 4)
Hueber, Eduard (archphoto.com): p. 72 1
Huthmacher, Werner: p. 78
Impremar: p. 99 h
InformationsZentrum Beton: p. 40 1
Judith Benzer Architektur: p. 162; p. 163
Junker, Beat: p. 19 4
Kapellos, Alexandre: p. 8; p. 151
Lutz Architectes: p. 52 1d
Max Frank GmbH & Co. KG: p. 113 3 b, c

MERO-TSK International: p. 63 3
Müller, Richie: p. 60 6
neutecswiss: p. 114 3
Naumann, Volker: p. 64 2
Niederwöhrmeier, Julius: p. 14 3; p. 16 2; p. 18 1; p. 22; p. 25 2; p. 28 1, 2; p. 31 4; p. 34 1, 2; p. 35 4; p. 39 5; p. 44 1, 2, 3
NOE-Schaltechnik, Süssen: p. 109 5
Ortmeyer, Klemens: p. 58 2
Pfeifer, Günter: p. 47 4
Pixelio.de/Kurt Michel: p. 129 3 (2)
Preuss, Uli: p. 62 2
Reeve, Edward: p. 116 1
Richters, Christian: p. 62 1; p. 67 8; p. 109 4
roadstone.ie: p. 102 3
Rötheli, René: p. 150, p. 153
saai Karlsruhe, Photo: Eberhard Troeger: p. 51 2c
Salzgitter AG: p. 56 1c
Schiess, Hanspeter: p. 124 1
Schmidt, Eckard: p. 101 2
Schweitzer, Roland: p. 75 3

Sozialwerk Bauhütte e.V., Aachen: p. 113 3a
Spiluttini, Margherita: p. 71 5
Stegmann, Dietmar: p. 14 5
Strauss, Dietmar: p. 60 4
Stylepark: p. 111 2b
TECHNOpor, glass foam concrete: p. 111 2c
Texton: p. 101 3
Thomas Mayer Archive: p. 15 7
VLB-Bregenz, Photo: Ignacio Martinez: p. 70 1
Wachsmuth, Henning: p. 122 2
Walter Lehmann GmbH & Co. KG, Mettmann: p. 112 1c
Walti, Ruedi: p. 38 1
Wasserhess, Theo: p. 15 8
Weis & Volkmann: p. 76 1
Wienerberger AG, Photo: Attila Polgár: p. 95 3
Wienerberger AG: p. 98 c
Xella Deutschland GmbH: p. 98 b, e
Zement + Beton Handels- und WerbegesmbH: p. 111 2a
Zimmerei Meyer, Weißenburg: p. 125 6

Editors: Alexander Reichel, Kerstin Schultz
Concept: Alexander Reichel, Kerstin Schultz, Andrea Wiegelmann
Authors: Henning Baurmann, Jan Dilling, Claudia Euler, Julius Niederwöhrmeier

Translation from German into English: Hartwin Busch
Copy editing and proofreading: Richard Toovey
Project management: Petra Schmid

Layout: Dan Kröning
Drawings: Dan Kröning, Anna Tomm
Design concept SCALE: Nadine Rinderer
Typesetting: Amelie Solbrig

The technical and construction recommendations contained in this book are based on the present state of technical knowledge. They should be checked in each case against the relevant instructions, standards, laws etc. as well as local regulations before applying them. No liability is accepted.

A CIP catalogue record for this book is available from the Library of Congress, Washington D.C., U.S.A.

Bibliographic information published by the German National Library
The German National Library lists this publication in the Deutsche Nationalbibliografie; detailed bibliographic data are available on the Internet at http://dnb.dnb.de.

This book is also available in a German-language edition (ISBN 978-3-0346-0039-2).

© 2014 Birkhäuser Verlag GmbH, Basel
P.O. Box 44, 4009 Basel, Switzerland
Part of De Gruyter

Printed on acid-free paper produced from chlorine-free pulp. TCF ∞

Printed in Germany

ISBN 978-3-0346-0040-8

9 8 7 6 5 4 3 2 1   www.birkhauser.com